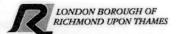
story . . . a stunning read that will resonate
with anyone who has ever loved.'
Latest Brighton

'Parents of autistic children will find it indispensable.'

What readers are saying about *A Normal Family*

'Thank you for inspiring me and helping me
through the "I can't cope" periods.' *****

'So special, so honest, so funny' *****

'Life-affirming, optimistic and generally
just rather marvellous!' *****

'Thank you for sharing your story, it has helped
me and my wife put into context what we have
been through the last twenty-one years.' *****

'A lot of love has been put into this book.' *****

'What a wonderful family!' *****

'Brave, moving, and utterly readable . . . they are real
heroes who have gone above and beyond to make their
family one that we come to admire and celebrate.' *****

'A testament to the love that he and his wife, Angela,
have for each other and their son Johnny.' *****

'Honest, moving, heart-warming, funny, joyful, sad' *****

'This book takes you off the merry-go-round of life and
makes you stop and look at what is truly important.' *****

Also by Henry Normal

A Normal Family

Everyday Adventures
With Our Autistic Son

HENRY NORMAL

and Angela Pell

TWO
ROADS

www.tworoadsbooks.com

First published in Great Britain in 2018 by Two Roads Books
An imprint of John Murray Press
An Hachette UK company

This paperback edition first published in 2019

2

Text © Henry Normal and Angela Pell 2018
Photographs © Henry Normal and Angela Pell
Poems © Henry Normal

The right of Henry Normal and Angela Pell to be identified as
the Author of the Work has been asserted by them in accordance
with the Copyright, Designs and Patents Act 1988.

All rights reserved. No part of this publication may be reproduced, stored
in a retrieval system, or transmitted, in any form or by any means without
the prior written permission of the publisher, nor be otherwise circulated
in any form of binding or cover other than that in which it is published and
without a similar condition being imposed on the subsequent purchaser.

A CIP catalogue record for this title is available from the British Library

Paperback ISBN 9781473656413
eBook ISBN 9781473656406
Audio Digital Download ISBN 9781473674035

Typeset in Cochin by Hewer Text UK Ltd, Edinburgh
Printed and bound in Great Britain by Clays Ltd, Elcograf S.p.A.

Hodder & Stoughton policy is to use papers that are natural, renewable
and recyclable products and made from wood grown in sustainable
forests. The logging and manufacturing processes are expected to
conform to the environmental regulations of the country of origin.

Hodder & Stoughton Ltd
Carmelite House
50 Victoria Embankment
London EC4Y 0DZ

Dedicated to our son Johnny,
who you may not be surprised to learn
has absolutely no interest in this book.

Contents

CONTENTS

Chapter 1
Introduction

Hello, my name is Henry and I am the father of an autistic boy. My son's name is Johnny and he's nineteen now. Together with my wife Angela we live by the sea in Brighton. For over thirty years I've worked in communication in one form or another – TV, film, radio, stage and books. These days I read poetry at literature festivals and often start by describing myself as 'a cross between Leonard Cohen and Daffy Duck. All the humour and frivolity of Leonard Cohen and all the spiritual depth of Daffy Duck.'

This is my family story. It is the most important story I have to tell. I'm only going to be able to tell it once. I want to do my very best. My intention is to write the book I wish had been available when Johnny was first diagnosed. That's when I needed most to understand something – and at times, with a certain desperation it felt like anything – of the journey ahead. I was forty-one when Johnny was born but very little in my life had prepared me for the challenge we were facing.

When I was approached about this book I asked Angela to help me write it, but at first she told me she felt it was something she couldn't face as it was too painful to remember those early days. Nevertheless, after she'd read some of the pages I'd written, and with a bit of encouragement and just the right amount of emotional blackmail, I did manage to persuade her to write some chapters. I'm really glad she did. For me her perspective and sensitivity adds balance and insight to this book that I couldn't possibly achieve alone.

You may wonder why we didn't just write each chapter of the book together. There are two good reasons. Firstly, Angela's perception and understanding is in many ways different from mine despite our journey together. Secondly, in a practical sense, when one of us is writing the other is very often looking after Johnny. Angela was a teacher earlier in life and is now a screenwriter. In a perfect world, she'd have written the whole book. Of course, in a perfect world the story would have been a lot different. But I'm glad to say Angela took to the task so well I began expecting my name would eventually disappear from the cover.

I read *How to Make Friends and Influence People* by Dale Carnegie when I was twenty. I'm not sure it helped me make friends or influence anyone, but I did become aware of the techniques used by other people who had read that book. I also read books on 'how to stop worrying', which didn't stop me worrying, but made me aware of the fact I was worrying, which I found worrying. I'm not averse to self-help books and I'm happy to seek advice on any subject. I'm always sceptical, though, as to whether such books are really able to fulfil the promise of their titles. This is not that type of book.

I wanted to include this disclaimer, therefore, to lower expectations and to state categorically – I don't have all the answers to parenting an autistic child. If indeed I have any. This is simply the story of our family told from Angela's and my points of view. I'm not saying any other family with an autistic member is like this. They may be. I don't know every other family where there is a person with ASD (Autistic Spectrum Disorder). I know some families on a similar journey, with either ASD or other special needs, and I've also drawn upon my direct experience of them.

I should warn you there will be poems, and jokes. You'll spot the jokes; there's big gaps between them. A sense of humour is vital at times but when dealing with some subjects it can often be frowned upon as being flippant. All I can say is the jokes and anecdotes here are told with love and affection and, given a choice between laughing and crying, I've found that, wherever possible, it's better to laugh.

We are all going to die. Sorry, I should have given you a spoiler alert there. There are two theories on the end of the universe. One is that the universe expands faster and faster and all matter disintegrates. That's the cheerful one. The other is that all matter contracts and forms a huge black hole and then explodes in a big bang and everything starts again. And so I imagine that all that annoying stuff you've had to do, you'll have to do over again. Either way you are buggered so you may as well enjoy yourselves. As my good friend, the late Linda Smith, once said, 'There were people on the *Titanic* that had turned down the sweet trolley.' There's also an old Russian saying that I love that goes 'Pain is the grooves into which we pour happiness.' I love old Russian sayings. My favourite is 'Your elbow is close but you can't bite it.' No idea what it means but it sounds profound.

I'm reminded of a recent incident when Angela and Johnny were visiting a church. Johnny likes churches. I think it's the acoustics. He has difficulty with communication, though I'm sure he knows more than he is able to get across. Occasionally, with gentle questioning, Angela will try to see what he remembers or has picked up. She began reciting the Lord's Prayer, 'Our father, who art in heaven, hallowed be thy name, thy kingdom —' And then she paused to see if Johnny knew the next line. 'For a horse,' he announced. We both had to laugh. Of course he'd remembered it incorrectly, but more importantly he was referencing Shakespeare.

In this book I've tried not to state what someone else thinks or feels, especially my son. Where I've guessed at something I've stated that it's a guess. How educated my guesswork is, I'll leave it up to you to judge. I've tried not to speculate wherever possible and practical. I'm particularly aware that were my son now able to tell his own story it would, quite possibly, be very different to my account. Although I've tried not to labour the point throughout, I'm keenly aware that he is the one with autism and that each moment of his life he experiences from his own perspective. As I can't begin to do true justice to his perception, or when I think of it, anyone else's perception other than my own, I can only respect that his experience exists and try as best I can to tell the truth of my own.

Reading this book back, it feels at times insensitive bordering on callous in parts that my role and thoughts are laid out in the foreground of events. I hold my hand up and admit my shortcomings here. These are my thoughts, my feelings and my observations as a man, a husband, a dad and the dad of an autistic boy – and to be honest I'm not even sure I've got these right. I don't represent any group or organisation and I'm not selling any philosophy or doctrine. I'm telling our family story in the hope that you might find it interesting and identify with parts of it. If you find it useful that would be great, but there's so much I'm still learning that I couldn't profess to offer this as some guide or template for family life with an autistic child.

I've tried to be as honest as I can without hurting anyone and I've tried to include everything I would want someone to include to give a 'younger me' a true insight. I've tried to be brave in looking at the pain and difficult areas of my experience as well as not shying away from celebrating the real moments of joy, however insignificant they might seem to others in the grand scheme of things. Angela and I have made mistakes and I have included those, as only by recognising them have we learnt anything. Our attitudes have changed dramatically and I've tried to explain how and why these changes occurred.

Though this is not a self-help book, I should say I have found compiling these thoughts and memories useful to me personally. Making sense of our journey has reaffirmed my commitment to those everyday lessons learnt, as well as a hard-won vision of our immediate future. Our distant future I am still coming to terms with, but I know I'm not alone in that.

Autism is a spectrum and our experience of my son's condition and his personality is in some ways unique. There may be people reading this book whose experience is different and that may make this book frustrating. I understand, as I've been in that position myself. There's little I can say to assuage such feelings, but the more genuine information there is out there the better chance that more people will connect with something appropriate.

I've read many books on autism, including the recent and excellent *Neurotribes* by Steve Silberman (which I thoroughly recommend). However, each time I read such a book my heart yearns for something that can tell more of the joy and humanity in the everyday adventure of living with a person with autism. A lot of the books I've read either concentrate on the difficulties (and there are enough to fill many books) or seem to leave me feeling like I'm reading about frogs being dissected in a laboratory. The most important and in some ways controversial statement I can make in this book is that despite, and in some cases because of, the difficulties we have a lot of joy in our lives. As a family we have many moments of fun and laughter as well as pain and tears. This wasn't always the case.

I can tell you categorically now that this is not a book about a miracle cure, but it is a book about how, through adversity, we found (and continue to find) this sense of fun and joy in our small corner of the world. Johnny is still profoundly autistic but despite his many challenges, he has grown to be a gentle, playful, calm yet often excitable, warm, curious, mostly confident, healthy, more independent, handsome and talented young man. He still has many problems with communication and learning. He is still overwhelmed at times.

Angela and I have learnt to view his autism as a different way of perceiving and interacting with the world. We are now more aware of his hyper-reactivity and are more able to see through his eccentric external behaviours to the person inside struggling to do his best. This was not as easy a lesson to learn as you might hope.

As you can probably tell already, this book is not written as a sleek story but rather in a stream of consciousness. While I've tried to organise the memories as best I can, looking back on our story so much is connected that it's difficult to remember it in a linear fashion. It's like trying to push a shopping trolley with a dodgy wheel. Instead, this book is thematic, like a series of articles and discussions or a scrapbook, and hopefully more interesting and entertaining for it. If this book is not for you I wouldn't want you to waste your valuable time. I hope you find something that works for you and wish you all the luck in the world.

I must say I was impressed when Two Roads approached me, as they are part of the John Murray publishing group. John Murray is famous for being the man who burnt Byron's autobiography. Considering what was already common knowledge about Byron at the time, I do wonder how much worse the revelations in the autobiography could have been. John Murray also published Darwin's *On the Origin of Species*. So I thought I'd be in good company. Then I noticed, looking further down the list, that they had also published Pam Ayres, so I quickly realised which end of the market I was destined for. I thought they might want celebrity anecdotes from behind the scenes of *Gavin and Stacey* and other shows I'd made, or a book on 'how to build a successful TV comedy company', but thankfully not. They'd heard the recent BBC Radio 4 show I'd recorded, called *A*

Normal Family, and urged me to expand on that as the basis of this offering.

As I type today I'm sitting in a room on my own in front of my computer. Angela is downstairs playing with Johnny. If I wasn't typing this I'd be spending time with them. I want this book to be good enough to justify my absence from these shared moments. Such moments are precious, so it's a hard task I've set myself. I hope you find our story interesting and engaging. If it helps or informs you in some way the effort will have been worthwhile.

I've included photos and poems as they are key to how this book came to be. The photos are family snapshots. They have no pretensions to be other than that. I purposely avoided anything that looked too professional, artificial or staged. My selection of these pictures was made on the basis of the emotion and inspiration they gave me as a catalyst to either the poetry included here or the text itself. I hoped that they would reflect the sort of photos anyone might have.

I also hope that, looking at photos from our family life, parents who are starting on a similar journey might see that 'normal' life continues, albeit with a little extra flavour.

Below is the first poem I wrote after a twenty-year absence from writing poetry. It is inspired by the photo below this chapter heading. You'll notice that quite a few poems in this book are inspired by the preceding picture from the relevant chapter heading.

PHOTOS WITH MY SON

Johnny is not interested in having his
photo taken

When prompted he will look at the lens
His hand is likely to move at any moment

I suspect he is not sure what is expected of him
'Smile,' he says

He doesn't smile
he just says smile

echoing the words
from behind the camera

Chapter 1a

And It's Hello from Me by Angela

As Henry mentioned, when he was first approached by Two Roads to write this autobiographical journey, he asked me if I'd like to work on it with him. My initial reaction was a very firm, speedy, absolute 'NO' – followed by a polite 'thank you'.

As an aside, I have always liked politeness. I find myself physically bristling when people don't use their Ps and Qs. Although I can of course forgive my son. Anything. It takes a lot of effort for Johnny to find the right words to say when he's trying to make even a simple request – expecting him to add a please at the end is a bit much. But when he's confident and looking receptive, I do try to encourage manners. I remember once when he was much younger, after he'd asked for something, saying to him, 'What's the magic word?' He looked up at me and innocently replied, 'Abracadabra.' He had a point.

So there I was, not really wanting to 'go there' with this book. Having no desire to remember and recount. I'm a screenwriter and autism is something I'd written about before, so it wasn't addressing the topic that was putting me off. It was more that I'd convinced myself that I didn't want to dig around in the past. Not when I'd spent so long training myself to live in the present. But it preyed on my mind. Why was it that I felt so adamant that I didn't want to relive Johnny's childhood? Which was of course all part of our gorgeous, funny, amazing son's life. It later dawned on me exactly why . . .

In the touching Nick Cave documentary *One More Time With Feeling*, there's a point right near the end where Nick is trying to articulate how he feels about the death of his teenage son, Arthur. He says that every time he attempts to discuss it, it feels to him that he's doing his son a disservice. Because although Nick and his family had to live through the tragic accident . . . it *happened* to Arthur.

And watching that was when it clicked for me.

Going back to the days when our child couldn't speak, couldn't make us understand any of his needs, kicked and hit and scratched, never slept, cried and screamed and retreated was painful for me – but what is more painful for me now is to think *it happened to Johnny*. He lived every second of it. His own particular brand of autism then meant that he was, I

11

suspect, trying desperately to fit into a world he didn't understand and was experiencing feelings and sensations far worse than the things that we were attempting to deal with. Even now I think he still is, but he is much more able to function in the world these days. I always describe 'back then' as 'challenging', but that's how it was for me. For Johnny I fear 'back then' was probably terrifying, frustrating, lonely and filled with despair, and basically just really, really hard. And that's what breaks my heart.

However, I decided I would take ownership of our past. I used to feel like my life had been divided into two sections. A big black permanent marker pen had firmly drawn (and gone over again and again, until it nearly went through the paper) a heavy line between 'Before Diagnosis' and 'After Diagnosis'. Everything that came before was carefree and everything that came after was the opposite of carefree. This was clearly nonsense but it was convenient nonsense. The line felt very real though. Maybe a lot of people imagine these lines when something happens in their lives to radically change what they feel is their place in the world – or their understanding of the world?

Almost two decades on, I still feel the demarcation but I no longer 'experience it' as that thick, black, terrible line drawn by a dislocated hand descending Monty Python-like from the sky. It's as though now when I think about it, it's a line that has been lightly drawn in the sand with a piece of driftwood, and my life 'after' is no worse than my life 'before'. It is just different. Not 'less' in any way. In many respects, it's 'more'.

So I thought I'd try to capture how that shift happened. There's not really one seismic event that brought it about, just a lot of little stories, strategies and realisations along the way.

Chapter 2
Childbirth

This is the only time my wife has ever evacuated her bowels on my foot.

Not a pleasant image but it sums up the raw, animal nature of childbirth. I think, being at the mercy of nature, not being in control, is what frightens me the most. We see it with death, illness and, I suppose, love. But more so with the birth of your first child, the stakes being so high – another human life, vulnerable, innocent, brimming with untold potential and, most terrifying of all, your responsibility.

Having seen Angela give birth to my son, I can forgive her anything now. Any amount of underwear on the bathroom floor, any amount of stain on the chopping board from turmeric . . . Oh, I've become so middle-class!

Angela's contractions started during an episode of *Coronation Street*. I remember this because I filmed them with a camcorder. Still a novelty at this time, and thankfully I'm glad to say I left it in the car, so the rest of the evening's events aren't committed to tape, and Angela has safely avoided reliving the pain over and over. It was the last time we were ever going to watch *Coronation Street*, or any soap for that matter. Not that I knew that as we gathered Angela's overnight bag and headed off to the hospital.

As though we weren't nervous enough, the maternity ward at Brighton Hospital is on the thirteenth floor. Angela's dad, Andrew, had followed us there and he and her mum, Sarah, were reluctant to leave. Well, I think probably more Sarah. Having been through it herself, she was naturally concerned for her daughter. For a moment I feared the prospect of all four of us together spending what was to be sixteen hours in a high-stress situation in this small clinical room. It was beginning to sound more like *EastEnders* than *Coronation Street*. Angela, now suffering with each contraction, tried the gas and air and immediately threw up into a grey cardboard bedpan. This may have prompted Andrew to persuade Sarah it might be about time to leave.

As the night stretched out before the two of us, we became accustomed to our surroundings. There seemed to be no concession to the spirit of children or the optimism of new life on the ward. It could have been any ward: Cancer, Cardiology, Accident and Emergency. I suppose they have to cater for those that don't make it too. It must be desperately hard to be surrounded by cute baby stuff when you've just lost your child. This lack of positive reassurance, though, only served to heighten the perceived risks.

I had been born some forty years earlier with water in my lungs and had almost drowned before taking a breath. It seemed strange then, that, as part of Angela's birth plan, she'd chosen a water birth. To this day I can't swim, so I was naturally nervous. Angela was confident. She can swim perfectly well and it was her decision. As part of her relaxation kit she'd even brought her own tape, Handel's 'Water Music', appropriately enough. Anyway, I wouldn't be getting in the pool so no rubber ring was needed.

The birthing pool was not the sort of thing you'd have in the back garden for the kids in summer. It had a military look to it. Like something American Marines would wash oil-covered porpoises in after a spill. Angela spent precisely ninety seconds in the pool before deciding that it wasn't for her after all. I was going to be supportive whatever she said, but was absolutely delighted inside when the pontoon went south.

We'd been allocated a midwife, I suppose you'd call her. I won't mention her name here. Not because of any protocol but because I can't remember it. I've heard some people say how they will always be grateful to the midwife and that they will remain friends for life, or will even name their child after this 'Angel of Mercy'. I wanted to punch the midwife and I'm not a violent person. I've never punched anyone in my adult life and the only person I can remember hitting in childhood was a big lad who ducked me under the water in the swimming baths after I'd told him I couldn't swim.

Part of me blamed this incompetent woman for some time for our son's autism. That's probably unfair but we'll never know for certain. On that basis, you'd have thought

I'd have remembered her name but I've never been good with remembering names. That's how my brain works and I suspect you choose what you feel is important enough to remember. The genetic argument for my son's condition, you will soon realise, is more than likely.

Angela was everything I would want her to be in this situation. She was strong, determined, patient, surprisingly civil and understanding. I don't know why I said 'surprisingly'; she's always like this. In anyone else I'd find this amount of virtue a pain in the arse, but Angela has a way of carrying herself and a quiet humanity that disarms. As the pain in her own nether regions increased she did ask for an epidural but 'Igor', as I'm going to name the midwife, reminded the mother-to-be, with the bureaucratic glee associated with the worst of the civil service, that she'd asked for 'no drugs' in her birth plan. It was at this point that I'd have gone nuclear, but, surreally calm, Angela conceded that was, in fact, the case and soldiered on. If it had been me, I'd have replied 'Yes, well I put "no drugs" in my birth plan because I didn't know it was going to be this fucking painful, did I?!' Avoiding any more gas and air due to fear of more nausea, Angela went through the entire procedure without any pain relief. Should I ever need a birth plan it would be simple. I'm sure it would be the same for any man – knock me out and give me a Caesarean, or kill me now.

Finding the right birthing position proved difficult as everything Angela tried became uncomfortable within minutes. We explored various options around our small allocated space, like trying out a mini obstacle course, and eventually she settled on squatting as the most efficient option. Let gravity do its thing. Angela tells me she has little recall of this night, but does remember walking off to the toilet fully naked, too tired to register, only to be called back to put on a gown, as there were men accompanying their wives on the ward. I'm not sure they'd have blinked an eye. Let me be frank, if there's one place men don't think about sex it's the maternity ward – well, only in the sense of thinking, 'What the hell have I done?'

The elephant in the room wasn't my wife, despite her protestations of being bigger than any mammal that had ever had a baby. She was absolutely fine for her height. The thing we weren't talking about was her dysphasia incident. This was something that had occurred a month previously. One afternoon, when nothing unusual seemed to have happened, Angela suddenly felt tired, had a terrible head-ache and began getting confused. She decided to call the doctor from the phone in the hall – we didn't have a mobile phone at this time, if you can imagine such a barbaric existence.

The doctor asked how long she'd had these symptoms and Angela couldn't form words into a sentence to explain. She was becoming upset as she tried harder to choose words that made some sense. I was listening in the doorway and I became worried. No, that's not quite right. I was worried, but I was also annoyed at her. 'You're talking rubbish,' I remember saying. I was fighting to quell my panic. I was powerless to stop this weird affliction. Useless with this loss of control to nature or science or whatever the hell was going on. I didn't know what was going to happen to her next. Was she going to collapse? Have a fit? I was scared. I'm not sure I've ever been so scared. I can't imagine how scared she must have been.

I took her straight to the hospital. Luck, grace or some-thing else saved us. Her confusion passed as quickly as it had come and the doctors did some tests. Up to this point Angela had never once spent a night in hospital in all her twenty-nine years and the fear that something like this would happen again haunted her for the next ten years. On reflection, the episode might have had some effect on our child; to me it seems quite likely. Meanwhile, back with Angela and the midwife, I was more concerned that childbirth didn't bring on this condition again, or worse, for the woman I love more than life itself. That's Angela, of course. Not Igor.

My middle sister, Valerie, with her usual categorical certainty, had told me that according to Angela's symptoms it was definitely a brain tumour. It wasn't.

On the thirteenth floor, the hours passed and contractions came and went, albeit escalating. Angela was getting weaker and weaker. Finding it difficult to push, difficult to squat even. It was at this point I decided I hated Igor. In my mind's eye Angela was a seal and this excuse for a nurse was clubbing her to death. I know I'm mixing my imagery here but impotent rage will do that to you. I was not even conscious of the consequences to our baby at this point. My complaints increased in proportion to the pain my partner was going through. I'd started politely and with deference, but as time passed you didn't have to be a brain surgeon or indeed a midwife to know something was wrong.

A 'proper' doctor was brought in and it was decided a ventouse would be needed. I helped Angela to her feet. She looked like she'd run a marathon in the costume of a pregnant woman. Her face was hot and industrial levels of sweat were pouring off her. I'd never seen her look so tired. Even in the trials since it would be hard to match this level of exhaustion.

I'd not heard the word 'ventouse' before. It's basically a big plunger with a vacuum, like something you'd use to unblock a drain. I stood holding Angela's hand at what you might call the 'away end' while down below the plumbing equipment got to work. After sixteen hours of pushing this contraption did the trick in a few minutes. Out popped our baby with the longest purple head I'd ever seen. He was like a Tefal baby who'd drunk too much Ribena. I said nothing of the sort, of course, not wanting to undermine the majesty of birth. The doctors explained that his appearance would 'normalise' very soon. So there he was, our baby boy. Whether vital oxygen was lost at any stage we were never told. It would not cross our minds for another two and a half years.

Johnny was nine pounds twelve ounces, giving some credence to Angela's beached-whale self-description I suppose. They'd had to cut her to save her from tearing. Not a pleasant thought. I'm reminded of the very old joke where a woman is being sewn up and she says 'Put an extra stitch in, for my husband.' Angela tells me this joke was definitely written by a man.

Angela settled down for a well-earned rest and I made my way home. I remember sitting in my car looking out at the sea and recording the moment on the camcorder. I shot a personal message to our son with our home in the background. 'We are going to bring you home,' I told him, 'and you are going to have a brilliant and beautiful life.'

Strangely, at this point, I didn't feel relief as I had thought I would. What I felt was resolve. I remember saying to myself that he was going to have a better life than I'd had. The things that had held me back wouldn't hold him back. I'd see to that. He had fought to get here. His mother had fought. Now it was my turn. Like a footballer picking the ball out of the back of the net and putting it on the centre spot. Game on.

It strikes me how overwhelming it must be for all of us, but especially an autistic child, coming into this world. This is a poem based on the photo of Johnny and his grandparents at the start of Chapter 13.

ESKIMO KISS

One hand supports soft scalp
another removes all obstacles
you are safe again
surrounded by family

There is warmth in this welcome
gravity embraced
eyes lock and focus as never before
generations whisper greeting

Biology reveals new sensations
a world now immediate and infinite
Face to face with creation
you breathe the same air

Tiny fingers realise a first grip
am I part of you?
are you part of me?
there are no extremities today

Skin touching skin
a most human hello
essential learning
you are connected still

Chapter 3

Before we Knew

Of course, when you arrive home from the hospital, there are no instructions. You're on your own, no doctors or nurses. You come home and – I'm sure all parents do this – you put the baby on the bed and you look at your baby, and you look at each other and you say, 'What do we do now then?' I remember for the first five nights Angela slept on the bed with Johnny and I slept at the bottom of the bed 'just in case'. I had no idea, in case of what.

On one occasion Johnny looked ill and seemed to be really hot and we didn't understand what was wrong, so we called out the emergency doctor. The emergency doctor arrived and as new parents we were all emotional and fraught and he said, 'Just open a window.' I remember thinking, 'Thank God I didn't go private, that really would be paying for fresh air.'

Like most parents, the very first time I saw my son was via ultrasound, but in my case I was working in Manchester co-writing *The Mrs Merton Show* so Angela (who was in Brighton) sent me a copy of the ultrasound scan by fax. I've still got it. Angela had drawn a speech bubble from Johnny's face saying, 'Hello, Dad,' which I thought was nice; not strictly speaking his first words though. 'Star' was his first word. I don't know if he was referring to my own qualities or his mum's. It was probably because we used to sing 'Twinkle Twinkle Little Star' to him.

Johnny did start to speak in single words, which at first made us feel he was on track. He learnt to walk by holding on to the side of the bath or the bed, then independently. I remember people saying, 'He will walk, you don't get adults sitting around who never learnt to walk.' I also remember using the same logic to calm and reassure myself that he would eventually use sentences.

In retrospect, a couple of memories jump out at me from this period. I was changing Johnny's nappy once and he struggled and I distinctly remember being pleased. I was conscious of the fact he hardly ever struggled and I was particularly aware that here he was asserting his own will. It's a strange thing to come back to me and I can only think it's because it must have been so out of the ordinary. This was the first moment I suspected something was different about him.

On a later occasion while I was changing his nappy I spoke to him and all I recall was the look on his face. It was a look of confusion, not mild or temporary confusion but the sort of look you'd expect from an Alzheimer's patient. It disturbed me. I never discussed this with Angela. I wasn't sure what it meant. I wondered if he didn't like me. Was I doing something wrong? It was as if I wasn't his dad. As if we weren't connected. As if we had never met.

With hindsight I now realise that the fact he never raised his arms to be picked up wasn't standard behaviour for babies. He never crawled; before he learnt to walk he shuffled along on his bottom. Also he would clench and unclench his fingers quite a lot, which could have been an early coping strategy to help him feel in control of his environment.

I knew Angela was a good mother and I was doing my best trying to be attentive and pragmatic and practical. Even though I was not the most natural of fathers, or particularly comfortable with familiarity, I knew I loved my son. Yet somewhere underneath the surface I could feel there was a strange emptiness in our lives. I didn't understand it and I would never mention it to Angela. To be honest I was a little embarrassed at the thought that it was me.

Johnny did have the MMR jab. Looking back I can't remember knowing anything about the reported controversy. Angela can't stand needles so she asked me to take Johnny to have the shot. I don't have a particular fear of needles so I was happy to take him. Only years later did I worry that I'd done the right thing. I should have at least understood that people at the time were worried about what they perceived as possible risks. It haunted me that he had struggled a little. Had I harmed my child through ignorance? Reviewing Johnny's development before and after the jab, I don't personally believe there was any difference.

I would say, hand on heart, whatever autism was affecting Johnny was there before.

I can see how it would be easy to cite MMR as a factor in your child's autism. It's administered around the time when developmental difficulties become most evident. From the articles I've read, there are persuasive arguments about the risks of any vaccination. I can only say that from my observation MMR didn't cause or heighten my own son's autism.

Would I have him vaccinated again now if I could go back? That's an interesting question. If I knew then what I know now I would probably already know my son was autistic before having to make that choice. Given the controversy at the time, I probably wouldn't have taken the risk of it affecting Johnny further and would have opted for separate vaccinations. But if my son was little now, in light of numerous research studies since, I'd have to say, on balance, that I would give him the MMR. Deciding whether to expose your child to any vaccination – not just MMR – is not easy though. I'm sure no sane parent wants to do anything that might risk harming their child. What you want is a clear, risk-free option, whether it's a vaccination or any other choice for that matter.

Occasionally we'd attend a get-together with others from our NCT antenatal class and here it was noticeable that Johnny was different. He was disconnected. He wouldn't play with other kids. He wouldn't interact with anyone unless confronted. Angela would say, 'There's something different about Johnny,' and I would say, 'No, he's just laid-back; he's like a teenager, he's so advanced that he's gone into that awkward teenage stage at the age of two.' I had this misguided notion that to admit there was something developmentally wrong was like a betrayal. Like giving up on him.

I tell a story on stage occasionally. The story goes like this.

'This is the only argument I've ever had with my wife. Now I know you're already on my side but reserve judgement. It's about twenty-five years ago and we are living in a small flat in Brighton. I'm watching the television and I'm wanting to tape something on the other side, only I can't do it, so I shout "Angela!" Anyway, she gets out of the bath, totally naked and dripping. She explains that the remote doesn't work and then proceeds to kneel in front of the TV, dripping on to the electrics, and starts to sort out the video recorder. So I'm laid on the sofa, and the thing is, she's in front of the TV screen. So I say, "I'm missing it now." She looks at me, doesn't say a word, gets up, walks across the room and just goes back to her bath. How selfish is that? Well, if that's her attitude, I thought, I'm not going to bother arguing again.'

Obviously I'm playing on my 'male' insensitivity in this incident. It is a totally true story in all respects other than it wasn't the only argument. There was another. One I don't like to admit to. Johnny was about two. He was crying for what appeared to be no reason. He wouldn't sleep. Unlike the other kids in his NCT class, he hadn't started to speak by this point, so it was frustrating. He wasn't affectionate in the way other kids seemed to be. Though I knew something was wrong, I was in denial.

While we were at home we could grit our teeth and get through the bouts of crying, the sleepless nights, the worry about Johnny's antisocial behaviour and lack of response; but the real problem was when we went out. We had a couple of friends who we'd known for some time and who had similar interests to us but no kids. We'd talk about films and comedy and other trivia young couples talk about when they don't have kids. I liked them both. In many ways they were us before parenthood. But when we visited them in London for a stopover with Johnny approaching his second birthday it soon became apparent that our lives were now so different.

Johnny cried continuously and nothing either Angela or I could do would calm him. No matter how we cared for him, nothing appeared to be getting through. It felt like the longest night of my life. I was embarrassed in front of our friends. I was confused and frustrated and at a loss. And I did the worst thing I could do. I blamed Angela.

It was like the moment in Orwell's *1984* where Winston has the rat cage on his head and he says 'Not me, not me, do it to her.' I was so ashamed. This might not seem a big thing to you here now reading this book, but I knew even then that I love Angela to her bones and yet here I was betraying her, betraying myself, betraying any notion of fairness or goodness, any notion of God even. Maybe this sounds over-dramatic but in that moment I had nothing to hold on to.

Angela doesn't argue, so she took my rant in silence and, driving away from London the following morning, all I felt was sick inside. I wanted to escape.

I can see why parents with an autistic child often break up. The idea of running away and starting a new life at such a moment could be more than attractive. There is a desperation. It felt like a whole midlife crisis had been packed into one day. Like I didn't know who I was. I was lost.

I'm not sure this story would go down so well at a live performance. This is the day I knew something was wrong with my son. This is the day I had to stop pretending it was all going to go away.

TELEGRAPH POLES AND SHIPS' MASTS

Telegraph poles and ships' masts
are hard to tell apart
from a distance

We are sitting on a wall
by the harbour

With my golfing hat on
you can't see the onset of grey
or tell that I don't play golf

With Johnny's arm around his mum
you might not tell he's autistic
even at 17

Although the wooden Pinocchio
he holds to his face
might make you question

If you look closely telegraph poles
are connected
whereas ships' masts aren't

as ships sail away in different directions

Chapter 3a

Soft Play Zones Can Be the Loneliest Places on the Planet by Angela

I have always thought a lot about dying. Perhaps growing up an only child of two only children, in the shadow of the sugar beet factory in the cultural vacuum that was 1970s Peterborough, gave me a penchant for pondering, 'Is this all there is?'

I am forty-eight years old now, so – to put my formative years in context – this period of intense searching for meaning happened at a time when the shops didn't open on Sundays, mobile 'devices' were only available on the starship *Enterprise* and an Athena poster of a female tennis player revealing her bare bottom (hung on woodchip wallpaper) was the height of interior design.

The majority of my friends lived some distance away and as I was vehemently non-sporty the idea of getting on a bicycle, or walking anywhere for more than half an hour, was so abhorrent that it meant I spent a good deal of non-school time alone. I was frequently bored – inspirational quotes like 'Only boring people are ever bored' hadn't been invented yet. Or if they had, they hadn't reached deepest, darkest Cambridgeshire. However, I consider now that all that boredom did me good. I relied heavily on my imagination. I contemplated my navel, eventually understanding that this thing I felt a lot of the time had a name and it was called 'being an outsider'. (Luckily, at a later date – I don't remember when; possibly after discovering The Smiths – I realised that 'being an outsider' wasn't necessarily a bad thing.) I read a lot. I began to doubt the existence of any God or any kind of moral justice. And to top it all, after realising that if I wanted something doing, I probably (annoyingly) had to do it myself, I became somewhat self-sufficient. All of these activities, as it turns out, gave me an excellent grounding for my later life as a Parent of A Special Needs Child!

Despite the immediate presence of the Grim Reaper and references to Nick Cave and The Smiths already, I hope that these sections of mine dotted throughout this book won't be too depressing. I am aware that, as you have been reading, an image of me may have been building in your mind. So far you know that

I am Henry's wife and Johnny's mum – a woman who has pooed on her husband's foot, has a clear disregard for the dangers of combining water and electrics, likes eating and doesn't get a lot of sleep. You should probably also know that I am usually quite upbeat. My friend Karen's husband Ian describes me as 'relentlessly cheerful'. So there really won't be too much focusing on darkness and oblivion. Just the other side of the right amount, I like to think. After all, you can take the girl out of the goth but you can't take the goth out of the girl. Said no Athena poster ever.

The thing is, there's some semblance of trying to recount events in chronological order here and so I should start in the early days. And they weren't all that sunny. When Johnny was very small, I remember feeling hopeless lots of times.

There are four occasions that really stand out in my mind.

1. I recall walking past a shop, perhaps Topshop, with Johnny in the buggy (a 'special buggy' we got given by the hospital around the time that Johnny was being assessed. It was slightly higher than your average buggy. I'm not sure how being higher was meant to help, but as Johnny was tall for his age even then, I guess it probably did.) The sign on the window in front of a glamorous mannequin said, 'Who Are You?' – at which point, I felt like breaking down and sobbing dramatically, 'I have no idea any more!' Instead, I bit my lip and held it all in, not wanting to upset Johnny or look like a mentally disturbed woman in the street. The irony is that I *was* a mentally disturbed woman in the street, but also that I actually *did* know who I was. I was an exhausted mother of a child I couldn't reach.

2. I remember when Johnny was around three or four years old, it suddenly struck me really hard that I HAD NO IDEA WHO

MY SON WAS. I knew very little of what he liked/disliked/ found funny/enjoyed doing/what his favourite colour was. These were all questions that my friends' toddlers could answer, but in relation to my own child were elusive. And I didn't think I'd ever know. There were lots of attempts at trying to elicit this type of information from Johnny – games that involved a basket labelled 'Things I Like' (with a smiling face stuck on it) and another one with 'Things I Don't Like' (with a grimacing face stuck on it), and encouraging Johnny to sort pieces of paper with single words on them like 'dog' (which was actually one of the few things we had a good idea that he didn't like) and 'food' (which we had a reasonable idea that he did like) into the relevant basket. But he wasn't able to complete these types of games. These 'tests'. I don't think it was a lack of interest (although he definitely had a lot of that too), or wilfulness – I just don't think he had any idea of the concept of like and dislike back then. What we like and don't like kind of helps define who we are. At least gives us a conversation starter. I felt like Johnny was a complete mystery to me. And at that time it didn't feel like there were a lot of 'ways in'.

As the years have gone by, I have gained more of an idea of Johnny's likes. And his order of preference! A few years back, I found myself explaining to him that I was going to be going away for a few days. I hadn't been away for a very long time. The conversation went something like, 'Mummy is going away tonight, and I will be gone Monday, Tuesday and Wednesday, but I'll be back on Wednesday night. I love you very, very much and I'm going to miss you. Will you miss Mummy, do you think?' I didn't want him to be upset. I felt bad about leaving him and was worried my absence might 'set him back' in some way. I held his hand and looked into his eyes. Johnny replied, 'pork'.

This was him checking that although I wasn't going to be there that evening, pork was still on the cards for tea. He's always had his priorities right. Meat in general we *now* know is a big motivator in Johnny's life. I once asked him, half joking, what he preferred, 'meat or Mummy?' The answer came back, 'Meat'. I had to laugh. I am confident these days, though, that I am somewhere in the running for the top spot in his affections. Still possibly below meat, but hey, he *really* loves meat.

3. When Johnny was about two, I remember watching other mums sitting around tables in Wacky Warehouse (our local 'soft play' facility, situated in a large side room of a pub) drinking coffee and laughing while their children ran off and played together in the ball pit. Johnny and I went there regularly. On reflection I have no idea why. It was awful. Possibly because it was what mums did (let's not dwell too long on my experience of some of the other things mums did, e.g. attempting to join Tumble Tots and being taken to one side after the first session and having it quietly suggested we probably shouldn't bother coming back or the many disastrous toddler music sessions, which I've also tried to block out).

Of course now I understand that all of these things were most likely a complete sensory nightmare for Johnny: the smell of coffee and popcorn, loud music, other children. Possibly his version of hell. He couldn't sit still, he couldn't follow instructions, he didn't understand what was expected of him. Knowing what I know now, I would never have subjected Johnny to any of this sort of stuff.

But there I was, climbing into the netted-off areas full of bright soft blocks in the shape of toadstools, trying really hard to get Johnny to engage with me. I was the only parent in there. I was the only one following her child around with a dazed, slightly desperate expression on her face, wondering why her son didn't look at any of the other children, and why I had to explain what you were supposed to 'do' in each section when all the other kids just seemed to get it straight away. And I was the only one running after her son, as he constantly tried to make a dash for the repetitive flashing lights of the slot machines in the pub itself.

4. When Johnny was around three, I had so many scratch marks up my arms that I looked like a self-harmer. I'd always try to wear long-sleeved tops because I was embarrassed at the state of my limbs. I remember one incident in particular for some reason. I was trying to put Johnny's coat on for him as we were about to leave the house. I was kneeling on the floor in front of him in the hall when he began hitting, kicking, scratching and biting me. Nothing I could do or say would calm him down or bring him any comfort. He wouldn't let me hold him in any way. For a three-year-old, he was very strong. Not knowing what to do, I remember not moving. Although I know now that this wasn't the best course of action, at the time I just sat there and let him hit and kick me. I figured that he would eventually exhaust himself and stop, plus I didn't want to just walk away because I was afraid he'd injure himself more than me. Every blow hurt mentally much more than physically anyway. In these moments Johnny was so far away from me. The fact that I couldn't help him or understand what was going on was extremely painful. I felt a failure as a mother.

It is strange revisiting these moments. It's hard to get my head around quite how lost I was at the time. I am sure that we also had some good times together in those early years – *I know we did* – but somehow they aren't as vivid in my memory. Maybe it's a bit like it is for famous people when they say they only ever remember the bad reviews (was it Andy Warhol who said, 'One should never read reviews, one should only weigh them'?) I imagine a lot of my feeling of helplessness probably came from just being worn out. Most of my friends worked and Henry was obviously at Baby Cow, his TV production company in London, five days a week, so Johnny and I spent a lot of time, just the two of us, out together. They were long days. He woke very early (sometimes at 2 a.m.) and finally went back to sleep around 10 p.m. He never 'napped' in the day – even as a baby. I remember our first ever full night's sleep. He was nine years old. Yes – you read that correctly!

Johnny still wakes up early. And I am still pretty tired most of the time. I can't imagine ever feeling wide awake again. But now I just try to keep on keeping on without thinking too much about it – and avoiding research posted on Facebook saying there's a direct correlation between lack of sleep and Alzheimer's and early death.

A BALL PIT IS NO PLACE
FOR A MAN IN HIS FORTIES

A ball pit is no place for a man in his forties
but as Johnny wouldn't play with other kids
Ange and I dived in

There's nothing soft about soft play
Brutality in prime colours
Polystyrene tea and dirty looks

Shrieks and quiet desperation
A vague smell of sick

Pity and time wasting away
A plastic purgatory
for the tired and the lost

Here's the thing about play
soft or otherwise

Johnny can kick a ball
and he will if you ask him
he just doesn't see the need to kick it
if you don't ask him

He can throw a ball
he can catch a ball
he can walk right past a ball and ignore it

Before we were told
I would have expected too much from him
now I'm trying not to expect too little

One of the first things I learnt
was that no amount of toys would save him
Buzz Lightyear was not coming to the rescue
Thunderbirds were not go
Spectrum was definitely green

This is in the days when I thought he needed saving
like a boy lost
and that one day the boy would find his father
and the boy would find his son

Chapter 4
Diagnosis

The first time I saw a leaflet for the National Autistic Society was in 1998. It had a logo on it of a crying child; not the most positive of images. The child was depicted inside a jigsaw piece. The logo was in black and white. Nothing about it was of any comfort. The new logo, however, is a

warm pink and purple with two stylised, fluid, almost femi-
nine, figures holding hands. It's certainly better. I think this
may be indicative of the change in people's approach to the
autistic spectrum generally over the last eighteen years.

In 2000 Johnny was two years old, reclusive, often
unreachable, and Angela and I were searching for help. He
wouldn't look at you if you entered the room, or acknowl-
edge your presence, and he fought against almost every
interaction. He was like this with everyone: adults, children,
his grandparents, even with me and his mum.

Events came to a head one day during that summer. Angela
had gone to a lot of trouble making a shopping game in the
garden. This was a game she'd always enjoyed as a child and
her enthusiasm can be quite infectious. She pushed Johnny
along in a plastic car, stopping at various shops she'd made
along the side of the lawn. A toyshop was one, a fruit shop
another. She encouraged Johnny to play but time after time
all she got was a blank stare. Later she confided in her friend,
Karen Gazeley, a mother of three children, the youngest being
Johnny's age. Karen quite rightly advised her to seek help.

Without Karen's honesty it might have taken a lot longer
for Johnny to get diagnosed and for us to then start working with him. When Angela mooted the idea that she was
worried about Johnny's development, Karen didn't brush
her off. The health visitor had done her checks and observations and thought there was 'nothing to be alarmed about'.
Karen, however, kindly but firmly told Angela she thought
we were right to be concerned and suggested we took
Johnny to see a paediatrician. When we talked to Karen
about this recently she said, 'I felt out of my depth and
scared you'd hate me for saying it but I hoped that it would
actually be helpful to hear someone say what you were

thinking.' That's the sort of friend you need at such times. Someone who has your best interests at heart and who won't pussyfoot around.

The doctor and the health visitor referred us to a paediatrician, who subsequently referred us to a clinic called the Jeanne Saunders Centre. It was a specialist unit based in a large Edwardian building in Hove, a little worn at the edges but clean inside. It had the feel of a community-run playgroup at a doctor's surgery, which, in a way, I suppose, it was. Johnny attended for several weeks while they assessed him. We had to leave him there so I'm not sure exactly how they did that. I presume they attempted to interact, gave him the opportunity to play and watched him. It was very difficult leaving him at first as we'd become protective due to his vulnerability, but we knew something needed to be done.

After several weeks they arranged for Angela and me to visit for a talk. This would be where we would start to put matters right, I assumed. A woman I had never met before and have never seen since took us downstairs to a room without windows. She handed us a leaflet for the National Autistic Society. On the front of the leaflet was the crying child logo and the word 'incurable'.

It's not easy to remember the exact words that were spoken that day. The main thrust of the conversation was the triad of impairments. Johnny had problems with 'social communication, social interaction and social imagination'. These were not things we didn't already know but now it was official, and these phrases certainly sounded official. What this all added up to, we were told, was autism.

We were told our child was 'mildly severe'. I still don't quite know what that means. One of the first poems I wrote when I started writing again was this:

SUMMER ON PLUTO

In a room with no windows
I am given a leaflet

The word incurable
is printed in bold on the first page

This is the only time I will spend in this room
This is the only time I will speak to this person

Autism is a spectrum
there are degrees

Your son is mildly severe
What does that mean?

It means he will always live at home
It means he will never have a job

never have a girlfriend
never be capable of taking care of himself

You will never have a proper conversation with him
Ever

It means you will worry about him every day
you will worry if he's happy

you will worry if he's lonely
you will worry what will happen to him when you die

Mildly severe
benignly savage

kindly cruel
none of this appeared on the leaflet

In that moment our future had changed. All the dreams we had for our boy had been broken and broken and broken, until all that was left in that windowless room was fear. A friend of mine at the time said glibly 'It's not an illness, it's a condition.' He was right, but at that moment I wanted it to be an illness, because if it was an illness it might be cured. There'd be hope. But at this point I felt beaten, without hope. I had lost my mother in a car accident as a child, I'd never had a close relationship with my father and now I was being told my son would always be distant.

When we got home I was numb, trying to take it all in. There we were again, alone as a family, like coming back from hospital after the birth, only this time with a task a thousand times more daunting. This wasn't the anticipation of an adventure. No one we knew had faced this problem before. There was no instruction booklet. We'd not been taught about this at school. We were totally unprepared. Immediately we arrived home I scoured the internet for more information.

There were still the everyday practical things of life to get on with. Angela made something to eat. She was very strong and resolved to do whatever it took. She came up to my office to see how I was getting on. I was collapsed over the computer sobbing with grief. 'I can't cope,' were the only words I could say. 'You can,' she said. I was more than embarrassed. This is not the image of the stoic hero I'd looked up to as a child. Clint Eastwood as the Man With No Name, seeing all but saying nothing. Showing no emotion, just defiance in the face of overwhelming odds. How could I let Angela down? How could I let my own child down? I had no choice; I would have to cope. No, it was more than that: I would have to fight.

Chapter 4a

Death, Name Dropping and 'In my Experience' by Angela

I should shamefully point out, before you continue reading more of my sections, that you may need a dustpan and brush, on account of all the names I'm going to drop. This is not by any means intentional, but there's nothing much to be done when your working world involves 'people of note'.

I am also very aware that when you are discussing any creative/ artistic or media-based project – which I will be doing – there is no getting away from the fact that you always sound like an arse. I am mortified if I have to use my mobile on the train to discuss a meeting, especially if it involves having to say the following words out loud: 'script', 'director', 'BBC', 'location' or 'they think the BFI might finance it.' I always imagine an enormous red arrow descending above my head, with the word 'twat' spelt out in flashing neon bulbs.

In 2006 I was on stage at my first ever press conference, sitting at the end of a long table with – amongst others – the lovely, remarkable Alan Rickman, Sigourney Weaver and Emily Hampshire (I warned you). I was terrified. We were in a large screening room packed full of journalists from all over the world. TV cameras were filming the event. It was, I think, immediately after the film *Snow Cake* had opened the Berlin Film Festival to an audience of 900 people (that bit was more enjoyable). As we entered the press conference there was that flurry you often see when 'celebrities' appear – the frantic flash of camera bulbs, the shouts of, 'This way! Over Here! Sigourney! Alan! Alan!!!' I felt like a rabbit in the headlights. All I remember thinking was, please, please, don't let anyone ask me anything. I hated public speaking. I felt sick. I still hate public speaking but, after several film screenings and subsequent Q and As during the months that followed (there's nothing glamorous about sitting in Nando's in Northampton while you wait to 'go on', believe me), I got more used to it. To cut a long story short, the conference was going well. The press only really wanted to hear Alan and Sigourney speak. All the questions were directed at them.

But then Emily was asked something. Then the director Marc Evans, then the producers, Andrew Eaton and Gina Carter. I was reminded of the old joke writers tell: 'A woman was so desperate to get on in Hollywood, she even slept with the writer!' – the joke being that writers are the lowest of the low in the film industry and no one is interested in them. At this precise moment I was rejoicing in this fact. Then it happened. A

German-sounding voice from somewhere at the back said, 'I'd like to ask Angela Pell a question,' and I actually thought I was going to be sick.

I have no recollection of the question. The point of me mentioning this story here is that I answered without thinking. I mumbled/rambled very briefly about Johnny (in the context of playing in the snow) and I said something along the lines of, 'Living with autism can be fun.' A few days later I googled the press conference (never google reviews, or anything the doctor mentions to you). On a particular autism site I saw a post that said, 'Fun??! Angela Pell clearly has no idea what living with someone with autism is actually like.'

There were several less pleasant comments – especially around Sigourney mentioning the words 'autism' and 'gift' in one sentence. One post stated: 'If I sent her a letter I think that it would be along the lines of telling her how very happy it would make me to have her experience this "gift" in her own life, i.e. by injecting her with enough toxins to destroy her body and mind.'

I'd got off relatively lightly, it seemed. But it did make me realise, from that point on, I needed to preface anything I said in a public arena with, 'In my experience'. Of course there are some people for whom living with and around autism is never fun. And their viewpoints are just as valid as mine. But I can only really talk about my own life. So this is just to make you aware that every sentence I write in this book (and every one of Henry's too) is prefaced, in capitals (and *italics* and **bold**) with the words 'in my experience'. You may agree with some of it, you may not. You may relate to some of it, you may not. I am not an expert on autism. I am only an expert on my son's autism. And even then, not every day. The thing is . . . I can only write what I know. (Although, as Henry sometimes jokes:

'They say "Only write what you know", but if we all did that, there'd be no *Star Trek*'.)

When you first get a diagnosis of autism for your child – or any kind of special needs, I suspect – there can be a period of mourning. Mourning for the child you'd imagined that you were going to have. The poem 'Welcome To Holland' is frequently mentioned or thrust into your hand. If you don't know it, I'll paraphrase it for you: when you're pregnant it's like you're going on a lovely holiday to Italy. You carefully prepare for this Trip Of A Lifetime – the prospect of experiencing all that exotic *Italian-ness*. You buy all the guide books, learn a bit of the language, but when the plane lands you find you've *actually* arrived in Holland. Supposedly, this is what it feels like when you realise your child is not the one you thought you were getting. (It's not a bad poem – it has its own charm. Maybe google it – make up your own mind.).

Anyway, in the real world, it feels like you're expected, almost immediately, to adjust. To open your arms and welcome the chocolate and tulips the Netherlands has to offer. (Strangely, there's no mention in the poem of hash cakes, which may well have come in handy in those early years.) Funnily enough, I don't think it did take me that long to 'accept' Johnny's autism; however, it did take me several years to fully 'embrace' it.

In my case, the child I'd always *imagined* we'd end up with was extremely cool. And would arrive fully formed at around fourteen years of age. Being an only child of two only children I had had very little experience of babies or toddlers. I don't think I'd even held one until I started my first proper job and someone brought one in. I had no idea what to do with it. So my imaginary son skipped all his cooing, first milestones, tantrums, etc. What/who I dreamt about was a 'little black cloud' kind of kid, one who had just the right amount of angst to write and then record quite brilliant songs in our basement studio (a basement studio, I hear you say! – well if you're dreaming, dream big), but not so much angst that they had to be medicated and worried the shit out of us.

In my head, Johnny would bring his friends over and I'd be the hip mum who swore and who they all found hilarious. I could even bake in these fantasies. Biscuits. FYI, I have never baked an actual biscuit in my life (and any attempt at following a recipe always ends badly because I have this weird 'anti-authority' thing going on that means that even being told what to do by a cookery book sticks in my craw and forces me to purposely alter given amounts – which of course leads to any finished product tasting . . . well, frankly, awful).

But those imaginary biscuits were delicious and made with love for this crowd of teenage boys with floppy hair and guitars, who were escaping their humdrum home lives to hang out at ours – because 'Mrs Pell gets us.' (There is no point, I think, in writing chapters in this book if I am not completely honest. However much of an idiot I end up revealing that I am). Basically, it never once entered my head that my son's classmates would pull up outside our house in a Sunshine Coach (which incidentally they do now a couple of times a year and actually we have A BALL – but that's a whole other story). And I certainly never imagined that I'd be my son's 'date' at his school prom. Although to be fair, I don't think anyone in this country had thoughts about proms back then anyway. Proms were what happened in imported American TV shows like *Happy Days* and *CHIPS*. We had school discos, which were much more 'low-key'. You certainly weren't encouraged to hire a gown for them. In fact a new belt from Chelsea Girl would have been seen as pushing the boat out.

The thing is, after getting our 'official' confirmation of Johnny's condition, I definitely had what you might call a period of grief. My daft dream had died a fast and Am-Dram style painful death (much wailing and flailing) and on top of that, I had nothing to replace it with. I had no idea what an autistic teenager would look like, for one thing. There just didn't seem to be any about. Although shortly after the word 'autism' entered our vernacular, I did see what I thought might be 'one' in McDonald's and promptly went home and sobbed.

Even though in reality Johnny hadn't suddenly changed when we got the piece of paper confirming his diagnosis – and he was exactly the same child we went into that paediatrician's office with – in my eyes, he came out 'different'. We came out 'different'. I was quietly dumbfounded. And full of self-pity. It didn't help that the majority of our first appointment with said paediatrician involved her gushing over the fact that Henry had written *The Royle Family*.

I don't remember how long the 'poor me' phase went on for. Once we started thinking about what we were going to do to try to help Johnny I'm guessing I became a little too busy to wallow, but I can't be sure. It's worth noting that nineteen years of inter-rupted sleep can do many things to you – in my case my memory is REALLY BAD.

Anyway, back to death and grief. As if we ever left it. I should say that even though I believe my centre of gravity shifted when we found out Johnny was autistic, I can't imagine that getting a diagnosis is really ANYTHING like losing a child. How could it be? There's no empty space. No vacuum where once there was a person. What the diagnosis really gave us wasn't a hole, but actually a space that was fuller than we could have imagined. We had a child who cried louder, hit harder, bit till he or we bled, kicked and punched, laughed and flapped way more than any other person we knew. Or had ever known. I should also point out here that anyone who thinks non-verbal means quiet is somewhat misguided. The thing was that at this stage we imagined that this was the way it was always going to be for us, for ever. A huge, all-consuming, challenging life.

Chapter 5
Our First Year of
Living with Autism

I remember the first time I met a punk. I was about twenty
and living in Hull. I'd seen punks on the television and I
was off to see Adam and the Ants, around the release of the
single 'Dog Eat Dog'. The venue in Hull had a fire scare
that night and the event had to be stopped half way
through. Police and firemen arrived and tried to get the
audience to evacuate the building. It did make me laugh
that the punk attitude was so hostile to the police that some
took a bit of cajoling to leave a supposedly burning
building.

I went with a friend to his punk mate's house. Punks weren't as clichéd in their dress at this time and, though this punk wore dark clothes and had black spiky hair, he could probably have passed for any disenchanted youth from any period. I remember opening the cutlery drawer to get a spoon for my tea only to find the knives in the knife compartment, the forks in the fork compartment and the spoons in the spoon compartment. I was surprised. I'd somehow assumed they'd all be jumbled together in a gesture of anarchy, but no, they were as orderly as anyone else's cutlery. It taught me a simple lesson – not to assume I could know someone from their outside appearance.

I was watching the author Alain de Botton recently on YouTube and he was saying how we view ourselves from the inside but others from the outside. Difficult at the best of times, but when the signals we are getting from the outside of someone are not necessarily a reliable indication of what is going on inside, it's even harder. With autism we don't always have a common body language, let alone a common verbal language.

The only reference I had to autism before Johnny's diagnosis was *Rain Man*. I liked *Rain Man*, but it's not the Tom Cruise film I'd previously thought would be most relevant to my future. I was hoping for something more glamorous, like *Mission Impossible*. Although the title 'Mission Impossible' did soon start to seem relevant. (At this point Angela's lack of sleep might have suggested more the title 'Eyes Wide Shut'.)

I must say, unlike Rain Man, Johnny has no savant qualities, though he does have a very good trick where he suddenly claps really loudly and gets us through queues very quickly. It's worth instigating at the right point in time.

We've been escorted all the way through airport security before now. They didn't seem bothered that we might be a security risk. I don't think they were anticipating an autistic bomber. Johnny's sudden loud claps in the bank are always interesting; bank tellers can get a little nervous.

When we first found out that Johnny was autistic, we looked at everything we could find that might help. We looked into PECS, which sounds like a gym for musclemen but is a picture-based communication system; ABA, which sounds like a boxing association but is a teaching system; and Tomatis, which sounds like tomatoes, but is a listening therapy. We tried oxygen therapy in a pressure chamber, homeopathy, music therapy, art therapy, a gluten-and casein-free diet, supplements, omega 12, some weird exercise that took him back to the womb and, of course, swimming with dolphins. Let's face it, like any parents we'd have skydived playing the ukulele if we thought it would help. (It wouldn't help, I'm fairly sure.)

From 2003, every Saturday morning I would sit down with my laptop and go through the Google Alerts for autism. I'd read about young autistic kids being helped by dogs or surfing, or suddenly speaking because they'd found an interest in music or art or video games. Angela and I were open to anything. We went to several conferences and listened to lectures on how the brain works and the latest theories on education. We wore our name badges saying 'Parent'. We bought the books and DVDs, read the leaflets, the magazines and the web pages.

I found out that the human body uses forty watts of electricity and the human brain uses half that, twenty watts. So if someone calls you a dim bulb they are not that far from the truth. That film *The Matrix* simply wouldn't work in reality; there's only about enough electricity in most families to run a fridge, let alone atomic energy, wind turbines or solar panels. Tell Keanu Reeves if you see him. They made three of those films. Unbelievable!

I learnt that the enormous quantity of connections within the brain that light up when we think are more numerous than all the stars you can see. The human brain is a wondrous thing and the more I found out, the more curious I became about how life started. I saw this TV programme with Brian Cox (I like him; he's like a clever version of Benny from *Crossroads*) where he was talking about abiogenesis. The theory that life on Earth arose spontaneously by natural means, and that all life, plants animals, us ... we are all descendants of that one initial spark. That's a lovely thought, that we are all connected to that moment. It means we are all relatives, all of us, with every bit of life.

Certainly the more we investigated and the more I thought about all the new obstacles we perceived we had before us, the more I felt connected to other people and their difficulties. We visited other families with autistic kids to see how they were coping. We had Johnny tested for minerals and allergies and intolerances. We tried all sorts of diets and regimes. I don't think anything we did harmed him but, looking back, I think only one thing in this first year really helped any of us.

Angela and I went to a lecture by an autistic woman called Ros Blackburn. We could see she was clearly on the spectrum. Her manner was sharp and uncompromising and honest in a blunt sort of way. I immediately liked her, though she did scare me just a little. She told us that she could only bear to talk in public if she could see the door she was to leave through. She talked about being non-verbal as a child.

She spoke about her relationship with her parents and her life now as an adult. For someone who didn't start talking till later in life she appeared to be making up for lost time.

This was the first time we had heard anything at all from an autistic person's viewpoint. There's something different about seeing someone tell their story in their own words with their own personality shining through. It affected me more than any written account I'd read or any reported account from a neurotypical observer.

Johnny was still very young at the time, around three, and I couldn't imagine how our lives would be as he grew older. Now, here in front of us, was a living person who had been where Johnny was. Of course, I know that there was no guarantee Johnny would ever be a fraction as capable as Ros in terms of communication or self-reliance, but this was the nearest we'd come so far to understanding Johnny's world. I longed to communicate with Johnny. Not with a text book or a theory or a program. Here at last was a person who could give me some clue as to what it was like to be him.

At the end of the lecture Ros agreed to answer questions. She explained that it was easier for her to speak to a group rather than an individual as it was distancing and she needed that. I knew I would only get one question so I asked the question that I most wanted her to answer. I asked, 'Do you love your mum and dad?' She had talked about how they had never used the word 'autistic'. She seemed proud of that. It's such a strange question to ask anyone, 'Do you love your mum and dad?', but that's how little I understood of what we were dealing with for our own child. Ros smiled and said, 'They were very useful.' It wasn't the words that struck me so much, it was the charm with which she said them, and that everything about her tone and manner told me that yes, she did.

I'd been brought up in a working-class Nottingham household. My dad never once told me he loved me in words. He'd do it in deeds, like taking me into town to buy the best top coat in the shop, or asking about something I'd been doing or making my sandwiches for work the next day before he went to sleep. In his later years if I talked to him he'd always talk about my brother or my sisters and how well they were doing. It would wind me up but my brother told me that all he would talk to him about was me.

I was lucky enough to meet Caroline Aherne and Craig Cash in my thirties and we created and wrote the first series of *The Royle Family* together. The first episode we wrote in one day. We sat down and Caroline asked, 'What does your dad say?' The first line in *The Royle Family* is 'Who's been ringing Aberdeen?', as it was clear 'being careful with money' was something all our dads had in common. My dad would say things like 'Are you in this room or that room?' And I'd say, 'I'm in this room' and he'd say, 'So what's the light doing on in that room then?'

We took a lot of phrases and dialogue from our own families in those original scripts. I once watched *The Royle Family* with my dad and his second wife Maureen. Maureen was a slim woman and despite being over seventy would always say 'Ooh, I've still got my schoolgirl figure.' It was such a good phrase I thought I'd give it to Sue Johnston's character of the mum. So I'm sitting with Dad and Maureen watching *The Royle Family* and Sue Johnston comes on the screen and says, 'Ooh, I've still got my schoolgirl figure.' Maureen turns to my dad and says: 'So have I, haven't I, Frank?'

The second episode took a fortnight to write. Then we had to wait two years to get the show on screen even though we never changed a word. When we presented the scripts to the middle-class TV execs they didn't get it. 'Can they be warmer to each other?' they asked. 'It's like they don't like each other.' We stuck to our guns. They love each other, they just don't go around saying it like in some gushy American show. When it aired on the BBC it was an instant hit. Working-class people could see the authenticity and they could see the love.

So when I saw Ros for the first time it was a revelation. Cutting through all the political double-talk and over qualified suppositions and watered-down best guesses, this was at last something real, something personal, something human.

The most important lesson I learnt the day we met Ros was 'There will be change'. This may seem obvious to you but at the time, the possibility of change was not clear to us. No one was talking to us about change or development. Everything was underplayed, undersold. No one wanted to raise our expectations, so rather than having expectations too high, as I might have had with a neurotypical child, I was being corralled into having expectations too low. In these early stages of coming to terms with Johnny's condition it caused a lot of heartache, a lot of anxiety, stress and even depression. So if your child has recently been diagnosed and you remember only one thing from this book remember this: 'There will be change.' It may not always be what you expect, it may not be on the timetable you want, but change will happen. Know it, plan for it, take comfort in it.

The other important lesson I learnt was: be useful.

IS MEMORY THOUGHT OR EMOTION?

Monkey bin
is a huge monkey head on a bin

It's not a real monkey
It doesn't move or make a noise
it has no arms or legs or body
just a head on top of a waste bin

This is Johnny's favourite bit of the zoo
Mine too

Johnny did like the penguins
It's a relief to know what he likes
or doesn't like
it's probably the basis of all
personality

He hates erratic noise
dogs and babies or
young girls who can't get what they want

I was drawn to the infant giraffes
awkward and strangely poetic
Johnny wasn't impressed
the moment came and went

The tiger intimidated
I could see in his eyes
he'd fuck me up if he could

I'm sure there were other animals
real monkeys and shit

but the only animals I remember
apart from monkey bin

are the giraffes, the tiger and
the penguins
and what I felt when I saw them

It's more the feeling I recall
and a yearning
for connection

Chapter 6

Cause and Effect

So you try to make sense of this condition and you try to work out what caused it, and for years I went on the internet and I looked at all the articles and there was a lot of fuss about MMR or an overdose of testosterone in the womb. I've seen reports citing Vitamin D deficiency, mercury poisoning and heavy metals generally. In one survey they said that the correlation in America was with the rainy areas and they concluded it must be caused by television. I'd love to blame autism on Simon Cowell but that's not going to help.

The truth is nobody really knows the cause. Experts tend to think it's genetic or that there's a genetic predisposition. The latest research as I write points to epigenetic causes, being the systems that turn genes off and on. We like to think of ourselves above the rest of nature but we share 50 per cent of our DNA with a banana. Not that we are two bananas. We share 96 per cent with chimps. So perhaps if you imagine a chimp eating a banana, you are fairly close. We don't even have the most complicated DNA; that belongs to a flower – *Paris japonica*, which has fifty times more DNA than humans.

From what I've read there are people all over the world working on DNA research into autism. It is the new frontier and there is a lot of money being spent. The chances are, though, none of that will have an impact on our particular family life. That's not to say it's not important to understand how any of us become the people we are. I'm just not holding out any great hope that someone will crack the DNA code and all matters relating to the human brain will be understood. I'm not even sure whether that in itself, in the wrong hands, would be a good thing for society. We are educated these days to respect biodiversity in nature. I'm sure differences in each individual brain have to be a good thing, generally. I'm very aware that different ways of thinking can be, and throughout history have been, undervalued or worse. I believe we certainly need, whenever possible, to look at the positive side of any differences. This may seem self-evident and even old news in some circles but I'm not sure it is in society's general approach to autism.

What experts will say in six months' times is anyone's guess. Even while writing this book I've read articles on ozone being a possible factor in causing ASD. If I tap 'autism' into Google today one of the first bits of information that comes up is a possible link to rubella in some cases and another site saying 'It is generally accepted that it is caused by abnormalities in the brain structure and function.'

The American politician Donald Rumsfeld once famously said: 'There are known knowns; there are things we know we know. We also know there are known unknowns; that is to say we know there are some things we do not know. But there are also unknown unknowns – the ones we don't know we don't know.' I agree with him entirely, although I wouldn't want to be stuck in a lift with him, that I do know. That is a known certainty. What we have in autism is a known unknown. Although there may be unknown unknowns on our journey to an answer.

What you do at first is you blame yourself. Was it the birth? Did we do something wrong? Did I have my bath too hot and shrivel my sperm? Had I worn my underpants too tight as a teenager? Ridiculous stuff. What really matters is what you do now.

One thing I know for sure is Johnny's autism wasn't caused by having a 'refrigerator mother'. Angela is naturally warm and loving as a mother and as a human. We know quite a few mothers of autistic children and I can't think of one of them who doesn't put their whole heart into caring for their child. The idea of cold parents as a cause of autism is a throwback to a misguided era, much like the misuse of electrocution for aversion therapy for the treatment of autism.

When we first found out about Johnny's condition (as I mentioned earlier) Angela and I went to several conferences and lectures. I remember a doctor explaining that there are so many brain disorders and that we categorise many of them purely through observation. She was at pains to point out that nature doesn't put different labels on such matters, we do, and these labels aren't totally useful.

You'll find that nearly every portrayal of autistic people you see in art, literature or the media is of a high-functioning person, and although I like the fact that through seeing high-functioning and Asperger's kids we get an insight into autism, the full scope of the autistic spectrum is often neglected. There's a phrase I've heard that may well have become a slogan in some parts by now: 'If you know one person with autism, you know one person with autism.' In my experience this is very obvious. Angela and I now know many families with an autistic member and the differences displayed are often more stark than the similarities. It is so difficult to generalise that I have to remind myself as I'm writing this book to stay in the particular world of our experience. I only hope that enough of the journey relates to enough people to justify the read.

I think the latest statistics for autism within the population figures are one in a hundred. In some parts of the USA it's said to be as much as one in sixty-five. Now if you think about it, there are seven billion people worldwide, so that's seventy million autistic people worldwide. Seventy million – that's the population of the British Isles. Can you imagine if the whole of the British Isles was autistic? What would the rest of the world do with that many people needing help? You'd need a bloody big carpet to sweep that under. Then again, thinking positively that's seventy million people from whom we can learn. Possibly up to seventy million undervalued assets.

Of course, when you are at home and you close the door and leave the world outside none of the labels or the attitudes of the rest of the world matter. There is only what you think of yourself and what you think of the other members of your family and what they think of each other and you. You can make your own rules, or lack of them. Nowadays, when Johnny is at home he's not autistic, he's just Johnny. This was not something that came naturally to us as a family at first and there was a lot of pain and tears along the way to find even this simple truth. It's not that such a thought wouldn't have seemed logical in the early days, it's that we weren't in a place where we could listen to logic. We couldn't see beyond the word 'autism', in the same way you can't easily contain or explain all your thoughts when you consider words like God or the universe, infinity or perhaps even love.

UNCONDITIONAL

His head is the size of my hand
I don't know what I'm doing
If I could I would sleep in that jumper

I don't know my son yet
I don't even know
how to imagine him

This is my boy
before we put a name to his condition
before I realised he had a condition

or thought of such a thing
as anyone
having a condition

Did I love him more or less?
I know that his condition means
that now

much more than before
I'm allowed to show him
I love him

Maybe
I've got a condition
or had one

Chapter 6a

Small Windows by Angela

For many years our days and nights were never quiet. There was no escape from the fact that this 'new' diagnosed Johnny was here in our lives. We felt his presence in every room of the house. And this terrible pressure to make use of the 'small window' when a child's brain is still pliable – to 'get rid' of his autism. Or at least reduce it.

'Getting rid of' was of course how we felt then. Not knowing anything really. Not understanding that Johnny's autism runs through every cell of him. It's in his DNA – wanting to banish it was akin to wanting to banish *him*.

Somebody currently working in education told me that the first two years of a child's life is the optimal period for listening and language development. Being given a time frame by professionals is meant, I think, to highlight the importance of input and support in the early years. But it makes many of us parents feel pressured and can give a false impression of a limitation on learning capacity – which of course continues, albeit at a slower pace, throughout our lives. Back then we were told it was the first five years that were vital and we were already on the clock.

I remember reading an analogy that described living in an autistic body as being like driving a faulty car: where the windscreen wipers come on when you press the brake pedal, and the radio intermittently breaks in, but there is no music – just announcers speaking a language you don't understand. The horn honks sporadically, the accelerator is the brake and vice versa, it keeps slowing down the harder you press on it, and the gear stick works in reverse. Oh, and the road is full of pot holes and the warning signs are written in Klingon.

Imagine not having any words, not understanding the world, or your own body – not knowing even where your own body begins and ends? Not knowing where you are going, even if someone is pointing to a pictorial representation of a place and saying, 'You are going here' because a) you don't understand the concept of following a point and b) the picture looks NOTHING LIKE the place you end up and c) what does 'you' mean anyway? Have you ever tried explaining 'you and me' to someone? It's a really hard concept – especially when you have to grasp pointing as well.

Chapter 7

Other Parents of Autistic Kids

It's easy when sitting in your own house to think you are the only one with a problem. I remember overreacting to cold sores as a teenager, thinking I was singularly cursed in the history of mankind. A bit of perspective at times is no bad thing.

When Johnny was three we travelled to America to investigate a new way of approaching our situation and Angela and I found ourselves in a room with another forty parents of autistic kids from all over the world. Part of the first session involved feedback from the audience, which gave me time to understand who my fellow parents were. The man I remember most was a six-foot-seven African-American dad who said that he'd been an American football player. I wasn't about to argue with him on that, or anything else for that matter. He told a story of someone in a playground calling his kid an idiot. 'He's not an idiot,' the dad had said, 'he's autistic; you're the idiot.' Everyone laughed, even though the session leader was at pains to point out, that was definitely too aggressive an attitude.

We were then asked to turn to the stranger next to us and do an exercise. The small, older woman next to me was from India and spoke very good English. She was to imitate her daughter for two minutes while I had to try to interact with her. The exercise started and the woman proceeded to perform in character. She asked, 'When is Daddy coming home?' I was a little fazed from the off but tried to improvise. For the whole of the two minutes she just repeated the same phrase, 'When is Daddy coming home?' Whatever attempt I made to answer the question or change the subject, she'd come back with the question, 'When is Daddy coming home?' That was a very, very long two minutes and it upsets me now to think about what that quiet but determined woman was trying to cope with. Like me and the American footballer, she was here in search of something. I don't know the full extent of her struggle but my heart went out to her and I still wonder today how she's getting on.

Roles were then reversed and I had to imitate Johnny for two minutes while she tried to interact with me. It felt so strange trying to be Johnny even for those two minutes. It wasn't something I would have thought of doing before. It did have a profound effect. By trying to see the situation from a different angle I realised it wasn't really about me. It was about how Johnny was going to interact with the world. I was just one part of that and it was up to me to decide whether I was going to be just part of the bigger problem or something more. *Something useful.* All around me people from all over the world were sharing this exercise. Angela was being Johnny to a fellow parent from yet another country with his own set of challenges. This was not just us with a singular problem in our house in Brighton. Looking around the room, there was a variety of people of all ages and backgrounds; we seemed to have little in common, and yet so much.

I thought of the American footballer again a year later when an incident occurred at our local garden centre. Johnny has always loved garden centres. They are usually spacious with high ceilings, and full of nature as well as the strange assortment of low-cost books, old-fashioned gifts and outdoor clothing that seems to have washed up on their shelves. The various seasonal fare always attracts Johnny. He likes the distinctive merchandise of Halloween, Bonfire Night and especially Christmas. An array of flashing lights, singing Santas, dancing reindeer, snow globes and glowing fairies adds a new level of attraction.

This was a normal summer's day though. Johnny was about four and he was standing with me in the queue to pay. He jumped about a bit at times around this age, rocking and moving his fingers – self-stimulation, or 'stimming', as it's sometimes called. Johnny must have invaded the space of the bloke behind us in the queue. The bloke spoke to him directly in a stern and abrupt voice. I confronted the 'idiot', as I'd now designated him. I explained Johnny was autistic and told the man in a similarly stern and abrupt voice to back off. I don't know why at this particular moment the anger welled up inside me, as I've never been a violent person, but I was incensed. I berated him more than I should have. He was a solid-looking man who probably could have knocked me out with one blow, yet my dander was up. I think I was trying to pick a fight but the truth is it wasn't with him. It was with the world, perhaps, or maybe it was with God. I just needed someone to fight because this fight with autism was too hard.

Of course my anger was all futile and luckily Angela was there and soon calmed me down. Later in the car I realised I had gone too far and felt apologetic. I think I needed to reach the brink of such stupidity to realise that anger and violence would never solve this thing. That's not to say resolve, persistence, fortitude and downright stubbiness aren't useful; at times they are essential.

I've heard people say, 'I don't want your pity.' It's a loaded word, 'pity'. I looked it up on the wiki-dictionary and it means 'the feeling of sorrow and compassion caused by the sufferings and misfortunes of others. A cause for regret or disappointment.' There certainly was sorrow at first in our experience of Johnny's autism. We grieved for the boy we felt we'd lost. Even now, after so many years, there are times when I feel that sorrow and part of me still grieves. I'm not sure if I will ever lose that. I'd like to, and I can tell myself all the positives of our experience and that I'm grateful for the life we have, and that's true, but it is hard not to succumb every once in a while even though you know it may not be helpful.

It always sounds a little selfish to wish for more, and feels like some higher element of character is lacking in not being content with your lot. That said, you need ambition to drive progress so perhaps the trick is to achieve balance, or a kind of Orwellian double think. To be happy with what you have but want more. This is part of the thought process they were trying to advocate at the American training course we went to. I understand the merits of this seemingly contradictory logic on an intellectual level. If you can choose what you believe and how you feel then it will serve you well. Emotionally though, I lack consistency and no matter how much I tell myself what I should feel I do lapse occasionally. In a strange reverse of logic I have told myself it is OK to lapse once in a while.

Last year I was given an honorary degree as a Doctor of Letters by Nottingham Trent University and was invited to make a speech in front of over a thousand fellow graduates. Most of these young men and women were not much older than Johnny. While I felt sadness that my son would never have the kind of life these young adults had in store, I think knowing that made me appreciate in a more profound way what great potential lay before this new generation. I was moved seeing the parade of fresh faces, some filled with optimism and some with trepidation. My heart went out to all of them and to their proud parents. For me the occasion encapsulated that we are all on the same team, whether we see that as humanity, or life in general. I try to remember that day when I think about other people's thoughts and feelings towards Johnny.

'Compassion' is a more positive word. To feel empathy and compassion for others is not usually presented as a bad thing. So when I am talking or writing about Johnny, when we are out and about in public, I am never offended by other people's compassion. I can't say I've ever experienced any negativity from others in the form of pity. Maybe I choose not to see it or choose not to let it affect me. I feel that more compassion in the world is a good thing. I'm certainly conscious in this book that as part of telling our story I am trying to enlist empathy and compassion at times. It would be a strange human story if it didn't. I've read *The Outsider* by Albert Camus, possibly one of the bleakest books ever written, and even there I found it impossible not to empathise.

I have recently had strangers ask about Johnny, saying, 'What's wrong with him?' To which I always want to reply: 'Nothing's wrong with him, he's autistic. What's wrong with you?' I realise even now I'm still a work in progress.

Generally, though, I find Johnny brings out the best in people. I know he brings out the best in me.

WHEN WORDS ARE NOT YOUR FIRST LANGUAGE

Any parent would sooner be ill
than their child

There is a helplessness

Johnny can't quite get the hang
of blowing his nose

His top lip gets raw
like bacon hitting the pan
I wince
and close my eyes to steel myself

Strangely he allows
more contact when poorly
he loses his edges
his lovableness is irresistible

Patience and distraction
are the only prescription

His mum throws her heart
into bamboozling him
through the worst

with such attention and diversion
we could call it just an everyday devotion

There are no words for what passes here

Chapter 8
Son-Rise

As I've said, when Johnny was first diagnosed we searched everywhere for information to help us. As I worked in television, I was able to get copies of all the available documentaries that had been made for British TV.

Angela and I watched them all hoping to find something useful. At this time most documentaries concerned themselves with the more 'high-functioning' people on the spectrum and a disproportionate number were about savants. The proportion of savants in the autistic community is far greater than the proportion in the neurotypical world but even given that, there was still too much interest in this small minority and very little about children like my son, who have no party trick to amuse or intrigue a TV audience. This sounds a little bitter and it's meant to. At this time I was feeling angry at the world, angry at the system that seemed to have no interest in our plight and angry at God or the universe in that illogical way you can be if you're becoming desperate.

Eventually I came across a documentary about a place in Massachusetts called the Option Institute running an autism programme called Son-Rise that seemed to be getting results with kids like Johnny. I was very sceptical at first but, when you think about it, if somebody's going to invent an in-your-face communication system, it's going to be the Americans. In my experience Americans are quite direct generally. I remember when I was in New York a few years before, I was sitting in a diner and was asking for food from a huge menu. Being English, I was trying to be polite so I started, 'Could I have —' and the waiter stopped me. He said, 'You got cash?' I said 'Yes'. He said, 'You can have any damn thing you want.'

There was a name on the back of this Son-Rise documentary that I knew. It was Jane Root, a lovely, intelligent woman who at the time was head of BBC2. Previously she'd been a producer and had worked on this particular show. I asked her if this place was genuine. She said she thought it was. So Angela and I decided we were going to go over to New England and give it a try.

It was a week's course for parents and it wasn't cheap. As we had never spent a day away from Johnny in his entire life at this stage, we decided to take him with us and enlisted Angela's mum and dad to take care of him in a local hotel while we were in the classes. We flew over to Boston and stopped overnight in the airport hotel. None of us had much sleep. Looking back, the nerve of even attempting an eight-hour flight with a three-year-old severely autistic child seems outlandish. The idea that we were all going to take the whole adventure in our stride, even more so.

The next morning I drove down the Massachusetts Turnpike to the Option Institute. As we drew near we passed a sign for the Moonie Church. I was very much on my guard. When I was twenty and living on my own in Hull I had been approached by followers of the Moonie sect and being vulnerable at the time had found the experience quite intense and unpleasant.

When we arrived at Son-Rise the next morning, I thought it was a bit 'culty', religious even, in a New Christian sort of way. At first to be on the safe side I held my phone in my pocket, ready, just in case. Then after a few hours I thought, 'Well, they might be after our money, and I don't mind that, as long as they're not after my soul.' I'm not religious at all. I'm C of E, which is not a religion, it's more of a dating agency for Henry VIII. The main thing was we weren't going to be abducted and held against our will. I didn't have time for that – we were on a mission, as the Blues Brothers might say.

Angela loved the food so much, I think even if it had been a cult, she was in. We attended the sessions during the day and went over to see Johnny at the hotel each night.

One of the first things we were asked to do was write a letter to our son. I thought it was a strange request at the time but I soon came to understand the benefits. Worried as I was that Johnny didn't understand, there were a lot of things I would have liked to say to him but had held back. Why had I held back? It's easier to say now but wasn't at all clear at that point. I was scared, first and foremost. Scared of being wrong. Scared of upsetting him or his mum or anyone close. Scared of making a fool of myself. Scared of losing control. That seems so funny now. Like I was in any way in control. I wrote the letter telling Johnny what I hoped for him, telling him how much I loved him, telling him not to worry, telling him that it was all going to be alright.

Whatever we took away from that first visit changed our lives. I can't remember all the details, but if nothing else Angela had a well-deserved break for the first time in years, albeit one where everyone talked constantly about autism. You don't often see that advertised by Thomas Cook.

A year later we went back to Son-Rise again, this time taking Johnny in to the sessions. The first thing they asked us, which quite impressed me, was, 'Have you told your son what you're doing here?' We hadn't. How stupid were we? They said, 'You don't know what he understands or what he doesn't understand. Tell him.' That one lesson alone was a game-changer. We try to tell Johnny everything now and he seems to understand, to some degree, most of the things that we're talking about. The important thing is to give him the opportunity to understand.

Years later Angela and I came across the book *The Reason I Jump* by Naoki Higashida, which was translated into English by the novelist David Mitchell and his wife Keiko Yoshida. Naoki is a teenage autistic boy in Japan who from an outside perspective would seem very like my own son. He flaps and skips and it appears he cannot construct a sentence. However, with the aid of a keypad he is able to communicate fluently, both in a written form and verbally. He says without the keypad he cannot constrain the words and they fly beyond his grasp, disparate.

Reading his book, the overall impression you get is that if a person is unable to communicate back to us, we cannot possibly know from our outside perspective what they understand or not. However, the possibility that they do understand should govern our approach. Imagine the frustration of being trapped in a world where you understand something but cannot communicate your understanding. Personally I believe it is better to assume a level of understanding. Even if you're wrong, it is likely to cause less of a problem than assuming no understanding. Every time you find this approach a success, that is a bonus. If you assume no understanding you are only setting yourself up for no possible gain, or even a negative effect.

You have to remember that at this stage, when Johnny was three, he wasn't interested in interacting. He was in a world of his own. So our first task was to establish contact. The Son-Rise programme taught us that the way people usually try to establish contact is like this: Imagine you're enjoying listening to the radio, and somebody next to you is saying, 'I'll tell you about this radio show. I'm enjoying this radio show. Here's something you can learn about this radio show.' Eventually you'd say, 'Sod off, I'm trying to listen.' What they said at Son-Rise was, 'If Johnny's listening, he's listening. Listen with him, be with him, join in with what he does, then when he turns and he says something to you, or he turns and just looks at you, or he gives you any attention, then you open yourself up and communicate and say, "Here's my world."'

This sounds simple and it applies to any activity, so in 'theory' I understood right away. In practice it is harder. It requires all the best attributes a human being can muster. I wasn't good at it. I wasn't equipped. My attitude was all wrong. Face to face with your own child and trying to genuinely engage him and win him over to your world is as naked as you can get. The pain I felt when I realised I just wasn't a good advert for life, reality, parenthood and humanity even, was devastating. Why would a kid want to live in a world that I represented? Generally at this time I was selfish, bitter, impatient, intolerant, self-pitying. I could go on but I think that's probably enough to make the point. It's not that I didn't have good qualities but the negative stuff was getting in the way. If I was going to help my son I had to sort myself out. The people at Son-Rise were experienced at this.

One of the things they teach is that *you* decide how you feel. No one can make you feel something, only you. Not your wife, not your child: no one. Now I know you might read that and think, 'Well, that's sort of obvious but how's that going to help?' It is obvious when you bring it to the front of your mind but at this time it wasn't at the front of mine. It's not to say you don't have feelings for your loved ones, only that you decide those feelings. It seems like a betrayal of romance or truth or some larger religious meaning to say you decide but when it comes right down to it, you do. If someone dies you can decide to feel grief at the loss or you can decide to feel relieved that they are not suffering or thankful that they are with God or with family. You can decide to be thankful for the life they had and celebrate that. You can decide to feel a combination of these things; but it is you that decides.

We'd work with Johnny hour after hour trying to help him connect, often to be slapped, bitten or, most crushing of all, ignored day after day. To decide to be OK was essential to making it work, essential to being able to go back into the room and try again, essential to doing your best when that flicker of an opening came.

When we were in the Son-Rise Centre we saw a psychiatrist. He said that he had been in the job for over twenty years and that everyone he had seen had come to him with the same problem. I was sceptical. How can everyone have the same problem? It didn't seem likely. 'Everyone,' he said, 'feels that they are not good enough.'

What a strange animal we are, us humans, that we should have such a problem. In my case he was definitely right, but if I wanted to help Johnny I needed to decide to do something about it. I needed to decide what I was going to do, what I was going to be and how I was going to feel. Only then could I be of use.

IF YOU SHOULD EVER CLIMB A TREE

I'm not sure how much weight
my head can support

but I enjoy the familiarity
the casual lack of boundaries

Without a word
we get a sense of someone

If you should ever climb a tree
I will be your low-hanging branch
I want that to be unquestioned

If my neck snaps
it was meant to be

It is the most important thing
to know

In the absence of sufficient language
I would rather seek out trees
to remind you

Chapter 9

In the White Room

This is the hardest section of this book for me to write. It was the most painful time of my life; but without it we would not be where we are today.

Parenting is not conducted in a vacuum. There are still bills to pay, work to be done. And all of this was going on not long after I'd set up Baby Cow Productions with Steve Coogan. We'd called it this after the first successful character we wrote together, Paul Calf. In the third TV outing for Paul he meets a young hippyish girl who introduces herself as, 'Dolphin, as in the mammal.' Paul replies, 'My name's Calf . . . as in baby cow.'

I had originally suggested the name 'Trans Global Ltd' as it struck me as funny having such a big name when there were only three of us sitting in a small bare office in Brighton above Spud-u-Like. I imagined someone calling and me picking up the phone and saying 'Trans Global'. The caller asking for Steve and me explaining that he was out doing some photocopying. This thought was inspired by when I worked in insurance. I had insured a firm called Dishot World Shipping who were based in Leicester. At the time they had two lorries and the policy was restricted to their use only up to seventy-five miles from base. So though they were called Dishot World Shipping they couldn't even reach the coast of England.

Steve and I had secured a two-year deal with the BBC and our first show *Human Remains*, with Julia Davis and Rob Brydon, had been a success. We had delivered on time and on budget and won awards and critical acclaim. Our second show *Dr Terrible's House of Horrible*, starring Steve, was not so well received. It was compared unfavourably with Alan Partridge at arguably the height of the Partridge fame. I still believe *Dr Terrible* is a great show but Partridge is a very high bar. What this meant was we were now under more pressure. Worse was the fact that to make scripted comedy for TV you need scripts and we didn't have any ready.

I looked at the accounts and at the options for production one day and I realised we were going to go bust. As a family we needed money. We'd bought a house we couldn't really afford and there were always costs. Not only that, but if I failed here that would probably be the end of my TV production career, before it had really got started. I came home and, exhausted, I went straight to bed, not even taking off my suit. I pulled the blankets over my head and I closed my eyes. My brain was buzzing from all these worries and I thought 'How am I going to survive this?'

The next day I went into the BBC and met Stuart Murphy, the head of the new BBC3 channel. I pitched him the idea of a new show, *How to Survive*. I realised I needed material that had already been written so I suggested we film over forty new stand-up comics and theme the material such that each show would have all the comics' material on one given subject. How to survive parents would be one, relationships another, crime, sex, holidays – as many subjects as you like. No one had a show like this and it would mean BBC3 showcased a lot of new comedy talent.

Stuart agreed but suggested I change the name. We called the show *Brain Candy* and we made fourteen episodes, putting forty-two comics on national TV who had never been on before, including Jimmy Carr, Alan Carr, Noel Fielding, Robin Ince and John Bishop. It was a success and we did a similar show with over thirty poets and then a further show with Shakespeare soliloquies performed by young actors and comics. With these shows I managed to keep the company afloat until we had more scripts, and the company survived. Having learnt the lesson, I ensured from then on that we would never find ourselves in that position again. In the next seventeen and a half years we made over four hundred TV shows, but on that day, when I fell exhausted into bed still wearing my suit, work wasn't my biggest worry.

Angela had embraced the Son-Rise programme and had gathered a few volunteers to help us work with Johnny. She'd put up posters at the local university and colleges with the heading 'Miracle in Progress'. For me, the first miracle was that people actually volunteered. In this cynical world, and especially having one foot in the selfish world of television, I had my doubts that anyone would turn up and even greater doubts that anyone would stay.

We painted Johnny's bedroom white, as we had been instructed. This was to avoid distractions. We even put stick-on frosted glass against the windows to stop Johnny just staring out and avoiding contact. We installed a two-way mirror in the door so we could all monitor the sessions and learn from each other. Angela drew up a timetable and we set about what you might call a home teaching programme. The object wasn't to teach facts; it was to encourage engagement and communication and then build upon that with whatever learning we could. Johnny's engagement was the hardest challenge and until we had that nothing else could happen. The old cliché, 'You can lead a horse to water but you can't make him drink' is at the forefront of this programme. In a series of one-hour sessions each day, we enticed Johnny to connect with us – but we couldn't demand attention; Johnny had to volunteer it.

What they taught us at Son-Rise was called 'joining'. So in the white room we would be with Johnny and we would join in with what he was doing. With Johnny at this stage being almost entirely non-verbal, this interaction would usually consist of flapping hands or banging a toy against a surface. The idea wasn't to mimic but to join in alongside him and try to enjoy the activity ourselves and see if we could understand what Johnny was getting out of the action. This would then give us both a starting point in Johnny's world at which to connect.

Invariably after a while Johnny would notice what we were doing and either investigate or alter his behaviour in response. The idea then is to spot this and use this invitation to interact and to build. Once your child responds, even in the slightest way, the aim is then to become the most interesting thing in the room. Why would you not want to play with the most interesting thing in the room? The theory is that by doing this again and again you eventually build trust and entice your child to interact in your more interesting, fun world rather than seek the safety of isolation and repetitive coping strategies.

It certainly made sense to me as a theory. You have to understand that our boy, even stood right in front of you, was in a world of his own. He avoided all eye contact; he was at times unreachable. It's very frightening when you have no means to help your own child, and the fear that it may become even worse haunts you.

Both Angela and I had decided that we were going to do this strategy and we would do it the very best we could. I can't tell you the resolve this took. There seemed to be very little progress; we were just battering our hearts against those white walls. The hours were long. Going back in took effort. Again and again we came out without any encouragement, any sign that it was working. Even when small moments of contact were made, in the next session we still seemed to be back at square one. This was no quick fix. No matter how much effort and how much thought and planning we put in and how much we wanted this to work, it wasn't going to be rushed. The main things it required were patience, stamina and never giving up hope. It sounds so easy to say these things but it was so hard to take the disappointment day after day, when nothing seemed to be working. The stakes were so high, for us the highest stakes there could be, and we couldn't fail. Nothing else in my entire life came close to this. This is where we were to fight or die.

One of the things they teach you at Son-Rise is that to ease communication you should always try to be lower down than your child. This helps with eye contact. It's harder for a child to look up, and takes more effort. If you are lower than them it's harder for them to ignore you. It also gives them power and demonstrates that you are non-threatening. It's just one of a number of little techniques we took on board and still used later. Of course, we have no choice but to use this now as Johnny towers above us at six foot three.

In the first year of our Son-Rise programme, working seven days a week, eight hours a day, every week, spring, summer, autumn and winter, without holidays, without breaks, we stayed in the white room. Johnny was potty trained in that room. We took food in, we took toys in, we painted, coloured, we built forts, buses, dens out of chairs and blankets, read books, enacted plays and stories. We took the whole world into that room with our imaginations.

If you were to go into that room after a year with that young boy you wouldn't say we had made progress. He was still very much isolated and displaying classic severe autistic behaviour. You would have had to have seen him a year before to know that we had made a little progress. It was minor progress but it was there. He trusted us and he knew what to expect. The hitting and challenging behaviours were disappearing. The rate of interaction was better, the length of each interaction a little longer. We had a long way to go but I knew we were a step along the right road. The fear he would regress was now less. Difficult as it was, we were now in a routine. We had a mode of operation and a plan.

My sister, Valerie, came to live near us and helped out in the room. Angela's mum and dad didn't go in the white room but helped in so many other ways. People who started as volunteers have become friends. We had a visit from Son-Rise and we recharged our batteries.

For three more years we carried on working in the white room as before, never letting up. Those four years in that small room with no place to hide, with everything down to us, and with so much to fight for, were the hardest days of my life. I can't imagine what they must have been like for Angela. She did by far the most work with Johnny. She bore the brunt of the everyday slog. How she kept going year after year without once complaining or feeling sorry for herself, only she can say.

I asked her what her worst moment was during this period and she said once she'd been running a bath for Johnny and, returning from fetching a towel, she found him sat in the bath with all his clothes on. Although this may even seem comical now, at the time such incidents only served to remind us both how far we had to go. What this experience was like for Johnny we will probably never begin to understand. All we could do was our best and hope that it was worth something.

After four years we decided we had done as much as we could in the room. We carried on using many of the techniques we had practised but now we felt it was time to move on and the world would be Johnny's room. Johnny was still very much autistic but at least we had a degree of interaction. We had built a relationship and trust. We knew Johnny a lot more than before we started the process. We knew his needs and we knew how we could help him overcome some of his challenges. We believed we could now cope with the world together in a way that gave Johnny a good life. What Johnny would have been like if we hadn't worked with him for four years we'll never know. What we personally would have been like is certainly less prepared.

A BED MADE INTO A CITY SIGHTSEEING TOUR BUS

On your left you will see
a boy who only plays with adults

Though he's sitting in the driving seat
he has his back to the steering wheel

Teddy bears are passengers
the wheels are paper plates

Someone has gone to a bit of trouble

But the bus is only visible from the outside
Inside it requires imagination

or the retention of the view from the outside
or is the little boy just sitting in his bed

behind a hand made barrier?

Chapter 10
Angela

I realise I am a total charlatan. Even before writing this book I was aware of the enormous amount my wife does to care for our son. Now I've had to give it more thought and investigate our lives thoroughly for this book, it is unavoidably apparent that she should be writing this. At best I am Plato to her Socrates, John the Baptist to her Jesus, Andrew Ridgeley to her George Michael, Schnorbitz to her Bernie Winters.

Of course, it would be my favourite book on Earth if Johnny could tell his own story, but as he can't I'll persevere. At least I've managed to persuade Angela to write something for this book now, which will give you another perspective.

I first met Angela in Manchester when she was at university. She'd joined a writers' group called 'Live Poets Society' that I'd helped set up. She tells me the first words I said to her were in a pub. Apparently I went up to her and said, 'I'm Henry Normal, can I buy you a drink?' I'm not sure how much I was hoping my minor self-deluded fame was going to impress her but it was weeks before I plucked up the courage to ask her out on a date.

I went round to her flat on spec only to find she wasn't there. Her flatmate told me she was in the launderette so I walked round and asked if she fancied going to Blackpool for the day. She agreed and as I drove we talked. As soon as we arrived in Blackpool she wanted to go in the tackiest gift shop I'd ever seen. 'Pants for a pound, knickers for a quid', I remember one sign saying.

We had chips and walked on the beach and she told me tales of her clubbing nights. She told me she would go to night clubs in just her bathing suit and dance all night. I looked at her youthful vitality and her beauty shining all the way through like a stick of rock and I wanted to be with her, but feared I wouldn't be able to hold on. I resigned myself to knowing that this was a good day but it wouldn't last. She was going to leave Manchester for Brighton shortly and that would be that. Ended before it had really started.

One year after she left I realised I was still thinking about her. It was impractical. She was in Brighton with a new life that I knew nothing about and we had only shared a few hours together. I was now living with a girl who, in truth, I'm sure would admit didn't love me. She was still in love with her ex. She was nice enough and creative and deserved better than I was offering at the time. It was like an early Woody Allen art house movie with not many laughs. Whenever a love song came on the radio I would realise that it was Angela I was actually picturing with me in my imagination.

I found myself my own flat and asked a mutual friend for Angela's address in Brighton. I drove the five-hour journey down from Manchester and knocked on her door. She was a little hesitant at first. She was working as a drama teacher at a local school for the deaf. She had a quiet but fulfilling life and – luckily for me – no partner.

The first time we went out together in Brighton we went to a party at one of her friends' houses. We danced and got drunk. Angela got exceedingly drunk. I ended up holding her hair back that night as she threw up in the toilet. Oh, the romance! I think after that she began to trust that I was committed.

One day when I came to see her she was making me something to eat. She'd tidied the flat and had set the table. I don't know exactly what it was about this moment, as it sounds so ordinary, but there was something. She'd made an effort and built a world for this moment, and I was part of her world and part of her moment. It seemed a way of saying 'I love you' that was more than the words themselves.

As we have a son, it'll be no surprise to you that Angela and I have had sex. I always find the importance of sex in relationships is generally overplayed in society. We've had sex many times over the years and enjoyable as it is, the individual moments don't spring to memory, but in this moment back when we first met, sitting together eating a simple meal, I could say something I'd not been able to say for many years: I felt loved.

Angela moved up to Manchester and got a job teaching juvenile offenders in a secure unit and we lived together while I co-wrote *The Mrs Merton Show* and *Coogan's Run*. After a couple of years we decided we'd move to Brighton together and start a family. It seemed strange when we decided to have sex to create a baby as opposed to just for the pleasure of it. Somehow, it was not as pleasurable. It was certainly not unpleasant but oddly enough it was different in my imagination. More functional and less romantic. The sight of Angela with her legs up against the wall afterwards, using gravity to coax the sperm in the right direction, did add to this altered perception.

We were both excited when we found out she was pregnant. I had a beautiful girlfriend I loved, a child on the way, a career in television. What could possibly go wrong?

There's an old saying, 'If you want to make God laugh, tell him your plans.'

After Johnny was diagnosed I must confess I did fantasise about running away with a younger (less tired) woman to a desert island where I had no problems. In these fantasies I'm somehow miraculously rejuvenated and virile, more handsome and with a better personality. I'd be lying if I told you I was immune to the stupidity and adolescence of most, if not all, men in middle age in wanting to hold on to my prime and recapture my youth. These frivolities are not easy for any middle-aged fool to attain at the best of times, but impossible when you have the sober responsibility of a child with autism.

I can understand why a lot of couples with an autistic child split up. Fight and flight are both natural responses. Autistic children can at times be hard to cope with and hard to love, even. If the parents' relationship isn't built on love it must be difficult to stay together as a family. Sometimes, even when there is love, the situation can become impossible. Both men and women can be selfish or can act in self-interest or out of self-preservation. Any way you examine it, it's a tribute to every parent and every relationship, to humanity even, every time any of us as individuals chooses the right way over the easy option. Of course, sometimes the right thing to do is to split up; and that too would have its difficulties.

Not that I want to break my arm patting myself on the back. I know both men and women must have faced these challenges and not all have been as lucky and/or received as much help as me in maintaining a close and functioning family. Others are yet to decide and even then it's not always just like flicking a switch. It can be ongoing, like with any relationship, only with the added weight of responsibility and the prospect of more challenges ahead.

In 2003 I found out that if you're not married, even if your name's on the birth certificate, you can't actually get your kid into a GP's surgery or even the dentist's. So I got down on one knee and I explained this to Angela. She was overtaken with the romance of it all and said, 'Of course, Henry, I'll marry you.'

We got married at Brighton Register Office and we chose Johnny's favourite music at the time to kick off the celebrations at the ceremony – the *Thunderbirds* theme tune. We kept the wedding and reception as simple and efficient as possible so that Johnny (and let's face it, I) could cope. We had nine people in attendance – including the two who functionally had to be there. We came straight back home after the ceremony for Marks and Spencer's sandwiches and a bounce on the trampoline. It may not be the best wedding I've ever attended but it was certainly the quickest and probably the cheapest. Luckily Angela was happy with all of this. Thinking back, the 'Pants for a pound' shop was a good omen.

Whenever I tell anyone about our life, Angela always asks me to point out that despite my maudlin tendencies we do have a lot of fun as a family.

One of the things Angela and I like to do most days is sit up in bed like Morecambe and Wise and have breakfast together. Johnny prefers breakfast in his own bed so he can ease into the day gently without him having to cope with any unnecessary social demands. Despite being up and wanting breakfast from any time after 4 a.m., he knows now that he has to wait. He has a routine of cereal and a drink of water around 7 a.m. followed by toast or pancakes at 7.30 a.m. This is usually served up by his mum. After this, if there's time, he will play on the computer upstairs or, if not, get washed and dressed and watch cartoons until it's time for college.

Angela and I use this time during breakfast to plan the day and talk about anything and everything. She often shows me funny bits on Facebook. My recent favourite was a photo of a 1980s soft rock band with the words 'bloody Foreigner, coming over here demanding to know what love is.' Other great lines posted are 'I hate those Russian dolls, they are so full of themselves' and 'The Flat Earth Society – members all round the world.'

Angela and I were drinking a cup of tea in bed a couple of weeks ago and Johnny was in the upstairs office, having finished playing on the computer, when we heard him shout to us one word: 'iPad'. Nothing else, just 'iPad'. We burst out laughing. He sounded like any other lazy bloody teen-ager. The thing was, this was the first time in his entire life he had ever shouted for something from another room. This was a good day. You have to celebrate these small victories, I feel, and little by little they all add up. I'm acutely aware that Angela and I are lucky to be able to celebrate these things together.

I AM NOT BELITTLED
BY YOUR CULTURE OF AMBITION

My wife has a moustache
It is plastic
It came out of a Christmas cracker

We are monarchy
in our paper hats

I am King Superman in his favourite cardigan
full of pud

It's not a thought-through image
we are ramshackle
a homely mess
like bric a brac
at a car boot

There is no sleekness to our design
no colour coordination
no concession to taste

Against all rules of fashion
and all aesthetic consideration
we are happy
at ease
daft in love

Chapter 10a
Henry by Angela

'Every old sock meets an old shoe' – Irish proverb

One day at the age of fourteen I turned a corner on my usual walk around the school grounds during 'playtime', only to fall crash, bang, wallop into obsession at first sight. I continued, for approximately five years, to give my heart to a sixth-former called Chris. If we were writing a timeline akin to one of those 'in the history of the formation of the planet, human beings have been around for approximately two minutes' things – I would say that out of those five years, Chris's interest in me lasted roughly three seconds. Possibly three and a half. After this time, my love was completely and utterly unrequited.

The upside of this was that it launched me away from writing the plays and stories that I had penned voraciously up to this point . . . towards a new genre. That of terrible poetry. Without this spur, I would never have turned up several years later in a side room upstairs at Manchester Poly, to investigate what the Live Poets Society was all about and tah dah! – have come face to face with my soulmate and future husband. They say no pain, no gain (plus – in case anyone reading this is young and currently going through a hard time – I now consider all the 'shit' that goes along with a broken heart, failed exams and loss in general to be just really, really good manure, out of which perhaps one day, many wonderful things will grow).

I remember a little about the night I first met Henry some twenty-seven years ago. I was sporting purple hot pants à la Kylie (all the rage at the time), which I had paired, seductively, with a blue hand-knitted woolly jumper. You work it out. I read a poem aloud – I don't actually remember which one it was as it could have been one of literally five million. It was undoubtedly pretentious, of that I'm sure. I listened to some other people read poems and then we all retired to the bar. Henry came over to me and said, 'Hi, I'm Henry Normal, can I buy you a drink?'. I thought – he's a bit cocky (never having heard of him before) but said yes please. And the rest, as they say . . . you've just read about.

It's been an interesting exercise writing this book with Henry. We have of course written our own sections separately and then read them through as a whole together. It's opened our eyes to some things we didn't realise at the time. I have been surprised to read about the depth of desperation Henry experienced during the early days of our life with Johnny. It's not that I didn't know he was upset at the time; I understood that. I think I was just too busy focusing all my energies on

Johnny to really see how badly Henry had been affected by the diagnosis. I do remember many times in those early years when we'd sit on the settee together, not speaking to each other because we were exhausted – but if Johnny suddenly walked past us, we'd both light up, talk to him in a jolly voice, then as he went into the next room we'd sink back to our previous positions ... and continue not speaking to each other. It was as though we only had limited reserves and we knew any energy we *did* have needed to be directed towards our son.

I know Henry has said that he thought about leaving at times. I did too (although Ryan Gosling probably wouldn't have been legal in those days). I remember feeling resentful that Henry got to head out of the house and go off and do creative things while I was left doing the lion's share of autism, even though I knew that we needed the money to pay the mortgage and buy all the resources I wanted to have at our disposal. Those inflatable ice-cream vans and alphabet floor tiles didn't pay for themselves.

I think back now and marvel that we got through it all pretty much intact. I know there were long periods when Henry and I didn't spend much time together. And when we did, the main topic of my conversation was always, of course, Johnny. I don't think Henry can have felt at all supported in either his sense of loss or in his new work venture. I didn't show much interest in the progress of Baby Cow at all, though I realise now it was at times a real worry for him. Whenever I asked him how it was going, he'd just say 'Good' anyway. Very reminiscent of Johnny's reply now when I ask him about college!

I remember a woman coming to our house in the early days of our Son-Rise programme to see if it might be something she'd like to do with her own child. She arrived in an agitated state, complaining that she'd had to push her buggy up the hill because no buses came near our house. I sort of knew that she was here under duress and it wasn't really what she was looking for, but I wanted to be open and show her what we were doing, because it was something we believed in – although we still weren't seeing any real marked 'progress' with Johnny.

She sat outside our play room and observed Johnny and me together through the two-way mirror. The session was a complete disaster. I remember Johnny was extremely anxious and bit my lip so hard it bled. The woman couldn't get out of the house quick enough, heading onto the street and barking back the words, 'This really isn't for us,' as I stood in the doorway offering to get her a taxi (blood pouring down my chin). I closed the door on the world, feeling that my life in that moment was best described as 'pitiful'.

I told Henry the above story when we were discussing writing this book. Neither of us remembered me mentioning this incident at the time. I think this is a good indicator of the distance between us in those days and that, possibly, we were both somewhat wrapped up in our own, individual pain.

But the good news is, we made it! I don't know how – perhaps bloody-mindedness. Actually, that's not true – we made it because the bottom line is we love each other. We have actually loved each other for over half of my lifetime.

I know that humour has also helped us over the years when things have been tricky. Henry is a very funny man. One of my favourite things written about him has always been that he's 'the funniest man you've never heard of'. He is the master of the quick one-liner and he makes me laugh every day. He has something several other comedians I've met over the years lack – he has a great sense of humour, of course, but he also has *a great sense of fun*. He can be incredibly daft. Here's a very quick example of the sorts of things I have to deal with on a daily basis. Just this morning I took him breakfast in bed. 'Crunchy Nuts,' I announced as I put down the tray. 'Must be the way I've laid,' he replied, wiggling his glasses like Eric Morcambe.

I also think Henry is a quite brilliant poet. His poetry has the ability to make you laugh out loud in one breath and move you to tears in the next. To me this is a very, very special gift. It's what makes Henry's work so accessible but also so powerful. It's Stealth Poetry. Just when you think it's all a bit of fun – boom, he whacks you unsuspectingly around the back of the knees and you buckle and fall to the ground.

I get on with the day-to-day running of the house. I make all of Johnny's appointments, tend to always be the one to see his teachers, take him to his various activities. However, if there is ever an issue – or something I feel I need advice on – Henry has this amazing ability to see the big picture. He will always think of things from Johnny's point of view. He often makes me see things in an entirely new light.

Most mornings, as you know, as Johnny sings and chats to himself over his two breakfast courses, Henry and I sit up in bed together for about twenty minutes and use this time to discuss what's happening during the day; tell each other ideas we've had for films and also talk over items I've heard on the news while in the kitchen. We also have other in-depth conversations that are random and varied, like discussing whether culture is influenced by climate or landscape and if free will exists. We have talked about time travel on many occasions, which neither of us can really get our heads around.

During our morning chats, Henry will also listen to my rather left-field conversation starters and never baulk. He'll always discuss ideas with me. For example I might say this sort of thing:

'I know that cherry blossom looks beautiful – but what if for that small window when the trees are in bloom, the tree itself is in pain? Maybe blossom for a tree is like a bout of acne – or hideous period pain? I'm always a bit sad when all the flowers fall off – but maybe for the tree, it's a relief.' We then debate the possibility that this could be the case, without any suggestion that I could just be an idiot.

We once had a conversation in response to the question 'Out of all the people we know, is there anyone whose life you'd rather have?' We thought long and hard about our friends and family. Some of the people we knew seemed on the surface to lead charmed lives – they had the kids, the house, the job – . . . but actually, on deeper reflection, they all seemed to have something else going on that we'd rather not have to have. Their own problems or issues or trials. It was an eye-opener, that discussion. We realised then that the old adage is true, that if we got together with everyone we knew and put all our troubles in a pile in the middle of the room with the proviso that we could take home someone else's, we'd all probably just grab our own back again. I think at least we know how to deal with our own 'shit'. Or if not deal with, develop strategies for coping with.

It may seem a bit daft to say, but I think these few precious minutes every day, putting the world to rights and exploring options, possibilities and ridiculous theories, really help Henry and me stay connected. It is interesting to see how much of our time together now *isn't* spent discussing, worrying, analysing and generally being preoccupied with autism.

We also now get most Saturday nights 'off' from being special needs parents, as my mum and dad look after Johnny for us. You can imagine how much we appreciate this and how lucky we feel. I am aware that not many other people in our situation get this

regular 'respite'. There are many, too, who have difficult relationships with their families. Who feel unsupported, or who just live
just too far away. We try never to take this time off for granted. I
often check in with my mum and dad to make sure that they want
to continue having Johnny stay with them. They are in their early
seventies now and I worry that it's a lot for them, especially if
Johnny is 'up and at it' very early. They tell me that having Johnny
is 'what keeps us going'.

Some people may think that because we work in the media
we lead a very glamorous life. I can categorically say – this is
not the case. We don't socialise with anyone in the industry.
Let's be honest, we don't actually socialise with *anyone* that
often. Our Saturday nights tend to go like this – I come home
from having dropped Johnny off at my parents' and having
done a big weekly shop at Sainsburied (as I affectionately call
it) at around 6.30 p.m. Henry is upstairs writing. I jump in the
bath. Henry makes us both beans and egg on toast (his
Signature Dish) around 7.30 p.m. We watch a film. I go to bed
around 10.30 p.m. Henry stays up and watches something sci-
fi-y or football or a history documentary. Basically something
he knows I have no interest in. Sad as these Saturday nights in
might seem to others, they are perfect in my book – as well as
being a lifeline. That we are both happy with this unadventur-
ous crashing out is a testament to the fact that we 'don't spoil
another pair', as my Grandma Norms used to say. That's about
as romantic as I get.

When Henry told me he was going to retire from Baby Cow I
was surprised. But I could see how tired he was from the four-
hours-a-day commute. He'd been doing it for seventeen years.
He'd also given his all. I used to sometimes feel that he didn't get
the recognition he deserved.

I continue to be proud of Henry every day. I love the fact that he has gone full circle, back to writing poetry. That he was brave enough to leave Baby Cow behind and return to his own creative endeavours. I met him when he was a struggling poet, with no arse in his trousers, earning £3,000 a year, performing up and down the country. I used to really enjoy going to his gigs. I'd get a kick out of him doing the odd bit of spiel about his current relationship. I'd stand at the back and think, yes – that's us he's talking about. Now, some twenty-seven years later, I continue to be there supporting him. The odd bit of spiel has become the backbone of the material these days of course and I still sometimes find myself thinking, yes – that's us he's talking about.

Recently Henry was given a special award by BAFTA. It was such a great night and I felt that during it, he finally got the recognition he deserved. It was one of the few media events I've ever been to that was actually filled with love and appreciation. Such thoughtful things were said about Henry. I was so delighted for him. He has an incredible talent and it was brilliant to see it so celebrated.

Most of our good friends and family had been invited but with the noise, waiting and number of people, it wasn't really going to be suitable for Johnny. My parents kindly offered to stay at home with him. The three of them, however, were there in spirit – and digitally! – being beamed in via a little bit of video taken on my phone the day before. Between John Bishop introducing Henry for the question and answer session and Frank Skinner doing a funny five minutes, my parents and Johnny gave Henry a message from the large video screen above the stage. To me it was the perfect example of how Johnny helps us put everything in perspective. My mum and dad were very sweet and funny and sandwiched between them was our lovely son. The entire room wiped a little tear away, I think, when Johnny said at the end, 'I love you Daddy.' Even though Henry and I knew this had been prompted, it meant so much to us. I think only other parents of children with special needs could ever really know how hard-fought-for, by the three of us as a family, such moments are.

Chapter 11
Commenting

Angela's mum, Sarah, took Johnny to see the flower show in Seaford Church a few years back. The arrangements were beautiful and Johnny always enjoys the tranquillity of a church, the high ceilings and the stained glass. He sat with his grandma in the pews and, seeing her hold her hands together in prayer, he copied. She explained that when you pray you can talk to God and you can tell him your troubles and that you can ask him for help and other things. They sat together for a moment in the quiet and then Sarah asked him what he was asking for. 'Ham and chips,' he said emphatically.

Johnny is now quite confident in requesting certain things he wants and answering yes and no to questions. He can make choices from a list, though we often check he's not just repeating the last word in the list. If he does request the last item in a list we will repeat the list in a different order to be sure.

He has a limited vocabulary for self-initiated requests, although it serves him and it is expanding with his experience. We have to guard against him just falling into a pattern of call and response. If we say 'What meat would you like?' he's more than likely to say 'pork'. So if we've just had pork we might then list all the different meats he eats. If he still says pork, we would talk about all the different ways you can eat pork and ask him to choose. Asking a second question is a useful way to try to draw him out and investigate a little of what he knows or is thinking about.

My biggest worry about asking Johnny questions or to make a choice, is whether he feels there is a right and wrong answer. There are at least two types of questions, of course. Those where there is a set answer and those where you are asking for an opinion or preference. I'm often not sure Johnny understands the difference at any one time, but at least now he is making unprompted verbal requests. This is not something he did in the early days and it has grown steadily over the last seventeen years.

It's difficult to say if Johnny ever comments. Maybe he does and we don't understand. I can think of very few occasions where I think he might be commenting and only two where I'm sure he did. The two I'm sure of were quite recently and I'm hoping it is something he is developing. The first was at Christmas in Portugal. Vila do Bispo beach is one of the most beautiful beaches in the Algarve and at times in my opinion one of the most striking beaches anywhere in the world. We tend to go there at least once when we are in Portugal even though it's a thirty-minute drive from where we stay. Johnny always looks forward to it. We generally walk along the beach and paddle, then sit in the cafe for a fresh orange juice or a hot chocolate depending on the weather.

As I walked down to the beach this December with Johnny, he declared, unprompted, 'The cafe is closed.' No one had used this phrase that day; it wasn't echolalia. No one had asked him a question. It was a genuine comment, perfectly audible and directed at me. This was the first time in his entire life I could be sure he was voluntarily communicating, verbally, an observation of the world without any outside instigation. Now Johnny is motivated by food and drink, so I'm sure that this was part of the drive, but it was certainly a breakthrough moment. He was comfortable enough with my presence and confident enough to speak.

It was another six months before I witnessed his second comment. Angela and I take it in turns to drive Johnny to college Monday to Thursday. I particularly like driving him the twenty-five-minute journey as it gives me some time alone with him. He knows the routine and he is generally happy. Like most men, I find it easier to talk to people while we are facing the same direction rather than face to face. Football is good for that. Two men won't say, 'Let's spend two hours together talking,' but during a match that's what happens and you can talk about anything. Often the game will bring out discussions on honesty, loyalty, commitment, fear and a whole range of conversations about life. If you said to most men we are going to sit down and talk about big issues even for five minutes they'd run a mile. There is something easier about sharing an experience without pressure, side by side, that allows communication to seep out naturally.

Some days in the car Johnny will request music and – we listen to a wide range of pop CDs – and some days he will most definitely want the music turned off. 'Music off' or 'Music on,' he will say adamantly. He often sings bits of songs, a little more repetitively than you might like for your own sanity. He doesn't like to sing at the same time as other people for more than a couple of seconds but he enjoys taking turns. So if you sing one line, he will sing the next line and a few of our journeys are a sporadic karaoke duet. Some days he won't sing and I'll talk to him about what's happening that week, and about incidents along the journey. Occasionally I'll ask a question and sporadically he'll say a line from a film he's watched or a non sequitur I often can't recognise.

A week ago, however, we had just set off and I was driving down towards the traffic lights when Johnny said 'Dead.' I looked to the side of the road and there was the remains of a fox or rabbit, I couldn't be sure which. It was a mess and had clearly been run over. I tried to extend the conversation. I asked him what kind of animal it was. 'Fox,' he said. I asked him how it had died but he didn't volunteer anything. I talked to him about death for a short while, then changed the subject, as it was a bright sunny morning and I didn't think dwelling on death was a good way to deliver him to college.

This was interesting, though, in that not only was he definitely including me in his observation of the world, but he knew enough to recognise death. Angela and I have spoken to him about relatives who have died and he's been to a couple of funerals. Several films and books he sees have death in them but, beyond fish on the beach or on his plate, served with the head still on, this was probably the first creature in the real world he had actually seen dead; pork and beef tend not to be served with the heads still on, outside of medieval banquets.

Angela has recognised various lines he will repeat when he's upset – 'White tunnel' was one he said when he was younger. We never got to the bottom of where that came from. Then for a time, when upset, he would say 'Red,' which could have several explanations including traffic lights. Red, of course, represents anger or danger or more generally to stop or not do something, which he might have picked up from lots of films and books. Recently, if he's ever upset he'll say 'Mr Potato Head,' perhaps from the *Toy Story* character, who is quite grumpy and in one line from the last film asks for his 'angry eyes'. It is never easy to be sure, though if Johnny says 'Mr Potato Head' repeatedly in an agitated manner you can be certain he is not happy. From the outside this must sound surreal.

Occasionally at home when we sit at the table waiting to be served food he will sing, 'Why are we waiting?' There is certainly an element of fun to the song and to his mum's mock outrage, which he enjoys. If Johnny is singing it is quite likely he is in a good mood. I must confess I am to blame for teaching him this song and there have been a few embarrassing times in restaurants when I've regretted it.

There are times when Johnny's sporadic non sequiturs seem relevant but we are not sure if they are actually meant. The year before last I'd driven Angela and Johnny from the

Algarve to Sintra in Portugal, just north of Lisbon. Lord Byron visited and is said to have fallen in love with it. If you look at images of Sintra on Google you'll see it is like a mountain with several castles and palaces giving the appearance of one huge bright ornamental folly. A perfect day out for Angela and Johnny, and with their shared love of art and decoration.

You are not allowed to drive your car to the very top of the mountain but can elect to walk or take a tuk-tuk, which is a like a golf buggy only faster. On the way down we paid a few euros for a tuk-tuk driven by one of the seasoned locals. There are no sides to these vehicles and no seat belts. The incline is in parts somewhere between thirty and forty-five degrees and is mostly cobbled. It's a bumpy ride even at low speed, but our driver was very much in a hurry, it seemed, and we clung on for dear life. Not wanting to frighten Johnny, Angela and I faked the best smiles we could and tried to make light of the tangible danger while gently reminding Johnny to hold on tight. Johnny was loving it. He has a great sense of balance and wasn't in the least bit worried. Halfway down the hill, seemingly from nowhere, Johnny started to sing the chorus of Kate Bush's 'Hammer Horror'.

I've no idea if he genuinely knew how funny it was. Angela and I laughed, of course, and he seemed to be enjoying the moment. I do wonder sometimes how many comments we may miss because we don't get the joke or the reference when he says something seemingly random.

A lot of his speech is either one-word requests or words reaffirming his timetable. So in the morning he will come into our bedroom and say what he wants for breakfast, like 'Toast and peanut butter'. We'll confirm 'Toast and peanut butter'. Then he'll say 'Watching *Tom and Jerry*' and we'll confirm 'Watching *Tom and Jerry*'. Now you can say anything you want when he says 'Toast and peanut butter', but he won't be happy until you've actually repeated the words. If you say 'Yes that's what you're having' he'll repeat 'Toast and peanut butter', as he wants you to say those words. He's very good if we have to substitute, say, jam or pancakes or whatever. No matter what the new breakfast, though, he will say it – 'Pancakes and jam' – and he likes you to repeat it. Then he'll say 'Watching *Tom and Jerry*' and he likes you to repeat that. Sometimes he seems to need further reassurance and he'll wait a second and repeat the request again, always in the correct order, like he's ensuring that you know the sequence.

If you talk to Johnny about his timetable he will repeat key words. For example if he's going to the shops on a Saturday morning he'll say 'Mummy's car, Lush, 42 juice, Infinity Foods, pizza.' Often the end of a sequence will be his next meal, as if he's only interested in planning his day up to his next food break. He always repeats the sequence in the right order. A lot of times once he's said a sequence he will repeat the first word in the sequence – 'Mummy's car' in this case. Maybe to fix the first part in his head or maybe to prompt action on the sequence.

Angela is very good in her intonation when responding to his repetition. Though at times it seems tantamount to 'nagging', Angela will either make light of it or answer as though it's the first request for confirmation. We often try to spin off into enacting other conversations but are seldom successful unless we ask a direct question. Often after answering the question Johnny will seek to reaffirm the sequence.

I've observed that the word 'why' is particularly diffi-cult for Johnny. If you use the word why in any ques-tion he can't seem to find any answer. I'm not sure if he quite understands the concept or whether he finds it difficult to communicate an answer. I've taken to avoid-ing the word nowadays. It strikes me that when ques-tioning motivation the question 'why?' can be replaced with two different questions. 1. What do you want (or want to happen)? 2. What do you want to stop (or to go away)?

For example, if Johnny is biting the back of his hand it's no use asking him why he is doing that. You'll get nothing. If you ask him what he wants he may tell you, 'Go in the car' and then you know he's frustrated with waiting. If you get no response from asking what do you want, you can then ask him, 'What do you want to stop or what do you want to go away?' He may then tell you, 'Noise,' and you can ask, 'What noise?'. Often it will be something like a window is open and he can hear the wind or the seagulls. Short easy-to-understand exchanges often get to the root of the problem.

I find it quite illuminating when looking at motivations to realise that it comes down to a basic choice of wanting something to happen or not and wanting it to stop/go away or not. To me this has made communicating with Johnny and, to be honest, with my own thoughts, much simpler.

Nowadays he's very good at saying 'yes' and 'no' but his 'no' can be quite firm, like when we offer him avocado or sweet potato. He even refuses to peel sweet potato, so don't try to slip one in with the 'white' potatoes. He does make me laugh sometimes when people politely offer him a lovely treat, and rather than a polite reply he says 'No' abruptly and then wanders off. I do envy his clarity sometimes.

Angela has just come into my office to tell me a story. She dropped Johnny off at school this morning in her car. As the school doors opened, all the other special needs children waiting in their respective cars and taxis started to emerge. 'OK, let's go,' she said to Johnny, who replied with the chorus from an early Nick Cave song from his Birthday Party days. 'Release the bats,' he sang cheerfully.

AN ACCEPTABLE USE OF AN EXCLAMATION MARK

Johnny looks good in a hat
not self-conscious

I'm always wondering if I should
take a hat off when I go in doors

Johnny is definite
if he's keeping it on, that's it

I'm guessing he's deciding what he wants
not what you think about it

He came over to me
yesterday

and put his arm around my shoulder
for a second

Then he said
'Daddy to go'

I said
'You came over to me!'

but those are my rules
not his

Chapter 11a
Language by Angela

Johnny is now mostly a joyful, bouncy nineteen-year-old man – with enough language a lot of the time, using single words, to get his needs met. He is also the most loved person I know. We laugh a lot every day. He has a very funny sense of humour and he really enjoys being squashed and squeezed and me shouting, 'Johnny! Have I told you how much I love you today yet!?' several times a day. It is a myth that autistic people are not affectionate. It is a myth that they all want to be alone. There is a section in the book *The Reason I Jump* about this. The author Naoki says that he doesn't believe anyone really wants to be left on their own. He says that he thinks that autistic people worry that they cause distress and trouble for others and that's why it's difficult for them to hang around neurotypical people. I remember a friend, the mum of another autistic boy, telling me that when she read this chapter, entitled 'Do You Prefer to Be On Your Own?', it made her weep and take to her bed for three days.

When Johnny was first being assessed, we were seen by a speech therapist at the hospital. She was great. Her name was Sue Crane and she was one of the few professionals we met at the time who I thought seemed to know what she was talking about. Subsequent speech therapists have come and gone. Henry and I would sigh to ourselves, as every single one seemed to start each session by delving into their bag and pulling out a bubble wand – as though this was literally some magic way of encouraging speech. It never seemed to work with Johnny. Not that we hadn't already tried it ourselves. Duh! Route one! (I am aware of the irony of writing 'duh' in a section about language.)

I expressed to Sue my concerns that Johnny would never speak. I distinctly remember she replied, 'Oh, I'm pretty sure he'll speak. It's just what he'll talk about . . .' The sentence was left hanging. I didn't really know what she meant and didn't feel in a position to ask. I'm guessing now that she meant his language would probably not follow a conventional path. It is fair to say that the majority of Johnny's utterances are seemingly random lines from songs and films, although sometimes he uses them as a way of expressing himself and they don't seem random at all. If we listen hard and are vigilant enough there are clues. For example, in the past, when Johnny was outwardly looking stressed, he'd shout, 'Harry hold on!' I realised later, while watching a film with him, that this phrase comes from a scene in which two characters are in grave danger and it's all very scary. His exclamation in those moments now made perfect sense to me.

Johnny is unable at present to have what you or I might call a conversation. I am hopeful that this might come. He isn't able to explain how he feels either – or tell us if he has any internal pain going on, although he can ask for a plaster nowadays, and show me where it needs to go. Having said that, he currently likes to put a plaster on different fingers every morning for no apparent reason, but this phase will come and go – like the one when he would (randomly to us) take all his sheets off the bed every Wednesday night, or when he wouldn't put his feet down on grass, or get out on any level apart from Level 3 of the car park . . . To any newly diagnosed families – in my experience, these phases can change. Don't think that they are fixed in stone. They may just get replaced by other seemingly mystifying behaviour!

Johnny often shouts out phrases and sentences from films, with great joy. He likes it when we join in. Many times Johnny has looked at me with expectant eyes and encouraged me to yell, 'May I introduce the Duke of Weaseltown' – which then has to be followed with a disdainful 'It's Wizzletown!' I must admit I am quite partial to this kind of activity, as I get to do all the Disney voices. We once spent fifteen minutes swinging on a country gate shouting, 'Prolix! Prolix! Nothing a pair of scissors can't fix!' which is a Nick Cave lyric. I had no idea at the time what prolix meant and I'm damned sure Johnny didn't; he just liked the sound of it. He also comes out with some amazing non sequiturs and song mash-ups, my favourite of which was a combination of the 1980s hit 'Einstein A Go Go' – Johnny sang the bit, 'You better watch out . . . You better beware' but then replaced the 'Albert said that E equals MC squared' with 'Santa Claus is coming to town.'

Johnny still occasionally gets distressed and can lash out or bite himself. He is a big lad now and I know that if he really lost it, he could easily put any one of us in hospital. Living with possible violence still feels like a taboo subject for parents of children with special needs. We don't like to talk about it. There is a great anxiety around it. The ultimate fear is, of course, that faceless 'authorities' will take our children away from us. The thing is, when it comes to autism I believe that every 'behaviour' we see is expressed for a reason. In my experience, there is never malicious intent. I don't like to use or hear the word 'aggression' in regards to autism – to me this implies a feeling that goes along with any acts of hitting out. In my view, violent behaviour exhibited by those on the spectrum is only ever a survival mechanism. A form of communication. A desperate last resort.

Chapter 12
Dads

Chris Bruce, an Australian I met when I was nineteen, was the first dad I ever saw really play with his child. Not only that, he cuddled his boy and kissed him on the head. This was 1976 and Chris was a new generation of father. He was somewhat exotic as well, being Australian. He was the first Australian I'd ever met and he worked as a salesman at my office, an old-fashioned insurance brokers where we had to wear suits and ties, even in the height of summer. He wore sunglasses all the time during the summer, even indoors sometimes. He dressed in well-cut, modern, lightweight suits and he had an energy about him that was different. I think it was optimism. Believing in a better future for your kids seemed in short supply in the council estates of Nottingham at the time. To me, Chris was a shining beacon of hope. He was the dad I wanted to be when I was older. Refusing to be brought down by England, he moved back to Australia and I never saw or heard from him again. He's the man I always think about whenever I see one of those mugs that say 'Great Dad'.

To be fair, as a kid I did once see Gary Carter's dad play football with his sons. Gary was a lad in my class at school and a good mate when I was around fourteen. We'd play football together for hours, with a burst ball, or a tennis ball if that was all that was available. I even remember once, the tennis ball split in two and we played with half a tennis ball. Every time you kicked it, the semicircle would curve like a Brazillian banana shot. We also played with a scrunched-up paper bag once. Whatever the ball, or substitute, if you could kick it a few feet then you could play football.

Gary was the lad most likely to succeed. He was good-looking, intelligent, good at football, sociable and he had a supportive mum and dad. It was just a council house like ours they lived in. Nothing special, but what was special was you could feel the love between them. It felt like a real home; something I'd missed since my mum died. I remember Gary and I were talking in his living room one day about superheroes; Batman and the X-Men and my favourite, the lesser known Doctor Fate. Gary's mum was listening in and said to Gary, 'Do you know who my hero is?' We both stopped and waited to hear. It wasn't usual for a parent to get involved in such discussions. 'Your dad,' she said to Gary. 'He gets up every day and goes to work to make sure we've got this lovely home.' I loved her for saying that. That was the sort of wife I wanted when I got married.

My own dad did once play football with me, when I was about sixteen. We were on holiday in Skegness or maybe Ingoldmells, on the beach one lazy sunny day. He rolled up his shirt sleeves and played in goal. I took shots and we both took penalties. It's a good memory. Why we'd never played before or since I don't know. I was told he once had a trial for Derby County when he was a lad, but when I was a kid he always seemed to be in work clothes, or Sunday best for special occasions. Like a lot of working men of his generation, he always wore a suit or suit trousers and shirt, often with a tie or with a V-neck jumper if it was cold. He would never wear jeans or T-shirts. I don't recall him ever wearing a polo shirt. A short-sleeved shirt without a tie was the most casual I ever saw him.

In the period before my mum died I can't remember having any interaction with my dad. I'm sure he was there, either driving the car or taking the photo, but he was more the ultimate authority figure, just out of sight. There was a TV show at the time called *Wait Till Your Father Gets Home*, obviously taking its title from a phrase mothers would say as a deterrent, and my relationship with my father up to the age of eleven was based on that thought. I had no idea of my dad as a person. Maybe being the middle child of five had something to do with this. Maybe being the second boy. Maybe it was me. I'm sure I displayed autistic tendencies.

I do see the possibility that my dad was autistic, but being from the north in those days you'd just expect such a bloke to get an allotment or a shed. He'd constantly stack small coins on the mantelpiece and had set habits and routines. From his diet to the clothes he wore, he chose the familiar.

He would study the horse racing forms for hours in forensic detail. He'd tell the same stories again and again and although he seemed to hold his own in company he would never seek it out. Certainly throughout my childhood he presented quite a lonely figure.

In comparison, my relationship with my mum had felt warm and close. Having had five kids, she'd been a big earth-mother type as far back as I can remember. I still see her face in my three sisters. My mother had a 'can-do' attitude. She was an independent woman, not the archetypal 'kept' woman, at home. She had established her own grocery delivery business and insisted on her own bank account, which she made sure she held in a different bank to my dad's.

I don't think my mum and dad's relationship ran smoothly towards the end. She did once talk to us about leaving and taking us with her. I wouldn't be surprised if she was having an affair at the time of her accident. I once saw her, as I happened to pass by, having a laugh with a man parked up near Bracebridge shops and she seemed a little fazed to see me. After her funeral, a bloke I didn't know kept asking if we were alright and wanting to help. It's not something I ever spoke about with my dad but then again he hardly ever spoke about Mum. In the forty years since her death he didn't mention her more than a dozen times and usually only when asked a direct question.

A year before she died Mum was very ill with jaundice and she asked me to go outside and check on whose roof a crow was cawing. It wasn't until I was older that I understood the significance – that crows are an omen of death. It wasn't our house; it was an old lady's house on the other side of Baythorn Road. I was able to give Mum the good news. I did wonder later if the old lady opposite had heard the crow.

When Mum died we went to the funeral at the local church, St John's, but none of her children were allowed at the grave. My dad never slept in their bed again. For years he slept downstairs on the sofa and my elder sister Linda recalls sometimes hearing him crying himself to sleep.

Years later when my dad was dying we asked if he wanted to be buried with Mum as he had bought a second plot at the time of her death. He said he just wanted to be cremated and he wasn't bothered what we did with the ashes. I could tell Linda was upset that he didn't choose to be with Mum.

When I thought about it, this was typical of my dad. He never really did anything wrong in his life, as far as I can tell, but there were things he didn't do. As a son or daughter, especially when you are young, you look to your parents to take charge in the way you see modelled on films or TV. I'd see JR Ewing from *Dallas*, who, though not a nice bloke, was a good dad, and he'd say to his son, 'I love you son.' He'd also take care of business. Only someone weak like Cliff Barnes would shirk responsibilities. The idea that 'a man's gotta do what a man's gotta do' was very much to the fore in those days. But that wasn't the nature of my dad, or maybe it was but he saw his duty as going to work. He could have stayed at home and claimed benefits, but he refused all such monies. Maybe it was pride. He'd go to work and he'd come home and watch TV, and as kids we would pretty much fend for ourselves most days. After Mum died, it seemed to me, we were leaderless. It was like Captain Kirk had died and Spock was not wanting to take charge of the *Enterprise.*

It must have been difficult for my dad. He had five kids all looking to him for help and he couldn't cope. At least when he remarried some twelve years after Mum's death, he inherited a grown-up family and no one placed any demands on him. I was grateful that his second wife, Maureen, had given him a new lease of life. I mention Maureen on stage occasionally as well as my dad. I tell a story about how we can see the same world so differently. My dad and Maureen were sitting with me and Angela watching the film *Titanic* one night. It was about an hour into the story and the ship had hit the iceberg and had started to sink. The stern was now high in the air and people were trying to cling on as men, women and children all around were falling into the icy water. Everywhere was panic, lifeboats were overturning, people screaming and crying. Angela and I were gripped with the emotion of it all. Maureen turned to my dad on the sofa and said, 'We're going on a cruise, aren't we, Frank?'

As my dad lay dying of cancer, Maureen didn't want to be alone with him through the night so I and others took it in turns to stay with him. My brother-in-law Tony was a real star and stepped up. He has a lovely matter-of-fact attitude to getting a job done. A good man to have on your team. Solid and no-nonsense, yet kind. The sort of man you'd want by your side should you ever be in that position. You won't be surprised to hear he's a great dad himself.

I got the train to Nottingham from work in London on a Friday night and slept on the sofa next to my dad's bed. We didn't talk much. I gave Dad a drink and lay awake listening to him breathe. The day me and my sisters talked to Dad about graves and cremation I went home to Brighton afterwards. On the train journey back a revelation occurred to me that seems so obvious now but I'd never realised before.

As I replayed Dad's words through my head it became clear – we were now the second family. Even though we were Dad's flesh and blood, he was so involved with Maureen's family they had now become his first family. This was quite a surprise. A totally unexpected new thought that seemed so fundamental to our relationship. I felt stupid for not understanding this before.

This was reaffirmed the next time I visited Dad to stay overnight. When I arrived he was being shaved by my stepbrother Ian. I like Ian; he's always been friendly and I feel he's an honest, helpful, straightforward bloke. I watched him shave my dad and was pleased Dad had someone like Ian to care for him. I think I'd been blinded for too long by this notion that he was the dad and that even now he should finally step up and take charge of his family, and so I'd not realised how old he'd become.

Looking at photos of him in his eighties I can now see he'd become the one who needed looking after. I have no excuse for any absence of thought I'm guilty of. The only reasoning I can bring to mind is that this was never role-modelled for me. As a kid I'm sure I didn't set the rules of the relationship. I certainly fell into this assumption of a lack of thought early on. Maybe in his later years he made an effort at times, but by then perhaps it was difficult for both of us. It seems too easy to pass this miscommunication off as autism in either Dad or me. 'Absent within the same room' is a phrase that comes to mind when I think of my dad in the later years. Though he was never diagnosed with anything, he showed signs of forgetfulness and would repeat the same stories and the same jokes again and again.

I certainly loved my dad and respected him, though I would have had him more engaged with his kids throughout his life. Odd for me then wanting to learn from that experience and be more involved with my own child, only to find my lad himself at first wanting no engagement and repeating phrases again and again.

I took Johnny to see his granddad several times but it was always difficult. Dad and Maureen already had plenty of kids and grandkids vying for attention. If I found it difficult at times to talk to my dad then the short period of time Johnny had with him, and Johnny's personality in the early years, all led to us expecting very little from the relationship. That's not to say there were not good moments and some happy memories over the years but I was aware neither I nor my brother had produced a grandson who would carry on the family name in the traditional sense.

I remember my dad came to see me perform once and he said to me, 'Do you talk fast in case people don't laugh and then it's not so far to the next joke?' Not my worst review. He was very proud when I worked in TV as that was a 'proper' job. He seemed very proud of the fact I'd bought a villa in Portugal, although he never wanted to go there. Strangely enough he had no photos of me in the house at all, but in the living room he had a photo of the villa.

His ashes were to be scattered in the garden of rest behind the crematorium. It always seemed such an impersonal place to me, but I wasn't in charge. If that was his wish I can respect that, but I can't help but find it a little sad.

The last time I saw my dad alive was a Saturday morning just after his ninetieth birthday. I'd stopped over with him on the Friday night. He'd reminisced about fishing with his dad when he was young. I think it gave him comfort to think of that. I didn't ask him what memories he had of the two of us when I was a kid and I couldn't offer any up. I was conscious that when I'm lying on my deathbed not only will I not have such memories of my dad to pass on, but my son may well not be interested in listening. It's almost comical if you enjoy dark irony.

As I left the house Dad told me it was cold out; and his last words to me were to tell me to put my hat on. That's the nearest he would ever come to saying 'I love you.'

Below is a poem I wrote for my dad imagining a conversation that never actually happened.

TINNED FRUIT AND EVAPORATED MILK

So it was last Saturday teatime when I called in at my
    dad's
He was sat checking his racing results
I ambled across the room and turned off the TV

'Just a second,' I said tentatively before he started to
    protest
'I've got something important to tell you'

I hesitated a moment, then bracing myself I came right
    out with it
'I love you Dad'

'Don't be so bloody daft,' he said

'It's not daft,' I said 'I love you'

'Err . . . alright, put kettle on then,' he said

'No, you're supposed to say – I love you too son – c'mon
   Dad you've seen *Dallas*'

'I've not got time for all this bloody nonsense, I'm off to
   the Legion,' he said

So I'm following him down the garden and I'm saying
'look Dad, I'm in my fifties now and I think it's about time
   it was out in the open
I love you'

And he's trying to shh me in case the neighbours hear

So I shout louder, 'I don't care if the whole world hears,
I'm not ashamed of my feelings, I love you, you're my
   dad'
And I give him a big wet kiss on the forehead
'What do you say Dad, what do you say?'

'Oh Henry,' he said, 'Where did I go wrong?'

Chapter 13
Maternal Grandparents

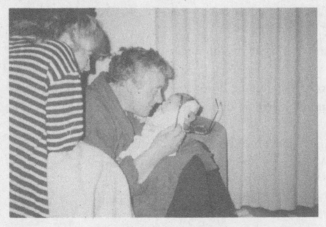

Of all the people who have helped us with Johnny it's Angela's parents, Andrew and Sarah, who have done the most.

When I first met Angela she lived with her parents in Peterborough, which, as every true football fan knows, is the home of 'The Posh'. So being working-class, when I first visited I was a little nervous. When Angela mentioned that her dad was quite fussy about table manners I was conscious I needed to be on my best behaviour. It mattered to me to make a good impression. I was in love with their daughter and I wanted Angela to be happy. I knew she was close to her parents and wouldn't be happy if we didn't get along. They lived in a neat detached house with a well tended garden on the edge of a quiet, newly built estate. Her dad was a tax inspector at the time. This was a far cry from the council estate where I'd grown up.

We sat down for dinner and the atmosphere was friendly but I was still a little nervous. Then for dessert Sarah brought out apple pie on which she'd placed a choc ice. I just had to laugh. I'd never seen that before – apple pie with a choc ice. They were as working-class as I was really. The atmosphere lightened and I began to relax a little.

The other thing I was nervous about was age. Angela is thirteen years younger than me; Angela's mum, Sarah, is only nine years older and Andrew is only ten years older than me. So I was conscious that they would be protective towards their daughter and I didn't know if this age difference would be a problem for them.

Angela had arranged for me to stay overnight. I naturally assumed we would be in separate rooms but Angela said 'No'. Her mum had set up a double bed in the back room downstairs. We said our goodnights and I went and lay in bed waiting for Angela. I finished my apple pie first; I didn't want to look too keen. Angela went to the bathroom, as women tend to do. The bedroom door opened and Sarah came in. She came round my side of the bed, wished me a good night and to my astonishment she tucked me in. I couldn't believe it. I was being tucked in, a man in his thirties. It was the best contraceptive I've ever seen. After that, I couldn't possibly get amorous that night.

When Johnny arrived, Sarah and Andrew were so happy. Angela's grandmother Norma, known as Norms, was alive then and there was a lovely warmth about Angela's family that felt safe and nurturing. When Johnny started to display unusual behaviour everyone seemed to take it in their stride. There were no big alarm bells ringing and although everyone was supportive, Angela and I were encouraged to sort Johnny out ourselves.

We spent the millennium night at Sarah and Andrew's new place in Sheringham, Norfolk. Andrew had retired and they'd bought a bed and breakfast establishment. Norms had moved to a seafront flat nearby. So there we were, at supposedly the biggest party night of the century, in this quiet East Anglian backwater. Angela and I sneaked out around midnight to see what the celebrations were like in the centre of Sheringham, only to find there were half a dozen teenagers hanging round the soon-to-be-closed Woolworth's. To all intents and purposes it was as if 1960 had finally arrived.

By the time we found out Johnny was autistic Norms had passed away. She was a quiet, kind, gentle soul who hated having her photo taken and had the patience of a saint with Johnny. Having a perforated ear from childhood, she wasn't able to fly, so Angela and I once took her on holiday with us and Johnny to an Art Deco hotel on Burgh Island just off the south coast. I wish we'd spent more time with her. Had she lived longer we had planned to go on a cruise. If ever I had a lesson on carpe diem, Norms's death brought it home.

Angela's grandma was the first person I ever saw in a hospice. Her ill health and death was a pattern I was going to see repeated. Not having seen the process before, I was surprised at how fast her health deteriorated. We joked with her about her meals of soup and ice cream. Then the last time I saw her we knew her death would be in days, if not hours. When I left her bedside I couldn't bring myself to say the word 'goodbye'. I didn't want it to be goodbye and saying the word seemed somehow like accepting it. I wasn't ready to accept it.

Norms used to tell stories of growing up being left-handed. She was made to write with her right hand. If caught writing with her left, she was punished and her left hand was tied up to stop her using it. This seems like something from the Middle Ages but was only two generations back. Even today in parts of the world there is prejudice against left-handed people; in Albania it was illegal not all that long ago. This seems like some Monty Python joke but it's true. The language we use today about right-and left-handedness still shows the attitude. We say someone is 'gauche', from the French for 'left', to mean awkward and clumsy, or 'adroit', from the French 'right', to mean skilful or clever and straight. It does make me wonder how people in the future will look back and judge our current attitudes and speech towards autism today.

As I mentioned earlier, when Angela and I went over to Son-Rise in Massachusetts we didn't want to be apart from Johnny for more than a day, so Sarah and Andrew came with us and looked after Johnny while we were at the training centre. They have been such a fantastic help above and beyond the call of duty. We go on holiday together regularly and they are so great with Johnny. They have their own relationship with him, to the point now where when we drop him off at their home he'll say 'Mum and Dad to go.'

They've moved to Seaford now, which is about thirty minutes by car from us in Roedean. A perfect distance in that we see each other regularly but not every day. Andrew especially likes to garden and he's been enlisting a very willing Johnny to help. Johnny loves going to the local tip, sorting the rubbish into each category and disposing of it. Johnny's a strong and able worker. It's a perfect combination for Andrew, who's now seventy. It has to be said that the tip is also Andrew's favourite place. There's that genetic tie-in possibly rearing its head again.

There is a joke I've told about Andrew on stage – how many fathers-in-law does it take to change a lightbulb? The answer is: One. And he'll bleed your radiators as well. You just have to pretend you don't know what you're doing and he will likely take over any domestic chore. You don't even have to pretend when barbecuing.

Sarah is a good cook and knows the way to Johnny's heart. He has his own room at his grandparents' and plenty of his toys and books and clothes around to help him feel that it's his second home. Nowadays, if it's convenient, he'll mostly spend Saturday nights at Sarah and Andrew's. They are always keen to have him and he's always keen to go, which helps Angela in particular feel she can have a well-earned break and a lie-in on Sunday mornings. On a Sunday, weather permitting, Andrew drives Johnny and Sarah to Eastbourne or Bexhill for fish and chips and a walk along the sea. They all enjoy the exercise, although I think it's the chips Johnny enjoys most.

Of course, grandparents do get older and frail and we know this happy arrangement can't last for ever. Angela's mum had a stroke and a heart attack at the same time last year. What was she thinking of? She was supposed to be looking after Johnny for us that weekend! Some people are so selfish. I have had a word with her, you'll be glad to know. She's on medication now, which she's taking some getting used to, and has to walk with a stick. Angela's dad now has a hearing aid and is on statins.

As with Johnny, we can't plan too much for a 'bright future' because very little is predictable and the things that are predictable aren't necessarily that 'bright'. So we enjoy these days we've all got together and just hope tomorrow will be as good a day.

THE WALKING WOUNDED AT LIDL

My psoriasis does not qualify
for priority parking

My wife eases her dodgy back
out of the vehicle

As eyes view us with suspicion
a blue badge authorises the windscreen

My father-in-law reveals nothing
of his need for statins

Only my mother-in-law looks the part
leaning heavily on her stick

A stroke and heart attack at the same time
qualifies her for a shorter walk to the supermarket

Earlier I saw her lift the weight from the world
Immersed in water

her limbs as free as summer
no time limitation in sight

Once inside the shop we are in public
A world of plenty is laid out before us

Fridges hum, tills bleep
Muzak underscores decisions made

A little girl with no physical ailments
squeals constantly for attention

She too has her story

My son wears his ear defenders
as the two of us sit back in the car
out of the way
and wait

in the disability space

Chapter 13a

My Folks by Angela

There were very few 'training' courses available to us as parents when Johnny was first diagnosed. As far as I know, there were (and still are) very few, if any, aimed at grandparents.

As Henry has said (without being prompted), we have been extremely lucky to have my parents around to help out with Johnny. To be honest, I have been lucky to have them around full stop. They have been very supportive of me. Which can't always have been easy.

My mum and dad always accepted and encouraged my early desire and rather obscure, outlandish notion of wanting to be a writer. They were absolutely fine with my hair being dyed every colour under the sun in the days when having bright pink hair was a real statement (especially in Peterborough). They didn't bat an eyelid when I got banned from my dad's golf club. In fact, I can only really remember my dad ever losing it with me twice. Once was when I came back from the hairdressers aged about thirteen with a large triangle shaved out of the back of my head (on reflection, what was I thinking?). And once when he was teaching me to drive and I took a cattle grid in fourth gear. The latter was the first time I ever heard him use the F word.

I think the reason they were so accepting is that my mum's family all are, or were, shall we say, 'characters'. The term would definitely have applied to Norms, and to both of her two sisters, Pearl and Val. My favourite story about my Great-Aunt Val is that she was married to a folk singer when she was younger, and once Bob Dylan phoned her house in the middle of the night to talk to her husband. She was heavily pregnant at the time. She asked him who was calling and in his characteristic drawl he said, 'It's Bob Dylan.' She replied, 'Well Bob Dylan – it's two in the morning over here, so you can fuck right off' and put the phone down on him.

Pearl was a member of the Communist Party, went on marches and also swore like a docker. I lived with her when I first moved to Brighton and continued to either see or speak to her every week until she died a few years ago. Norms worked as a proofreader on the local paper in Peterborough. I remember visiting her at the print works when I was little. It was loud and exciting and smelt of ink. She'd tell me lots of funny stories. I recall her saying how one day she couldn't find the weekly horoscope prediction to put in, so she just recycled that week's from the previous year. My granddad Lefty died when I was twelve. When I think about him, I remember him as a cross between Leslie Phillips and Spike Milligan.

We often went on holiday together to Norfolk. These weeks away mainly involved being huddled behind a windbreak on Cromer beach and buying classic rude postcards (which I collected and later proudly displayed in my Prince Charles and Lady Di wedding memorabilia photo album. I was an odd child). We also spent a lot of this time in the car visiting other tourist spots and my mum, Norms and I would wind down the windows and whistle at handsome men on bikes. We'd also pretend to throw bombs at every golf course we passed. I was about seven or eight years old and I found all of these shenanigans hilarious. I had no idea what my dad, who was driving, made of it all.

When I was about fifteen, Norms was living in a bungalow a stone's throw from the centre of town. For the next few years I would crash at hers on Saturday nights after I'd been out with my friends. I'd roll in, often quite drunk, and she'd be in bed snoring with the TV still blaring out. Sometimes she'd be silently sleeping with her mouth open and I'd worry just for a second that she was actually dead. I'd creep in, check she was still breathing, then turn her TV off. I loved staying with her. When I think back, I remember the green blanket on my bed there and the smell of her talc. I remember her cracking open a pale ale at 6 p.m. every night and the sound of Radio 4. I remember her efforts to take on board my new-fangled vegetarianism by making me a full roast dinner and replacing the meat with a large lump of cheese on the side. She still covered the entire meal in gravy. And her gravy was so good that I'd eat it all, convincing myself it was unlikely that Morrissey would ever find out.

Every Sunday morning, Norms would want to know all the details of what went on the night before. Who had snogged who, who had thrown up and whose turn was it to end the evening crying in the toilets. Once when she was in her seventies, she came home to discover a man in her bedroom rooting through

139

her cupboards. She chased him out of the house towards the garage a few doors down, whereupon the mechanics working there locked the man in a side room. Whether this was to detain him, or to keep him safe from the screaming pensioner brandishing a stick at him, we shall never know. When the police finally arrived, they told Norms in no uncertain terms to stop swearing. It made the local news.

We scattered Norms's ashes on the beach of her home town, Lowestoft. It was a stormy, grey day and the wind blew so hard that Norms flew back in our faces and Johnny's buggy took off down the beach (with him in it) and Henry had to run after it. I think she would have found the whole thing really funny.

So, given this family history I suppose, if I'm totally honest, my mum 'getting' Johnny is less of a surprise than my dad accepting his condition. My mum is a hugely generous, non-judgemental woman – with, to quote *Snow Cake*, 'the emphasis on the mental'. She is into 'healing', angel card readings and Australian bush remedies. When I was growing up, she was the only mum I knew who wore fake leather trousers and shopped pretty much exclusively at the health shop. She drove a Mini and looked like the redhead from Abba. I used to walk to her office on my way home from school to get a lift back with her. I don't think she'll mind me saying I suspect that, as a part-time secretary for a chartered accountant in pre-computer days, she was solely responsible for the success of the Tipp-ex company. But because of her sunny disposition (and the fact that she looked like the redhead from Abba – in fake leather trousers) she got away with murder at work.

My dad has always been the 'conventional' one. He grew up in a Plymouth Brethren household. His dad left when he was four and he never saw him again. His mum didn't remarry. When he was fifteen, his grandfather died in a tragic accident, falling down the stairs and breaking his neck. About eighteen months later, my dad's mum died of cancer.

My dad met my mum around this time and they eventually moved in with his grandma, who was still in shock from losing her husband. My parents married when they were twenty-one and I was born a year later, the fattest baby you've ever seen. The four of us continued living in my dad's grandma's house. My parents looked after her there, until she died when I was four. My dad can come across as very reserved and I think it takes him a long time to feel comfortable around people. I wonder if this is partly because he had to face such a lot of loss and responsibility at an early age. However, once he 'lets you in', he's one of the most generous people I know. He hates being idle and he will fix/build/fetch anything for you. He likes a project. He will also run people to their appointments, give away vast amounts of the vegetables he grows in his 'market garden' and has even been known to bestow, on some lucky people, a rare glimpse of his rather mean Elvis impersonation.

It has been a complete joy for me to see how comfortable my dad has become around Johnny. His slightly bossy method of giving his grandson thousands of jobs around the house and garden, and his own love of routine and order, means they are pretty much like two peas in a pod. You can often find the two of them in the evening, sitting side by side in silence at the kitchen worktop, slicing up mushrooms in preparation for breakfast *the next day*.

However, it's the times when we have had Johnny's class over that I am most in awe of my parents. They both excel at being welcoming, open and easy-going; they throw themselves into playing daft games like 'the Dressing-Up Game' and treasure hunts, and my dad has even been roped into being Father Christmas more than once. Neither of them has been remotely fazed by the often quite surreal behaviour and questions thrown at them from the range of special needs kids who Johnny has had the fortune to get to know over the years.

There is an air of lightness, fun and acceptance about my parents that I'm pretty sure every child who has been over to ours has picked up on. I am so proud of them and, of the many, many things I'd like to thank them for in my life, it is this that I am currently most grateful for. Their being 'unfazeable', always finding the joy and emphasising the positive, are priceless gifts to us all.

Chapter 14

Walking Round the Block

When we first moved into Roedean we felt like the Beverly Hillbillies. We'd previously lived in the nearby Kemptown district of Brighton, which is more bohemian. We couldn't actually afford the house and I was hoping I could earn enough money before my next tax bill came to catch up with myself. A lot of the houses in Roedean were far bigger and certainly looked more grand than ours at the time (and to be honest, still do).

I remember parking my car with two of the tyres on the grass verge to allow for cars to pass easily, only to find an anonymous note on my windscreen. 'We don't park on the grass round here,' it said, 'we're not Whitehawk.' Whitehawk is the local council estate. I did think, that may be so, but at least in Whitehawk they would tell you to your face rather than hide behind an anonymous note. (The funny thing is that when I first looked at the plans for this mock-Tudor house, built as were many of the houses along this road in the 1930s, I noticed the area was referred to as East Brighton Council Estate.)

Within the first couple of weeks we did receive a couple of visits from our neighbours at the time. They seemed pleasant enough but there was a phrase that they all seemed to use. I remember it because I'd never heard the phrase before, so to hear it repeatedly was odd. 'We don't live in each other's houses,' they said. Did they say this to everyone, I wondered, or just to us?

When we came to view the house originally there was a sign on the door next to the number declaring that the name of the house was 'Cobwebs'. Inside the spiders were indeed making themselves at home. The curtains were so full of dust they could stand up on their own. On one wall dead birds were displayed as decoration. The whole place was dark and dank and reminded me of Miss Havisham's house in *Great Expectations* but a bit more down market.

The sight of the coast always reminded me of family holidays when I was a child, and warmth and fun. Being from Nottingham, which is about as far from the sea as you can get in this country, I was determined above all else to have a sea view. On that first viewing of the property I walked out into the back garden and there it was, the simple beauty of the horizon. I looked back at the house and decided that over time I could change everything about it that needed changing. Then I looked at the sea again and crossed my fingers that we could make this work.

Angela was pregnant with Johnny at the time and felt physically sick every time she saw the plastic yellow tiles in the kitchen, so they had to go. This was to be the house in which we would bring up our child, and by the time Johnny was born we had settled in and the house was functional. We'd put a wire net over the pond in the garden and removed anything with sharp edges, in anticipation of him being a toddler.

Even when he was a tiny baby I remember us walking Johnny round the block in his pram and, fairly soon after, in his buggy. Collapsible buggies seemed to be the latest thing back then; 'based on the undercarriage of a Spitfire,' I remember all the dads saying to each other at the time. There seemed to be two basic options: you could have your baby facing you or facing the direction of travel. I remember that we chose facing forwards, wanting Johnny to see the world. In retrospect even this appears a questionable decision.

Even before we moved to Roedean, Angela and I would walk along the front by the pitch and putt and enjoy the sea air, look over to the Downs and then walk back along the crescent daydreaming about living in one of the handsome houses. As Johnny grew, a walk round the block at least a couple of times a week became a natural activity; in spring enjoying the cherry blossom, then in summer whiling away the long afternoons, in autumn watching the leaves turn brown and even in winter enjoying the snow.

When I lived in Nottingham or Manchester, just going for a walk didn't seem to be on the agenda unless you went somewhere specific like a park. In Brighton, perhaps because of the sea, it seems natural to go for a walk. Johnny loves walking and requests a walk round the block more days than not. He could probably walk around the block unaccompanied but neither Angela nor I could bring ourselves to risk it. He only needs to encounter one dog or something unexpected en route and there could be trouble. If approached by a stranger who knows what might happen?

It seems such a simple pleasure, and almost mundane, but Johnny appears to get a lot of pleasure from it and I must admit I do too. He likes to run his finger over the gate numbers as we pass. Most of the neighbours now recognise my six-foot-three son with his bright red ear defenders and my wife with her wild hair, though they probably wouldn't recognise me in a police line-up.

If I walk anywhere with Johnny I find even people I don't know will sometimes say, 'Hello Johnny'. He has become visible in his local community. There is no question of hiding away from the world, no timidity in embracing his local surroundings. Brighton is the only community Johnny has ever known; and as we've now lived in the area for twenty years, even I no longer feel like an outsider. I've resigned myself to bringing up a southerner.

Johnny has only ever lived in Roedean. The chances are, certainly for the foreseeable future, he will only ever live in Roedean. This is his home.

This poem is based on the photo at the start of this section taken on Brighton beach.

KING CANUTE SHOULD
HAVE CHECKED THE TIDES

Taking your own chair to the beach
is a commitment
fleecy on
hood up

Better to keep your limbs moving
some might say
but sitting is a definite statement

We are not just passing through
we are making a stand
sitting firm

Day trippers we are not
nor ill prepared tourists
We are stones amongst scattered pebbles
rocks amongst shingle

Bring on your highest wave
the glory is ours
we live here
we own this weather

Chapter 14a

Sweeping up Crisps in a Portakabin by Angela

Here's a story to give you an idea of how sometimes life lived under the dual umbrella of 'special needs family' and 'working in the medja, dahling' can be surreal. Most days during his years in education I have found myself dropping Johnny off at school or college in the morning, surrounded by the open, excited faces of his fellow students and their equally friendly and upbeat taxi drivers and escorts. It's usually a bustling, chaotic scramble for a parking space involving manoeuvring around loud, slightly 'out-there' children. Several times a year, after dropping Johnny off I have to hightail it up to London on the train for a meeting.

That really quite bonkers drop-off in the car park contrasts sharply with the world of Soho House or some other private members' club in the heart of TV Town (I use the term 'bonkers' in a completely complimentary way – as in the Mad Hatter's 'You're entirely bonkers. But I'll tell you a secret – all the best people are'). The most striking contrast between these two worlds happened to me when Johnny was three.

In 2001 we had just embarked on our Son-Rise Programme but we were also looking at other practices that might complement it. Someone mentioned a communication system called PECS, and there was a two-day course on it at a special needs school just up the road from us. I enrolled Johnny and me on it.

It turned out that the course was run in a Portakabin that, much later in Johnny's life, became his first classroom when he transferred from his longstanding school to a new one. I often find little connections like this weird. But rather lovely. Like when you meet a new person for the first time and you have no idea how they are going to impact on you and your life. As it turns out, Johnny had the worst year ever in that classroom. This was through no fault of the teachers, who were amazing – but, on reflection, down to the fact that the change of school affected him much more than we imagined it would. He was in a new place with people who didn't know him – and was in with a group of children who he found difficult due to several of them being very unpredictable.

This is the age-old problem with special needs children and schooling – in particular, I feel, with autistic kids. They are mostly put in classrooms with other autistic children who all have their own issues and challenges and foibles. For Johnny, having to spend all day in a room with a young girl who might squeal when she's agitated is like putting an asthmatic person in a room with a smoker. It may well, of course, work the other way round too.

Putting the young girl in a room with Johnny, who can stamp loudly, shout and hit out when he's stressed, may cause her to squeal. You see the problem. Anyway – that 'year from hell', as I affectionately call it, involved Johnny breaking a class room assistant's finger, a year of night terrors (so bad at one point I thought he was fitting and took him to an epilepsy consultant), and he was also biting his hands so badly that I frequently had to take him to the nurse to have them dressed and we were referred to a skin specialist, who provided special bandages infused with seaweed. We were also getting hit a lot at home.

Anyway, back to the PECS course. There were about seven children and their parents on it. I recall in the playground talking to another parent who had a much older child. She wasn't there for the course. I think maybe they were visiting the school. Her child was about nine. I asked the parent what she was 'doing' with/for her child and she told me that they weren't really doing anything much. I distinctly remember being aghast. How on earth were they 'not doing anything much' ... how could they sit around and let their child on the spectrum just 'be'? No interventions? No dietary investigations? Didn't they want their child to 'get better'? Looking back, I see now that they had reached the place we are currently at, just much earlier than we did. Apart from the odd bit of omega oil, a gluten-/casein-free diet, some cranial therapy and of course always striving to help Johnny engage and cope with the world around him, we don't 'do much' now either in terms of finding a 'cure'. We don't feel that keen urge to change him any more. To 'make him better'. We love and accept him for who he is. As I believe we should.

Several hours after the first day of the PECS course – having learnt all about laminating and constructing written sentences on Velcro – I was in London. Henry and Steve had written the film *The Parole Officer* and it was the night of the red carpet premiere.

There were a few 'stars' there. I got talking to Helena Bonham Carter in the queue for the toilets. She said she liked my dress and my bag. I was rather thrilled and informed her that they both came from TKMaxx. She smiled the smile of someone who had no idea what TKMaxx was. Undeterred, I went to the auditorium to find Henry. To my amazement (and slight horror) I found myself seated and about to watch the film next to Hugh Grant. To put this in context, it was at the time when Hugh was at the height of his fame. He had just done *Bridget Jones's Diary*. I mean, he was A Very Big Name.

I felt like Cinderella – a few hours earlier I'd been sweeping up crisps in a Portakabin and now here I was, all dressed up, sitting next to – well, 'him'. Prince Grant. Henry was of course sitting on the other side of me. On the other side of him was Jenny Agutter. I turned around to see various members of our family excitedly pointing and mouthing the words 'HUGH GRANT!!!' at me. As if I had no idea who I was sharing an arm rest with. I did that wincing face back – the one that means, 'I know! Tell me about it!' The lights went down and I then spent the duration of the film thinking, 'OMG, what on earth do I say to him when the lights go back up?' Fortunately I'd seen an edit of the film before, so it wasn't like I was missing any of the action as my mind wandered over my Hugh dilemma.

The thing about spending the day on the PECS course was that I hadn't really had a chance to eat much and my stomach let me (and everyone around me) know. The film lasted for an hour and a half. If I was hungry at the start, imagine how much hungrier I was and how much louder my stomach was towards the end. No matter how I sat, whether I leant forward or back, tensed, tried to relax or held my breath, there was still a rumbling underscore.

When the final credits had rolled, I turned to Hugh, knowing I really needed to say something. All my rehearsed witticisms and flowery descriptions of our joint viewing experience abruptly left me – and the first words out of my mouth were, 'I'm so sorry about my stomach – I've only had a Dairylea sandwich all day.' And there it was. I had said the word Dairylea to Hugh Grant. I pride myself on the thought that I don't know if anyone else has ever said the word Dairylea to Hugh Grant.

I went back to the Portakabin the next day, and began day two of encouraging my son to communicate with me by handing over a small picture of a toilet.

Chapter 15
School and College

For most parents choosing the best school for their child is important. It is even more of an issue when your child has special needs. Of all the topics we've spoken to other parents about, this is the one that causes the most stress.

As we did the Son-Rise programme for four years, it wasn't until Johnny was seven that he entered the state education system. Looking at possible schools, it became clear that Johnny couldn't cope in mainstream school even with a one-to-one assistant. They were far too formal and restrictive for a boy who wanted to move and whose concentration and attention span wouldn't have survived even the first lesson.

We looked at several special schools catering for a range of abilities. Looking at Johnny's peers was a wake-up call. On his own Johnny can seem to fit in with the landscape of family life because we are geared up and have adapted, but seeing a class of five to ten autistic kids, all with their own personalities and challenges, initially looks like anarchy. Once you become accustomed to it you learn how to relate to each individual, but on first sight from the outside it looks daunting. I worried about how my son would cope. At each school they had a good ratio of teachers and assistant teachers to give each child personal attention, but even this initially looked to add to the anarchy. It's natural to be protective towards your own child and I must confess I worried Johnny wouldn't find the right level and fit in around other his classmates. Some seemed way ahead of him in terms of communication or ability while others had more difficulty.

I'm in awe of teachers of special needs children. Every one I've met seems to put themselves wholly into bringing out the best in the kids. I once taught poetry at a regular secondary school for three days and had to lie down every day when I got home, I was so exhausted.

The main thing I cling on to is that Johnny was almost always happy to go to school and now always looks forward to college. He's happy when he gets home and shows no sign of stress, though there was a year when him adjusting to a new school took time and caused considerable tension.

We have a system now where we have a book that is carried to school and back in Johnny's school bag every day and is passed between ourselves and his teachers. Each college day we write in the book anything we feel that the teachers might need to know and they do the same. Any recent behaviour or health problems are noted. Anything that might affect his mood, like not sleeping well or being overtired due to any physical activity. This is very helpful and it's comforting to know when he's had a good day. He usually has a good day, which indicates that there is nothing fundamentally wrong with his routine, and that is equally comforting.

The biggest problems we've had with Johnny's schooling over the years have been with his hitting teachers, pushing and hitting fellow pupils, or biting the back of his hand so badly he still has scars. He even had a phase of night terrors and Angela did wonder if he'd developed epilepsy, but it was just the transition from one school to another. Nearly all these problems come down to sensory overload. If people get too in-his-face or sounds get too loud Johnny needs a coping mechanism. We are lucky that his schools and now the college have instigated a quiet room for him; when overloaded Johnny will choose to go in there and when he is feeling able he chooses to rejoin the class. With a little gentle persuasion Johnny will rejoin his classmates before too long, even if he requests his ear defenders. As much as we can, at college and at home, we try to minimise the ear defenders. He usually wears them most times in the car but certainly at home he leaves them at the door. We are geared up in the house to avoid noise and are conscious of even the slightest irritation.

Angela and I have friends who have had a worse experience with their autistic kids and their relationship with school or college, and I know it can be worrying. I'm convinced that logically teachers want to find a solution just as much as parents do. I look on them as just part of the bigger team. This trust has come slowly though; I do remember in the early years dropping Johnny off at school and being so worried for him. Letting him out of my or Angela's sight was hard; I sat in the car and cried several times. Not the best start to the working day.

Nowadays when I drop him off at college, he gives me a hug and strides in confidently, never looking back.

AS THE GROUND ACCELERATES
TOWARDS YOU AT AN ACUTE ANGLE

If I tilt my head to the side
you are perpendicular
and the rest of this unholy mess
is at a slant

Italic trees in parallel
mark the degrees
ten past the hour

Dry leaves defy gravity
There is no slide to the east

Shadows brave the slope
The sun no longer certain
of its position

Toes grip for balance
Legs lengthen or shorten
to compensate

Fire-engine red you stand out
amid the muted woodland

You lean against the sky like Atlas
carrying all on your back

Chapter 16
Placements

'You might as well just put him in a cupboard for three years' I couldn't help blurting out during a recent 'consultation' about Johnny's options for further education. I'm sure Brighton isn't the worst council for special needs provision. I'm absolutely sure there are plenty of people all over the

UK trying to do their best given the resources and the system. As a parent or carer though it is frustrating and sometimes infuriating to hear generalisations or platitudes, jargon and political clichés and excuses when you are struggling to get the best for your child.

Last year Johnny was leaving his existing college to start a new one. The council had three possible options for his next placement, one being a mainstream college, the second being an established special needs facility and the third being a new special needs unit. As you know by now, Johnny is noise-intolerant with learning and communication difficulties and clearly isn't capable of coping with a mainstream college, which left the two special needs options.

The established college was a few minutes from our door. A large set of brick buildings set back from the small local roads and sufficiently high above them to lessen any traffic noise. The area in which it was set formed our local neighbourhood. One Johnny was familiar and confident in.

The new facility was essentially a Portakabin that adjoined a mainstream school situated behind the busiest main road in town. It was over forty-five minutes from our home in an area we never visited.

The established college had plenty of light open space and large teaching areas that would be perfect for Johnny's physical needs. The established college also had a good experience and established relations with the local community in the areas of both horticulture and art – the two activities in which Johnny is motivated and shows promise. The facilities and trained teaching staff were already in place.

The new facility had a room for art that looked like an ordinary classroom but with all the tables together facing each other. Horticulture was available but only with a forty-minute drive from the college there and a forty-minute drive back.

The new facility also had a dog. However well-behaved the dog was, this would be a problem for Johnny, whose biggest difficulty is noise and especially unpredictable noise and more specifically dogs, babies and young children squealing (particularly girls, due to their higher-pitched voices).

So you might think the choice would be obvious. However, the decision was made that Johnny was to be sent to the new facility. Angela and I were naturally concerned and asked for a chance to put our case to the council. We worried that the reason Johnny was being sent to the new facility was that it was half the price of the established college. I understand the wording now used is 'appropriate'. The council were obliged to find Johnny an 'appropriate' placement. There are ways you can interpret that word, 'appropriate', but I'm sure I'm not alone in thinking the way we shouldn't use it is to mean 'the cheapest' or 'the bare minimum'. We are all better than that.

One of our main worries was the dog. We'd been trying to solve this fear for almost nineteen years so it wasn't like he was going to suddenly get over it. It seemed bordering on cruel to send Johnny to a place every day where he would have to face his worst fear. More disturbing to us, although it perhaps sounds strange, was the fact that the dog wouldn't be there every day. So now there was the added stress that Johnny would never know when he turned a corner whether there was going to be a dog or not!

Angela and I spent four hours in discussion with the local council. I can't tell you any details of that discussion as we both had to sign a non-disclosure agreement. I can tell you that as parents we were passionate and strident in putting across the logic of our arguments and what we saw as the correct way forward for Johnny. To be fair the council must have listened, because within a week Johnny was reassigned to the established college, much to our relief.

Our particular story has a happy ending and shows that positive outcomes are possible, but it's hard and stressful nevertheless and not every parent has the time, the communication skills, the stamina and the ammunition to achieve the best result.

I don't believe anyone would want to send a child to an 'inappropriate' place. I do believe that generally people who work in special needs and for local councils have children's best interests at heart. The whole system is underfunded and often understaffed though. Certainly in the south-east speech therapists are like gold dust, and I wouldn't be surprised if they're scarce in other parts of the country too.

The stress of finding the right help for any child – or adult – with special needs can be crushing. Very often parents and carers can feel helpless. Angela and I have several friends with children on the spectrum whose battles with local authorities are constant and seem to drain these parents, who are already stretched to the limit by their everyday battle to do the best for their vulnerable son or daughter.

I'm conscious when I read poems and talk on stage about our life with Johnny that there are possibly people in the audience, and certainly out there in the rest of the world, whose lives are harder. On top of all the other troubles and complications that can affect any one of us, the added pressure and anxiety of coping with special needs and navigating a positive outcome for an autistic child is not at all a laughing matter. Several times I've done a book signing at the end of a reading and parents and carers have told me of their own stories. Sometimes, no matter how public the arena, they can't hold back the tears. I know it is serious and important and can take the breath from your body, which is why I feel we need to communicate more about this world.

Perhaps the most important thing I say during a reading (which I mentioned earlier) is that when we found out about Johnny I said to Angela, 'I can't cope.' I know there are a lot of people who feel that helplessness at some point, or even for years. To know you are not the only one feeling this helps. I'm sure it does. That's always been my experience. A lot of what people have to contend with is hard and seems beyond understanding. Sometimes there is no logic and sometimes it just seems unfair.

I believe that openness is the key. If I can't understand something I have to say so. More often than not someone will try and explain or help me find a way of understanding. If I can't do something I say I don't think I can. Once that is out there I can try and find an answer. To bottle these things up and suffer and be tormented in silence is not good for any parent and certainly won't help their child.

I don't think I could just get up on stage and deliver

serious statements about autism. It would miss the point for me. It has to come back to an understanding of, or an attempt to understand, the individuals affected as people. I don't want anyone, whether it's an autistic child, a parent or anyone else, to have to put up with the bare minimum. I want to make joy and happiness and human connection as important as facts and figures. If we forget that then it's an easy step to dehumanising others and before long we are putting people in cupboards and forgetting them.

ACADEMIA AND THE
COMPULSION TO COMPETE

Too small to be a snowman
this could be a snow child

I hold onto your hands
partly to warm them
but partly not

Two brussels sprouts
a lemon for a nose
scarf and cap

We are not going to win any prizes
This is a family photo
of family
for family

It need be of no interest to anyone else
If you saw it in an album
you might well flick past without comment
a little embarrassed
that we would consider this worth presenting

Whether we are on a downhill slope
or uphill
is a matter of perspective

Our faces white as hoar frost
haunt these early learnings

When you were a baby
I put your name down for a school place
paid a deposit

The money is no loss at all

Chapter 17

Growing up, Food and Other Stuff

Johnny didn't like getting his first pubic hair. 'Get it out,' he said to his mum. We both explained the process of puberty to him. We explained sex and more urgently we explained masturbation. Like most lads exploring themselves, Johnny began to occasionally fiddle with himself in public. We explained, each time, it was something he could do in the privacy of his bedroom, and pretty soon it wasn't a problem. He does occasionally get an erection but no more than any teenage boy. He just doesn't disguise it as well. We have always encouraged him to have a healthy and balanced view of his body. He's not inhibited in the least but he knows to wear clothes around other people.

With this book, Angela and I were clear that we didn't want to write anything we thought Johnny wouldn't want us to. So although I think it's honest to mention masturbation, I don't want to say too much on the subject. Each parent, not only parents of children with special needs, has to decide where they draw the line on all sorts of privacy issues. For example, I would never put a photo of Johnny even semi-naked on the internet or social media. I know how conscious of their bodies people can be, and so even a shot of Johnny with his shirt off is off-limits as far as I am concerned. Other parents will have other lines and other concerns on a whole range of issues. With Johnny, because he's not able to articulate his thoughts in the same way as a neurotypical boy his age I err on the side of caution every time.

During puberty Johnny started to grow quite tall and put on weight. He's now six foot three and sixteen stone. He wears XXL clothes. Even though he is active, swims and exercises and walks regularly, he does like his food and we do have to watch his weight.

In our favour is the fact that he has never had a fizzy drink in his life. He doesn't like the bubbles. Apart from mints Johnny has never had a sweet either. Very occasionally he will have a square of chocolate. Johnny's diet is gluten-and dairy-free. When we were investigating causes of autism we came across the theory of leaky gut syndrome. A Doctor Shattock in Sunderland had been working with autistic children and thought there was a prevalence, amongst children on the spectrum, of problems caused by gluten and casein. The theory is that we get drowsy after eating because the system is dealing with peptides in our food. In people with difficulties, with either the stomach or the blood–brain barrier, more peptides can reach the brain, causing problems.

There was an easy test to be carried out that just meant sending a sample of Johnny's urine to a clinic in Sunderland. The test came back positive so we decided to err on the side of caution and embrace a strict diet for him. Angela's mum is gluten-intolerant and my brother David always had stomach issues, so it did seem possible that our child could have a problem. Of course if Johnny did have a problem we had an added difficulty in that he couldn't always communicate any internal pains like stomach ache to us.

It's only anecdotal evidence but both Angela and I feel this has helped Johnny's behaviour. I do remember once giving him something containing gluten by mistake and seeing a change in him. It was as though he was on drugs. He was spaced out, not really there in a much more profound sense than his usual level of withdrawal at this time. It was genuinely frightening. I never made that mistake again.

Angela tells me of a time when she was in a parent and child class with Johnny and several other families. They were doing PECS, the Picture Exchange Communication System that teaches a child to communicate by selecting a picture card and presenting it to the parent or carer. As part of the training the class was using treats to spur the children to engage. As Johnny doesn't like sweets or fizzy drinks Angela had taken fruit, hummus and carrots. She and Johnny sat quietly at his desk while the majority of mums and dads struggled to keep their sugar-high kids from running around. Thank God for Johnny's unusual tastes.

I know that a lot of autistic kids do restrict their diets, which can cause problems. Luckily that's never been the case with Johnny. In fact it's quite the opposite. Over the years we've introduced Johnny to a variety of foods. He enjoys Singapore rice noodles, crispy duck and seaweed from the Chinese takeaway. When we moved back into our new home after having the old one rebuilt, Angela wanted it to feel welcoming on our first night, so she made sure Johnny had his favourite meal – chicken biryani followed by Christmas pudding and dairy-free custard. He's always liked a variety of meat and he'll eat most vegetables with a bit of gravy or tomato sauce. He'd eat tomato sauce on its own if you let him! He won't eat avocado; I don't know if it's the texture. I won't eat mandarin oranges as the segments remind me of slugs, so who knows for sure what puts people off certain food? The gluten-free range at the major super-markets is getting much better, although it's quite often full of sugar. Hummus and apple or carrot is a great snack standby. I can't bring myself to eat gluten-free cakes though; they're usually too dry.

It's no wonder Johnny's so healthy. If only I'd have had his diet I could have been a top sportsman . . .!. Unfortunately I was part of the working-class generation that ate Vesta curry or beef risotto from a packet, boil-in-the-bag cod in butter sauce, pot noodles, pop tarts and Nesquik.

For Johnny, I sometimes think life is the bits he has to get through between meals. He does like his food and it is a great motivator. That's not to say he's greedy – most of the time he will not let you add extra food to his plate once he's started. He will eat what's presented and that's it. He tends to like everything separately (although he likes gravy and sauce on food) and will usually eat each aspect of the meal in sequence. More often than not he will start with the meat or fish, then eat the potatoes or chips, then whatever else is on the plate. The idea of having two different tastes on the same fork is not on the menu. I think sometimes he eats each food in accordance with his preferences, eating what he likes most first. Not a bad mode of operation; if he needs to stop because he's full, then he's had all the best stuff. He will sometimes leave vegetables, though adding gravy or tomato sauce can produce a more favourable attitude. We try never to eat in front of him if he's not eating. If there's no gluten- and dairy-free option at a particular cafe then we avoid it or we all stick to drinks. This seems only fair and respectful and there's no point in courting problems.

Johnny's a stone overweight at the moment so we've joined a gym. He's mastered the treadmill easily and will walk for twenty minutes at a brisk pace without complaint. He then goes over to the swimming pool and does a few lengths. Exercise too has taken persistence. When he was a younger, about five or six, he did a poo in the local pool one day. Everyone had to get out. Angela's word to describe it is 'mortifying'. For a time she was quite fearful that it would happen again, but she made herself take him back and keep going. She'd made a point every time of ensuring that Johnny went to the toilet before entering the pool, but even then she kept a constant vigil for several years, still a little on edge; thankfully it never happened again.

It's certainly important to us to ensure that our son is the healthiest he can be. Your child being ill on top of being on the spectrum is a complication you don't need in your life. In fact, you being ill is not going to help your efforts either. So keeping everyone healthy is just good planning. Johnny has taken a range of supplements over the years to help his brain, but unfortunately neither I nor Angela took them so we can't remember what they were called. He used to have a lot of omega fish oil tablets in drinks and mixed into food when he was younger. I'm not sure if they helped his brain. I'm sure they didn't help his appetite. He still takes some fish oil and omega tablets despite their horrible taste. His mum often mixes them into a healthy shake with fruits and vegetables. I think she calls them nutri-bullets these days.

Johnny also has probiotics to help his gut bacteria and for a few years when he was younger we tried homeopathic medicine and he even had what was called homeopathic chelation. I couldn't tell you if it made any difference to anything other than our bank account. Today Angela mentioned a nutritionist she wanted to approach. 'OK,' I said, 'so long as it's not one where they ask you to push against them and tell you to stick almonds up your arse.' I have become a little sceptical over the years.

The problem is that whatever path you take, it's difficult to know what difference another path might have made. Any change, for better or worse, could be down to a single source or a combination; and it's not always easy to define with any part of the body, let alone the brain with its complicated nature. I remember being worried once and going to the doctors saying, 'I've got a lump in the middle of my chest.' 'Yes,' said the doctor, 'we all have that, it's called the sternum.' Another time I went along convinced I'd got earache, only to be told it was an abscess on my back teeth.

Probably the best example of getting it wrong was when I started feeling dizzy when I stood up. I thought I'd got a brain tumour. I must have been channelling my sister Val. I lived with the dizziness for a few days, not wanting to alarm anyone, then finally told a work colleague in London, who immediately took me off to Harley Street. They did all sorts of tests and took my blood. They suggested I have a CT scan, which would cost me a few hundred pounds. I was covered at work by Bupa but needed my local doctor's sign-off for the paperwork. I went in to see my usual doctor, who told me it was my ears. Some fluid in my ears had crystallised and he gave me a simple head-turning exercise that cleared it up in about a week and cost nothing. The bill came in from Harley Street at over one and a half thousand pounds. That's enough to make anyone's head spin.

When Johnny turned sixteen we were told he wasn't legally ours any more. Because he's officially 'mentally incapacitated' he became a ward of the state. We had someone from the government visit our home, and they came in, and went to talk to Johnny. The woman asked him two questions, then, realising he wasn't able to answer, she came and talked to me and Angela. I don't mind admitting I was scared by this visit. I didn't know what was going to happen. I had this terrible feeling that our ability to protect and nurture Johnny was no longer in our control. Everything we had built and put in place to help him seemed under threat. Well-meaning as she may have been, this woman didn't know my son. Did she even like him?

Even now we are still wondering what this all means. Do we have to ask someone's permission to take him out of the country on holiday? We've been abroad several times and not been stopped at the border. Do we have to ask permission for medical treatment? Well, he goes to the dentist regularly and occasionally to the doctors and nothing seems to have changed. Can we even cut his hair or his nails? Stupid as it sounds, these are questions that have occurred to us over the last couple of years.

How could I tell this woman (or anyone else the state may send), what our son is like? How can I explain the journey we've been on? The challenges he's overcome, the progress he's made and continues to make, albeit almost imperceptibly slowly at times? She doesn't know his routines, the extent of his noise intolerance, his favourite foods, his artwork, the people he gets on with, his love of walking, his trips to the tip with his granddad, his dislike of scarves, his favourite books, his films, his love of music, the fact that, every once in a while, without any warning he won't walk on a bare hard floor in bare feet, where he enjoys getting his hair cut, what he can do himself and what he can't, what he means when he says words that don't seem to make sense to anyone outside the family. She doesn't know he will put his arm around you while watching television, that he can swim in the sea, or take his shoes off and walk with you along a beach as though everything in the world was perfect.

I can't remember what exactly we said at that meeting but in the years since, we have never seen that woman again. We've never had anyone else from the government visit and have had no further contact with any government department. It was following that meeting I started writing poetry again, after a gap of twenty years.

This is a poem I wrote for anyone involved in working with people with special needs.

VANGUARD OF AUDACIOUS

Kindness is bravery at its brazen best
Its boldest and most ballsy

It empowers all it touches

To put your heart in the line of fire
Is as heroic as it is honourable

To be gentle you offer up a vulnerable underbelly
Empathy and humanity are gifts that entail risk

No matter how everyday it may seem
To dare to act not in self-interest
Is valiant

To demand dignity for others undaunted is intrepid

To find strength to confront and challenge prejudice
    requires courage
However uncool to cynics

To make a stand for justice, equality and even love
Is never unfashionable, never untimely

To insist that tenderness endures and that mercy is
    victorious
You put your body above the parapet

To face injury, loss, ridicule or one of a hundred fears
But still have resolve and compassion
Is a testament to an indomitable spirit

On whatever scale
The matter-of-factness of such nobility
Is a quiet but magnificent defiance

Chapter 18
Social Life Differences

I can't pretend we had a whirlwind of a social life even before we found out Johnny was autistic. Like any parents, our lives in the early years revolved around baby routines and hoping that there'd be light at the end of the tunnel somewhere in the not-too-distant future. We tried to stay in touch with old friends, many of whom didn't have children. We made some new friends and became closer with those who did. Family helped out a little and tiredness often curbed excessive ambition. But when Johnny's ways became apparent, even before he was diagnosed, self-limiting often seemed the safer option. We stayed home or went to places on our own as a family of three.

Once Johnny was diagnosed it was easier to make strident decisions on what he could or couldn't cope with at this stage. Meals out and family gatherings were pre-planned, with a plan B if problems occurred. We were not thinking positively about Johnny's development but rather looking at containment of our family 'difficulty'. We were fraught with anxiety at the thought that we might be burdening others and selfishly interrupting their fun. Once Angela and I had got our heads into gear to think more from Johnny's point of view, decisions became clearer and easier. Still very much trial and error but with less and less error as the years progressed.

The friends we socialise with now know what to expect from Johnny and what not to expect. The more comfortable with Johnny in company Angela and I have become over the years, the more comfortable our friends, and Johnny himself, have become. We don't make a big fuss over hellos and goodbyes. Johnny will either engage or he won't. Friends are encouraged to talk to Johnny directly and know if he doesn't want to answer their questions, or can't, then that is the way it is today.

I think when people first meet Johnny there is naturally a curiosity. The expectation that he is going to 'perform autism' is soon dispelled, as Johnny has no intention of being anything other than himself. More likely than not, if under observation, he'll just walk out of the room. Most people accept Johnny as he is very quickly. Let's face it — the options are take it or leave it and Johnny isn't particularly fussed either way. In a way I think it gives people permission for them to be themselves. I think it would be hard to have pretensions for very long in a room with Johnny. It would take a high level of self-delusion.

What we tend to do nowadays is to socialise mostly with family and a few close friends who to all intents and purposes are extended family and know Johnny very well. There is a scientific principle called the Dunbar Number, which states that human beings given their brain size can only sustain a meaningful relationship with around 150 people. Think how much brain space you can allow each person if you narrow this down even further. One hundred and fifty is about the average size of an English village. I recall the old saying 'It takes a village to bring up a child.'

It really brings it home to you which relationships you value when you have to write a will. Who do you trust enough that you would ask them to care for your child after your death? This is perhaps even more worrying when your child is autistic. Angela and I sat down with a solicitor to do this recently, as we know attending to such matters is important. Going through the whole process and the implications of what happens when each of us dies (either singularly or together) was one of the most depressing conversations I've ever had.

At least writing this book means we can pass on information about Johnny should everyone who loves him die in a car crash. I suppose it acts like an extended letter of wishes.

SAND BETWEEN THE TOES

This is what constitutes an action shot in my world

The thinning at my crown is conveniently out of frame
The avalanche under my chin obscured

If I have a best side, this is it

According to my father-in-law's socks it's Monday
The mid-west easiness to his attire betrays no irony
other than that he's from Peterborough

Johnny shows the least interest in having his feet cleaned
He'd make a good Pharaoh
Nonchalant during de-sanding
Ear defenders and fiddly bit of plastic now part of the ensemble

I use his red sock like a shoeshine boy
Buffing the digits

My mother-in-law relaxes leaning forward
Her walking sticks hook the bench
like stabilisers

Autistic Family Robinson

Even behind a camera my wife is the centre

If she dies first
we will be buried alive in her tomb
we just don't know it yet

Chapter 19
Routines

Johnny wakes up early. Too early for me. Usually between three and six o'clock. Nowadays Angela can usually persuade him to go back to sleep but he is still ready for breakfast by 7 a.m. Angela is a light sleeper and wakes at the slightest noise from Johnny's room. Sometimes he will go to the toilet in the small hours and Angela will ensure he's alright and return to our bed once he's safely back in his bed. This can cause a little worry if we have guests, as he's not too conscious of noise levels and will wander to the toilet sometimes without pyjamas.

I am blessed with the ability to sleep through a nuclear holocaust, although strangely enough, if Angela is away and I am listening for Johnny I can't sleep at all. When Angela has been away, once a year for four days on a well-earned break, I am so glad to see her back. She also acts like a very efficient burglar alarm. If she's sleeping next to me I think nothing of safety beyond ensuring all the doors and windows are locked before going to sleep. I know it's psychological but I somehow feeler safer when she's with me. When she's not there I sleep with a hammer next to the bed. I mentioned this at work to a friend called Ted, who quite rightly asked: 'What is Angela, some kind of ninja?'

Before Johnny, the prospect of an early night would usually mean sex. Nowadays not even sex comes before the opportunity for a decent sleep. I do a joke sometimes on stage. I say, 'Now I'm semi-retired Angela and I get to spend more time together; the other afternoon she said to me "Johnny is at college and we have the house to ourselves, let's have sex." "That's all very well," I said, "but when do I get some me time?"'

Now although it's a joke, it does play to a truth that many parents of autistic kids face. What with planning, preparing and anticipating, or even reviewing or tidying up and putting stuff away, there is never enough time to just chill. Stacking the dishwasher or watering the garden are things I enjoy just for the escape of a mundane task that doesn't tax the brain. Mindless television or even staring out of the window can seem a luxury at times. Angela told me today that going for a mammogram meant she had a lovely quiet fifteen minutes to herself.

This may seem a little over the top and Angela and I both try to take each day as it comes. You never know though when even the simplest of things could present a problem. There was one day when Johnny was about seven; he must have been thirsty. Turning our attention from him for a few moments, we didn't see him take a bunch of daffodils out of their vase and drink the water. We spent the rest of the day in hospital with Johnny being treated for poisoning.

Johnny's breakfast starts with Chocolate Stars or cornflakes in bed and a glass of water. He usually prefers water to any drink. He's never had a hot drink other than a couple of cups of chocolate made with non-dairy milk to see if he enjoyed them. As he is gluten-and casein-free we do try to find variety in what can sometimes be a limited selection. Johnny doesn't seem to mind though and is always happy to have old favourites.

Uncannily, as he doesn't consult a clock, he will always wander into our bedroom at 7.30 a.m. and request 'toast and peanut butter'. This may be replaced with crumpet and honey, or on occasion raisin bread. Johnny does take reasonably well to alterations to his routine; the main thing is he's getting food of a similar ilk. As soon as he's finished his toast course he's ready to get washed. Angela or I usually supervise but he knows what to do. He even shaves himself now. He cut himself a couple of times to start with, but then so did I when I started shaving. Angela usually supervises him getting dressed but he knows what he needs and he can choose what he wants. He can do buttons and zips. Occasionally he'll put his button in the wrong hole but I've done that before and not realised until hours later. I've also spent the entire day with my fly zip undone – but luckily without getting arrested.

On a college day he will then go downstairs and watch cartoons. Now this may seem childish for an eighteen-year-old but there's not much choice in the mornings, and I don't know any autistic person – and very few non-autistic people – who actually enjoy breakfast TV.

Johnny's choice of viewing and his choice of bedtime books may betray something of his thought processes. He likes Cirque du Soleil, which he'll happily re-watch over and over. He often requests a documentary series called *Food Factory*, which is usually about factories in Canada making food in bulk and has lots of shots of ingredients going into hoppers and packaging machines. *How It's Made* is a similar show but with a wider brief than food. As well as lasagne and Gummy Bears, I've recently learnt how to make a windfarm and a kayak.

The bulk of Johnny's TV-watching is animated films. He likes movies like *Elf*, *Charlotte's Web* and the Harry Potter series. We do try to introduce more grown-up films but the animated films these days are so well made and bear repetition. It is hard to find live action films that can compete. The Tim Burton *Alice in Wonderland* and *Alice Through the Looking Glass* combine live action with animated characters very well and Johnny particularly enjoys these.

Films with a lot of talking are difficult and he displays no curiosity for more mature themes. I think we will continue trying films like *The Addams Family*, as he likes comedy, light horror films, or *Star Wars* and fantasy superhero films like *Spider-Man*. We are also trying to introduce nature films like *Planet Earth* and *Blue Planet* but they don't seem to keep his attention for long.

TV and films are a great way to have a little communication and interaction without being too interruptive. Johnny can navigate the Sky TV menu with the remote and we encourage him to take control. He likes the Vintage TV channel for music, instigated by his mum, who still likes all the old 1980s videos. At least he's not watching soft porn music videos.

His bedtime books are again quite juvenile. We ask him to choose a book and it's usually a short kids' story with pictures he likes. This is something we have to keep working on. He can read and understand a lot of basic words, but his comprehension of a story is difficult to gauge as he won't always answer our questions directly. Whether this is part of the communication difficulties or to do with his understanding we can only guess. We try to stretch him a little when reading, while still trying to keep it fun. There are some books I'm sure he knows by heart. If I ask him the next line he can recite it, often without even glancing at the page.

After watching some cartoons, at 8.15 a.m. he'll clean his teeth and get his coat on ready for college. Angela and I take it in turns to drive him there and back. Sitting in the front seat of my Land Rover, Johnny always wears his ear defenders to lessen the engine noise. He can still hear me talk to him and I find this a lovely way to have a chat one to one while driving about anything that's going on. If we've got something like a holiday coming up or if he's been biting the back of his hand, this is a good way to talk in a quiet and non-threatening way. Until he started school we had hardly ever had Johnny out of our sight other than at the Jeanne Saunders clinic. Even now outside college he is always within sight of myself, Angela or Angela's mum and dad. On Mondays Johnny takes photos into college from his weekend to use as a 'show and tell' to the class about his activities. The teachers tell us this is very useful in order to get him interacting.

Johnny arrives back from college at around 4.15 p.m. He takes his coat off and asks for cornflakes. This is something he'll eat on the purple settee in his art room while playing games on his iPad. I say his iPad; it used to be my iPad but he's seconded it. He plays various games and watches YouTube videos. A lot of the videos are animated songs or things like domino runs. The games are either quite basic jigsaws or word games. He chooses to watch these and it is a chill-out period for him, so we don't worry too much about moving him on to less childlike versions. It's an area we do need to revisit regularly though.

Also on Mondays Johnny likes to go to the local garden centre for a look around and invariably there'll be something to buy or something of interest. As I write, the Christmas decorations are in. A few weeks ago it was Bonfire Night and before that, Halloween. There's always something different happening in the garden centre whatever season it is. All the staff know him and say 'Hello Johnny' as he passes.

From Tuesday to Thursday once he's had his cornflakes he'll enjoy a walk. Living in Brighton as we do, we are lucky to be able to walk along various parts of the seafront, down by the pier or just to the shops or round the block. We all love walking by the sea and, a bit like in the car, it's a great place for casual interaction.

We've usually got a jigsaw on the go at the kitchen island these days and it is sometimes a good distraction from the job of waiting in the lead-up to dinner. Johnny sets the table with knives, forks, spoons and glasses of water. Under instruction, he likes to help with preparing the meal where he can. Also during this period he likes to draw and colour various figures on his own. These comprise line drawings, often a self-portrait (head and shoulders), a pirate or a Christmas *Nutcracker* soldier. By now he must have done well over a thousand of each of these.

When he's finished he'll cut out the figures himself and stick them with the other figures on a specific wall or blackboard. At his grandma and granddad's he sticks these figures up on the French windows, entirely covering them. This gives the house the appearance of being occupied by someone with a level of obsessive behaviour that must help deter cold-callers or religious zealots.

Johnny is getting better at just waiting, whether it's for food or whatever. When necessary, we always start by trying to explain to him as simply as possible the need to wait. I'm sure there's still an element of frustration but that's something we all have to come to terms with. These stressful situations require either avoidance or management. Avoidance is often preferable but if it's not possible then we just have to manage them. It's useful for us to teach him about coping in this supportive atmosphere, and we can but hope it carries forward to other situations. It doesn't always follow with autistic learning but then, though it's more likely, it doesn't always follow with any learning.

A little distraction we've employed recently is using the countdown facility on Angela's iPhone. We'll set it for five minutes and give it to Johnny so he knows how long he has to wait. He can see the time in digital display counting down. When the countdown reaches the end, some 1950s-style elevator music plays, which always makes us all laugh and we do a granddad-type dance to it. I think Johnny enjoys the music and dance so, as well as the distraction, he gets to anticipate the fun. We use this only occasionally but it does give a little breathing space if we have our hands full.

At 6.30 p.m. we have dinner – or tea, as I used to call it when I was still a working-class northerner, and as I still think of it in my head. We always sit down at the table and eat together, Johnny in his usual chair at the end of the table with Angela and me either side of him, sat opposite each other. I've learnt that if my voice is too harsh on a subject it causes Johnny anxiety. It doesn't matter what I'm talking about – Donald Trump or British Rail – whatever has aggravated me, Johnny picks up on the mood. He may not understand the argument but he is conscious of the atmosphere. So we try not to discuss anything annoying. Instead Angela and I use the occasion for modelling interaction and try to include Johnny in the conversation as much as possible. We discuss things of common interest to us all and just concentrate on enjoying our meal. Occasionally Johnny will stop eating and put his fingers in his ears and we'll quietly try to identify the noise that has upset him. It might be the dishwasher or the fridge, or just that we are talking too much. Sometimes it can be the clatter of cutlery on the plates, or even perhaps the sound of chewing within his own head.

Johnny then watches TV in the living room until bedtime. After about forty-five minutes he will have some fruit and yogurt. Sometimes he'll play on his iPad while watching TV; he'll do it without turning the sound off, but not if I'm in the room, as it drives me barmy.

Unlike most teenage boys, Johnny is always eager to have a bath and go to bed. Usually he's too keen, so we have to try to keep him up till at least 8.30 p.m. He loves bath bombs and bubbles and doesn't seem to mind the sound of the water too much. He'll normally go to the toilet first. He's very good at going to the toilet in time nowadays. If anything, he'll go to the toilet too often. I think he uses it as an excuse to get away to a nice quiet room for five minutes without any pressure.

When the bath is full he will test the heat and then get in. He'll wash himself and fifteen minutes later be ready to get out. When he was little he went through various stages. One was that he wouldn't sit in the bath at all. This reluctance came out of the blue, appeared sporadically without warning, and disappeared without trace, although we did put special plastic sheeting at the bottom of the bath for a while and that seemed to help. Another strange quirk he has is that on the odd occasion he won't walk on the wooden floor when he gets out of the bath, so we've now put a mat down for him. Problem solved.

We now leave his light on and ask him to turn it off when he's ready. Wherever we can we like to give him as many elements of control as he can cope with. These are only small things but they can build. Once in bed he will usually settle down to sleep. Sometimes though we'll hear him shouting or laughing or clapping in his bedroom or in his bathroom. One of us will pop upstairs to ensure he's fine. Mostly he is and will eventually settle.

It's usually around 9 to 9.30–10 p.m. when Johnny goes to sleep, by which time Angela is too tired for anything other than an hour's TV and bed, ready to start again in the morning. I'm more of a night owl so I'll sit up writing or watch football or anything else like sci-fi or boys' action movies I know Angela wouldn't want us to watch together (then I regret it in the morning).

QUINTESSENCE

Yesterday was quite ordinary

We went through the usual wake-up routine
Cornflakes, toast and peanut butter,
time on the computer, the iPad,
washed and dressed, word-search

The morning came and went without
much conscious thought
Johnny set the table for lunch
Filled three glasses with water

In the afternoon we went for a walk in the woods
Making something out of nothing
Angela used slowmo and time lapse
and we created little films for ourselves

Driving home we listened to music
Johnny set the table for dinner
Filled three glasses with water
and we all sat down together

I looked over to him, an eighteen-year-old
with what might pass for designer stubble
Six foot three, muscular
a new haircut and suntan

and for no reason
I noticed
he was handsome
Hollywood handsome

We were eating dinner
quietly
like an ordinary family
I can't even remember what food

and there it was
a glimpse
unexpected
This was the man Johnny could have been

'Isn't Johnny handsome?' I said to Angela
wanting to include her in the moment
It was all I could do
to stop myself weeping like a fool

After
when I stacked the dishwasher alone
I broke like death

Unexpected
I hadn't glimpsed
the man Johnny could have been
The mourning was for a different loss

one known
but not understood until now
for there in this moment
was the beauty of the man he was

Chapter 19a

Bedtime by Angela

Our routines in general are quite rigid. When I write the word 'rigid' I feel it has negative connotations. But actually rigid routines can be far from negative. Take bedtime, for example. It is actually my absolute favourite part of the day. Any day. It is forty minutes of unadulterated fun and the time when I feel most connected with Johnny. He is incredibly 'present' and basically we spend the majority of our 'countdown to bed' laughing together.

Johnny likes going to bed and will usually ask to get ready around 8–8.30 p.m. This means he's actually all pyjama-ed up and wanting lights out around 9.15 p.m. This is ridiculously early for a nineteen-year-old and is no doubt one of the reasons he wakes up very early. However, it's what he likes and it does mean that Henry and I can get a little bit of time at the end of the day to crash and watch TV together. On a good night, we are able to delay the start of bedtime until a little later. Although it doesn't always follow that the later Johnny falls asleep, the longer he'll sleep.

Johnny has a bath every night, a lot of the time using the bath bombs that we buy on a Saturday. We have a good ten minutes of messing around while the bath is running and he gets undressed. This involves Johnny pressing my face/chin (as is his wont) and me shouting things like, 'Monstrous Villainy!' and 'Outrageous Behaviour!' at him in a gruff pirate voice. The bit he likes best is when he looks like he's going to go for my chin again and I tell him that if he does, I'll spray him with cold water from the tap. He laughs and laughs in anticipation. Then he can't help himself and basically grabs my chin once more. At which point I shout a loud 'Right!' and fill my hand with cold water and throw it all over him. The shock of it makes him laugh like a hyena. He prances around the bathroom, dripping and giggling. Sometimes he laughs so hard he gets the hiccups. Often he's bent double, unable to stop. I love this. This activity can carry on for another good five minutes.

We have had an issue with Johnny's 'grabbing' for years now. It is often done in jest – an inappropriate attempt to play or inter-act. Occasionally, when he is stressed, it is done in an impulsive 'No, I want this to stop' kind of way. It is very easy to tell the two versions apart. During the former, he has a huge smile on his face and a twinkle in his eye. With the latter, he looks cross and some-times makes harsh-sounding noises. He might also be stamping his foot. Neither is ideal and both tend to be quite painful, although when he is playing, he is able to stop himself if he can see from my reaction that it's starting to hurt and I need him to cut it out.

Knowing how to respond to or change this behaviour is tricky and we (and his teachers) have tried all sorts of things from underplaying, distracting, saying an outright 'No', trying to take the playful grab and turn it into something more 'appropriate' like a high five etc. None of these approaches has really worked. It's complicated – for example, by offering up a high-five (or an even more exciting alternative i.e. 'Ooh you want to play now – great – let's go and shoot some hoops!') reinforces to Johnny that when he grabs, he gets an alternative offered. Maybe he then thinks – I need to do the grab in order to get the basketball? Whatever the theory, I am not sure that shrieking 'Monstrous Villainy!' and then upping the fun and drama is a good idea if we want to reduce this conduct. But in the real world it is sometimes hard to be consistent – and fun is important.

As a parent, when you're getting such amazing, fully engaged interaction, it's asking quite a lot of us to forsake it. To 'not give it any energy'. We spend so long trying to get this level of engagement that we don't want to waste it or discourage it. We don't want to jeopardise it. So although we know it's 'inappropriate', it feels precious. I hold my hand up in this instance and say I really don't know what's the best thing to do.

I *have*, however, discovered what works in the car to prevent grabbing while I'm driving. A slightly more serious prospect. I am not sure how much Johnny understands about the prospect of pain. Or even death. And therefore I employ the old advice, 'Use your child's motivation'. Instead of giving Johnny a list of all the awful things that could happen if I crashed the car because he was busy grabbing my face and I got distracted, I take another tack. There's little point in telling him we might get hurt, have our legs broken, have to have an operation or, worse, be killed. These are abstract concepts. Instead I inform him of something more immediate. More tangible. It's well documented here that Johnny likes his food; so I tell him that if we crash, we will have to go to hospital and we'll be there for hours because it's always so busy – which means we won't be home in time for tea. He stops grabbing in an instant.

Once in the bath, Johnny has a good soak, sometimes playing with squirty foam or using plastic utensils to sculpt soap. I go and get his pyjamas and book ready. He will have already chosen which book we will be reading. I still, despite him being a grown man now, read Johnny a story in bed every night. He has all his books on display on his bedroom wall on a shelf-like structure I got years ago from a schools equipment magazine. It looks like something you'd find in a library but it means he can see all his options. Johnny's books are still all children's picture books, and although every so often we try to introduce books that are a little more 'grown-up' he invariably picks his old favourites. He has been reading these books for years. I think he must find them comforting. I equate it to imagining if I had spent all day in a foreign land where I don't really understand a lot of the language and customs, where everything feels quite inaccessible (say for me, somewhere in Japan) and then I randomly bump into an old school friend on the tube. The sense of relief because I know this person, I know how they speak and what we're likely to talk about would be palpable. I guess it's the same for the films Johnny chooses to watch again and again as well. Familiarity is a warm blanket. It's undemanding. Happily predictable. Reassuring. Safe.

After his bath, Johnny lies on the bed snuggled in towels and I massage his feet with almond oil and liquid melatonin, then put his socks on for him. Johnny has always had a passion for all things circus. Even though my back is shot and my joints ache, we then play a game where he lifts me up on the flats of his feet as though to make me fly. I wobble about a bit shouting, 'Ladies and gentlemen, I give you The Great Pelletiers!'

Johnny then gets up and puts on his night gear and we lie back down on the bed for his story. I have to admit that I suddenly become taken over by the spirit of a hammy old actor at this stage in the proceedings. I read every story as if my life depended on it. Oscar-worthy some might say, if they were passing. I've even given myself a sore throat on longer books that require a greater level of dramatic range.

My favourite books to read are Ivor the Engine stories (I do all Ivor books in a Welsh accent. I've explained to Johnny they are all set in Wales and this is how a lot of (clichéd) Welsh people speak, but whether or not he understands I'm not sure. He may just think, Why in God's name is it that every time we read Ivor The Engine my mum puts on this even more ridiculous voice?). The best story in my humble opinion is 'Ivor and the Dragon'. It's very funny and has a lot of loud exclamations which Johnny really enjoys. 'No! No! Not water! Water is certain death to dragons!' is a particularly fun line to shout in a poor Welsh accent. I also love Roald Dahl's *The Enormous Crocodile* – it's beautifully written and great for reading aloud (although quite long). We are both fans of Dr Seuss too (as though the world weren't surreal enough to explain at the best of times). All books are read with the odd bit of squeezing/chin-grabbing creeping in, at which point I playfully tell Johnny he has to sit on his hands if he wants me to continue. He sits on his hands for all of three sentences.

Once the story is finished, we have a hug and then Johnny heads off for a wee. Briefly, and a little off topic, but someone recently asked how we eventually got Johnny 'toilet trained', so here feels like a good place to answer that question. We did a lot of modelling action, sitting and waiting – while 'playing' on the toilet with toys or looking at books. We had a lot of mishaps on the way and Johnny was in nappies until he was about six or seven I think. Looking back now, though, the best bit of advice I can give is not to get too stressed about your child not doing stuff 'they should be doing by now'. I believe that kids pick up on parents' anxiety way more than we think they do. Giving yourself and your special needs child a 'timetable to complete' any tasks is a fool's errand. It puts pressure on everyone and few of us are at our best when we're under pressure. Be persistent and believe you'll get there, but try not to make it the be-all and end-all. Hope for the ideal at each attempt, but if you can, let go of any attachment to the desired outcome. This sounds really hard, and it can be.

I recall thinking Johnny would never be out of nappies. But he got there in the end. He still needs help toileting, though, even now. He rarely flushes. Maybe this is because he doesn't like the noise; but I've learned to stop worrying too much about it. He could still be smearing his poo all over the walls, but he's not. He has come a long way. Of course, there are no guarantees you will succeed in any given area. There are many people with special needs who never get out of nappies. Some I know who still manage to function pretty well in the world, it has to be said.

Johnny then comes back from the toilet and tells me to go. I say goodnight and 'Don't forget . . . I love you.' He tells me he loves me back. Sometimes I also say, 'Don't forget how great you are!' or 'Don't ever forget how fantastic you are!'

We have on occasion asked Johnny to describe people to us. He finds this very difficult. However, when we ask him to describe himself using five words he is always more than able to do so. He usually says, 'Clever, brilliant, great, good, gorgeous.' I guess we can tick 'building self-esteem' off our list of things to do.

Johnny invariably replies to my extra 'don't forgets' with one word: 'Cornflakes.' This means 'I'd like cornflakes for breakfast please, now you can go.' I'm sure you're thinking it's hard to decipher who actually likes this bedtime routine more. I'll admit it could be me.

I don't know how we get into these habits, to be honest. One thing leads to another and before you know it a new routine has taken hold. Johnny likes to go to the garden centre on a Monday night, for example. We have been going up there for years, regular as clockwork. He's very insistent that we head up after college. However, once in the building, he just does a quick circuit, then he wants to come home again. I think sometimes he just needs to do these things because they are a means of getting to the *next* thing, i.e. once he's been to the garden centre he knows he comes home and watches 'the circus' (a Cirque Du Soleil DVD) while peeling the potatoes. And peeling the potatoes means the countdown to tea. I don't like to mess with his routines if I can help it;. I think they make him feel safe and secure and that he has some control over his life. I can't imagine what it must be like being at the mercy/schedule/whim of other people all the time. Which is probably how many people with special needs have to live their lives.

Chapter 20
Friday/Saturday/Sunday

Johnny has never attended school or college full-time. He has always had one day a week being 'home educated'. On these days, we like to ensure he's engaged in meaningful, learning activities. Since last year he's been involved with a farm project via the organisation Farm Buddies. Johnny enjoys the physicality. He mends fences, clears ground, feeds pigs, plants trees and does whatever labouring jobs are asked of him.

On a Friday afternoon twice a month, a musician called Tom Cook comes round to the house and works with Johnny for an hour. He been coming now for five or six years and encourages Johnny to sing, often using a microphone, which Johnny enjoys. They make up their own songs like 'Don't Bite Your Finger' (a punk classic), and also play and sing covers of 1980s songs. Tom also encourages Johnny to play along with various musical instruments – drums, maracas and other percussion instruments, mouth organ, guitars and anything Tom can lay his hands on. Johnny gets plenty of enjoyment out of these sessions. He often puts great energy into the songs and smiles and laughs and sort of sways and dances throughout the session. Angela has made a couple of videos of them singing and while I was working at Baby Cow one of my colleagues animated a song Johnny had made up and sung about Kung Fu Panda (using a drawing by Johnny). Seeing Johnny's face light up when he first saw the video was priceless.

Johnny likes physical activity. He likes nature. So if you combine the two you're on to a winner. He helps his granddad and grandma with their garden. His granddad has an array of vegetables and for most of the year there is stuff to be done. His grandma has a herb garden and lots of flowers. There's also a large lawn and a few hedges, so all in all a six-foot-three strong helper is always very useful when you reach seventy. Johnny is happy to get involved for short periods, with the added incentive that at some point he's going to be eating some of those vegetables. Jobs like taking waste to the tip and dividing it into the right skips he enjoys. He often requests 'tip'. Any job with a clear instruction he'll give a go.

Once a month on a Friday afternoon he goes to a different farm to work alongside a lovely woman called Dido Fisher with her horses Dylan and Magpie for an hour. He brushes them, picks out their hooves and on occasion washes them. He walks them and feeds them. He sometimes cleans their stables. One of the main things he's learnt is to be gentle with them. Johnny's been going there for about four years now and the difference is marked. Nowadays he calms himself down and concentrates while setting about his tasks. He has gained such a lot of confidence around these quite large animals. As someone who is still a little nervous around horses I find it inspiring. Angela often reminds me that the key to any of these activities with Johnny is to persevere. He may not at first show signs of taking to them, or any competence, but little by little a relationship grows. You find the level he can cope with and build on it.

Also on a Friday he goes to a group run by Jo Offer called Rocket Artists based at the Phoenix in Brighton. All the Rocket Artists have special needs. Here he's had the opportunity to try new things like weaving and printing. They also have exhibitions constantly up in the building, which he enjoys visiting.

When Johnny was younger a woman called Persephone Pearl taught him trapeze for several years. Johnny has always loved being high up. Dangling precariously in an old church in Lewes, he got to do just that. Percy, as we all called her, was particularly patient with Johnny and over time got him to interact and do exercises and moves on the trapeze that, when they started, we never thought she could possibly achieve. As Johnny grew older and larger, though, it became apparent that, like those of his parents, his body just wasn't built for the trapeze.

On a standard Saturday morning, Johnny and his mum go into Brighton. They visit the same shops and generally buy more or less the same items. Johnny looks forward to this and could probably do the entire shopping trip blind-fold by now. Being so distinctive, Johnny is welcomed into each shop as a regular. We have the pizza they buy for lunch when they get home and Johnny will paint a picture. If Johnny has any spare time he often opts to paint a picture. He has always enjoyed art but over the last few years it's become something special for him.

His paintings are now mostly large in scale and he has several recurring themes – 'hills and trees', 'the villa' and 'the pavilion' are the main three. He gets a lot of enjoyment from painting. I can see him really concentrating and making choices. He's very confident and bold. He likes to paint and draw the same scenes, although each time he uses different colours and the overall effect can be very different. A little bit like David Hockney painting the same rural scene on different days of the year.

'Hills and trees' is Johnny's favourite theme, which at times looks like a depiction of the crucifixion. It usually consists of three trees that resemble crosses and a variety of hills that vary in both size and number. There are never any figures in these paintings. He now paints with such confi-dence that the later versions are clearly different from his early works. Sometimes now he uses Posca Pens to add detail on top of the picture once the paint is dry.

Once a month Angela takes him to a Saturday-morning art class for children with special needs called Mymarc, run by Sue Winter. He's been involved in all sorts of different activities here – mask making, sculpture, printing and even painting with his feet. To encourage widening his painting scope, he's occasionally asked to choose a painting by a famous painter from a book and paint his own version. I love the fact that Johnny's version is always so surprisingly different. I don't think I would have the imagination to find such difference. Johnny's choice of colours is quite striking and many people, including seasoned artists we know, comment on it.

Angela has made a postcard book with some of Johnny's paintings. She has also had some of his work printed on mugs and T-shirts and caps. I used Johnny's paintings to illustrate the covers of both of my recent poetry books *Staring Directly at the Eclipse* and *Raining Upwards*. When the first box of books arrived, Johnny seemed genuinely happy to see his work reproduced. We have framed several of Johnny's paintings and hung them throughout the house. There are also paintings hung at his grandparents' and his aunties' houses.

Angela has even put up his paintings on Facebook. 'Art By Johnny' if you want to check it out. I'm a little suspicious of Facebook in that I've got 1,700 likes and 1,701 followers. That's one person following me who doesn't like me. That's basically a stalker. Anyway Johnny is not far behind me now with Facebook followers. I'm hoping once this book comes out his painting will be seen more widely. From the comments I know he inspires people.

A local framer recently asked if she could display some of Johnny's paintings and when we showed him them in her shop window his face lit up. I think Johnny enjoys people liking his artwork. I can see by his reaction and the way he holds himself that he takes pleasure from the appreciation. He's also had a few of his paintings in an exhibition in Wales. We took a short break there; I drove Angela and Johnny and Angela's mum and dad over to see the exhibition. There were over fifty paintings on display. I asked Johnny which was the best painting. Without hesitation he pointed to one of his own. I had to laugh. He had certainly become a true artist!

Watching him create art, I'm struck by his deliberation. He is making decisions by himself for himself. The act of painting and drawing is something he seeks out and requests. While painting he always appears happy, engaged and content. 'The villa' is another of his standard themes. It's a view from his painting table in our Portugal villa, on the patio, out across the pool to the garden. He once painted the pool black, which really surprised me. It's not a colour I would ever have chosen for the light-blue-tiled pool. Again, these paintings have no figures in them.

Johnny does paint and draw figures, which are often quite haunting. He went through a phase of drawing a particular character he called 'Kung Fu Panda'. They were always in black and white and the ears seem to hover detached from the head. One of Johnny's self-portraits I particularly like is a black and white drawing where he has coloured himself black. I do love that it would most likely have no political or racial meaning for Johnny; his world view seems to represent the ultimate in equality.

Johnny has painted tables and stools around the house. He will paint anything that that doesn't move – or, to be honest, anything that doesn't move too quickly. Art has become part of his life. Part of who he is. I can't imagine him without his painting now. It would be like imagining myself without my writing or Neil Armstrong without his having walked on the moon.

Johnny paints virtually every weekend now, and every day on holiday. When he started we got him these 'colour by numbers' books but he doesn't like being restricted. These books tell you which colour to put in where and they show

you the edges to colour up to. Well, Johnny was not having
any of that; he put what colours he wanted in, and he decided
what edges he wanted, and I loved that.

BEAUTY WITHOUT NUMBERS

Presented with Colour By Numbers
he chooses only what colour he wants
only what borders appeal

The figurative made abstract
The shape of the world embellished

New edges imagined
The palette reinvigorated

A choice is braved
A universe decided
Personality shaming mathematics

Lines enhanced as never before
to create
a map of self-determination

Chapter 20a
Art By Johnny by Angela

There is a quote that goes around the parent blogs and pages of online special needs communities: 'I thought I would have to teach my child about the world. It turns out, I have to teach the world about my child.' I am pretty sure that through his art, Johnny is also doing his bit to educate people about expectation, expression and communication.

I suspect that Johnny was always going to be a creative soul. Realising that he was autistic and beginning Son-Rise meant that we spent four years of his early life focusing on inventive, fun ways to establish meaningful relationships and interaction; these often involved dressing up, music, dancing, drawing and painting and other creative activities. This practice of engaging creatively became a shortcut – a way to put across meaning and build human connections that didn't rely so heavily on spoken language, as spoken language was – and still is – an area of challenge for Johnny.

It was an intense time for all of us. As well as being very emotional, it had practical implications. We stopped seeing people, lost touch with old friends, didn't spend much time with family. But looking back now I am so glad that we did it. During those formative years when Johnny had no verbal means to express himself, every time he looked up and came back from being in another world he was met with a smiling, non-judgemental face, offering him up the chance to partake in a joint activity that was always based on his own passions. Not a bad way to start life.

Perhaps, therefore, for Johnny – when faced day in, day out with adults dressing up as characters from his favourite books or TV shows; turning his playroom into the surface of the moon or an underwater scene; transforming an upside table into a magic carpet (with accompanying Disney soundtrack); squirting paint across lining paper à la Jackson Pollock while dangling from a hammock, etc. etc. – it was just a case of him holding his hands up in a 'Well, if you can't beat 'em . . .' kind of way.

The key idea of Son-Rise is enticing your child. I am aware that reading the previous paragraph, you may get the feeling we bludgeoned Johnny into engagement! This isn't the case really, although one of the funniest memories I have of that time is of my sister-in-law Val, arriving at the house (having driven to us) all ready to 'play', dressed from head to toe in a giant 'chicken coming out of an egg' costume. I also, incidentally, remember her sitting on the potty and demonstrating to Johnny how to use it (grunts and all), while the man who had come to fix the playroom window waited outside, watching her through the two-way mirror. She wasn't in the egg costume at the time (and she was fully clothed), but I am still sure it's a sight he will never have been able to unsee.

I think labels are very problematic, for autistic people especially. It's actually difficult to refer to anyone as one thing or another. In the case of autism, there are such overlaps that 'severe' and 'mild' feel inadequate at best and often misleading.

Johnny, like most other people on the spectrum, displays a variation in ability. He still struggles with verbal communication. He can get most of his needs met using one-or two-word requests, but is unable to hold an actual 'conversation' or really tell us what he's feeling or thinking (at the moment. Who is to say that this won't change?). Currently, he doesn't understand a lot of the complexities of how the world works in the way that a neurotypical person usually does. He is often overwhelmed by sensory input. Noise in particular he can find challenging. He dislikes the cries of both seagulls and young girls who can't get what they want. He is fearful of dogs. However, he knows a million songs; he can groom a horse from top to tail, swim twenty lengths without stopping and it is very clear that he can choose, mix and apply paint in a way that I am reliably informed leaves other 'regular' professional artists 'feeling intimidated'.

Johnny's paintings are full of energy, movement and emotion. I know there's an idea that all good art comes out of chaos and struggle and I do wonder if Johnny is constrained by how his own specific autism impacts on him. For example, he always paints the same subject matter when in a particular room, and a totally different subject matter when in another room. He will always start one kind of painting with the same colour ('Hills and trees' always begins with yellow). He will only ever use a felt pen once (biting around the top of the lid as a way of identifying that that pen must now be discarded, i.e. given away to friends' children. I joke that he has a serious 'felt pen habit'.) He will never use a certain brown or a certain red that come in the packets of paint we buy at the discount store. Yet he is never constrained by any fear of 'getting it wrong'. He paints with confidence and always with a total delight in colour. Which he seldom uses naturalistically. And even if he is adamant in choosing one of his four current favourite subject matters, every time he paints he manages to make each picture look and feel different and fresh. He is not so tied that every painting has to be the same colour as the last. Far from it. Each has its own unique energy. To me, that is one of his greatest talents.

Johnny generally walks through life, all sixteen stone, six foot three of him, boldly and with great joy. He has a self-belief that comes out in his brush strokes and the definiteness of his outlines. I suspect we can also see, though, in some of the figures and faces he draws, how overwhelming life might at times be for him. They can be quite haunting. They can seem expressionless. They appear to loom in front of you with their arms outstretched. This may just be us projecting, of course. Henry wrote a poem about this.

WITHOUT TRESPASS

Your hands are together
as though in prayer

The image before you
has his arms raised
as though wanting to be picked up

Without trespass
I try not to project my hopes
and accept all possibility

Your hands might be caught mid clap
The image might be exalting the sky
You are more than my perception

You may be warming your hands
against the weather
The image may well be waving

You could be rubbing chalk between your palms
The image could simply be trying to surrender

Johnny paints quickly and with no pretension. He delights in squeezing out the paint. Often he moves around while painting – dancing, singing, talking, laughing to himself – and mostly, he has no real interest in the work once it's finished. This is a great lesson for me, as a precious writer. A great lesson for us all, I guess: live in the moment; engage fully in what you enjoy, don't worry too much about 'getting it right' and don't dwell on past glories.

Johnny's interest in art as a child was limited. When he was very young it took a lot of encouragement for him to even pick up a pen. But I guess I persisted because it was a field I felt able in myself. If I had been any good at maths, I might well have used numbers to try to engage with him; instead I used paint and glue. We did all sorts of stuff in the early days. We began by drawing on the walls of his playroom. I used to just patch it up. Eventually we got a whiteboard. Now Johnny paints on a wall protected with B&Q builders' tarpaulin, held up by staples. When I first set the 'studio' up for him, I covered half the room in plastic sheeting. It seriously looked like a 'Kill Room' from the TV series *Dexter*.

The best bit of advice I was ever given in relation to creating art was from my old A-level teacher Mr Giles. On our first day he told us to all get our pencils out, which we dutifully did. He then threw them in the bin. He said, 'From now on you draw with your paintbrush. If you make a mistake – just paint over it.' After our initial shock, we all began to realise that this was incredibly freeing. I have encouraged Johnny to do the same thing over the years. We don't really have any pencils in the house. I like to think that this has assisted Johnny in developing his style of painting, perhaps best described as, 'big/bold/definite'.

We've recently been given the opportunity to put on a month-long exhibition for Johnny at the prestigious Phoenix Art Gallery in Brighton in April 2018. This is a real achievement and we are so proud of him. He is a prolific artist and a talented one – but more than this, it's a testament to how far he has come and everything he's achieved. He's become 'known' for his art. In a way, people define him by it. If I think back to him as a little child and me not even knowing what he liked, this puts in perspective just how far he has travelled.

Another parent of an autistic child was talking to me about Johnny's exhibition recently and she admitted she felt 'jealous'. Not because of the opportunity he's been given, or the art, but jealous of the fact that our son 'has found something he loves doing'. When Johnny was growing up people used to pass on cuttings to us from newspapers and tell us stories about how various autistic children had been miraculously made more verbal or interactive by the addition of a pet dog/horse-riding/surfing/* (*insert a random activity here). These articles had headings like 'Horse Boy' and 'Surf Boy'. I used to find them really annoying. Partly because I couldn't see any of these examples working for us, partly because I felt this pressure to find 'the thing' that would unlock our son so we too would be able to move forward with his amazing newfound abilities. I remember thinking, what if it's something we'll never find – what if Johnny's 'miracle' is just too obscure, like rearing bats in Papua New Guinea? I woke up early the other day and thought – could Johnny now be seen as 'Art Boy'? Perhaps from the outside, that's the way it might look to some people, but the answer is a definite no. Art is a big part of his life and for the minutes he spends doing a painting, he's relaxed and happy. But I can't say it's made him more verbal or more interactive.

You may have guessed that the musician Nick Cave is a bit of an idol in our house. I am a member of a few 'appreciation' sites. One Saturday, Johnny painted a picture of Nick (who we listen to a lot in the car). He really enjoyed 'interpreting' a photo of said Rock God on the iPad, carefully looking at the photograph and then back at his painting as he worked. When he'd finished it, I posted it up on one of the 'fan' pages. Lots of people commented and eventually the picture even got selected by the group to go into a birthday book from the 'disciples' to Nick, for his sixtieth. There's a photo of Nick receiving the book. I got super excited, knowing that he'd seen Johnny's picture. We bought a copy of the book and when I showed Johnny it in the flesh and told him the birthday gift story, he positively beamed. He may well of course merely been swept up in my gushing, slightly histrionic, motherly pride – who's to know?

Originally Johnny's exhibition was going to be a joint one, along with his peers at the Rocket Artists studio. However, Rocket Artists decided that as Johnny had so much work and the work was strong, they'd like to curate the event. In doing so, this would give their artists the opportunity to learn what it takes to put on an exhibition. Although excited and proud, I was actually in two minds about Johnny having a solo show. I didn't want us to be seen as 'pushy' parents – that type of mum and dad who thrust their (reluctant) child into the limelight or into participating in an activity they have no real interest in. I wondered if Johnny would actually *be bothered*? I know he likes the gallery space, because we visit it most Fridays and he loves running around in it – I think he is especially keen on its echo-y acoustics. But I imagined that he'd go along to the private view, enjoy bouncing around and seeing his art for five minutes, then be more interested in getting back home for tea.

When I mentioned my 'pushy parent' worry to my friend Terry, she just looked at me and said, 'But no one's ever likely to push Johnny into doing something he doesn't want to do, are they?' I laughed. How right she was. When Johnny's not having any of it, he's not having any of it. And, as Henry said when I questioned the whole thing, 'Well, why not? Johnny may or may not be moved by or engaged with it, but we'll only know if we give him the chance.'

Chapter 21
Work Ethic

When we found out about Johnny being autistic I felt guilty going to work and leaving Angela.

When I was a kid my dad had worked seven days a week at Raleigh Industries as a maintenance mechanic. He worked a full day Monday to Friday, Saturday till 2 p.m. and Sunday till noon. He'd leave the house at 6 a.m. and during the week arrive back at 6 p.m. From what I've heard he was good at his job and well respected.

I often wondered if he was using work to hide from his problems. There, he was just like everyone else. His problems at work were easy to understand; he was equipped and he knew what he needed to do. Being at home, bringing up three young girls and two boys, was something scarier. Something that not many men of his generation had experienced before.

I worried that with Johnny I was taking a similar path. We needed money, probably more than we'd thought before, if we were to gear up for the challenges ahead. Love, patience, resilience and pragmatism are without doubt the most important attributes to have as the parent of a child with special needs, but not being able to afford treatments or resources was a fear. This was my thought process, my pragmatic approach and my game plan. Though I couldn't help but be aware that this also sounded like an excuse to hide from problems at home.

The only way I could justify this to myself was by being efficient. By earning as much money as possible at work in reasonable hours and spending as much time at home with Angela and Johnny as that would allow. I was lucky in that I was in a job that could be flexible and paid well, so it did feel like we were building a war chest. I accepted that Johnny was probably never going to work for a living. He was always going to live with Angela and me and we had to prepare for that. Then there was the bigger fear – what would happen to him when we died. I wanted to leave him with a fighting chance of a happy life.

From the start, my dad had instilled in me a work ethic, and I understood and enjoyed work. My first part-time job was stacking shelves at Fine Fare on Bracebridge Drive, Bilborough. Fine Fare was a fairly downmarket supermarket and the wages were low. I used to look at the people coming in to shop and think they were looking down on me for working in such a place. As we lived on the council estate and didn't have much money, we also shopped there, and when I entered the place to shop I used to glance at the people stacking shelves and think they were also looking down on me for shopping there. Either way I couldn't win. I used some of the money I earned at Fine Fare to buy a stereo system. I used to swap the price tags on the LPs at Fine Fare and buy all the latest albums I wanted, like Deep Purple and Led Zeppelin, for 72p rather than £2.50. I do feel guilty sometimes that some poor bugger paid £2.50 for Acker Bilk or Herb Alpert and the Tijuana Brass.

My friend Nigel's mum and dad ran a disco once a week at the local pensioners' club. I used to take my stereo and records along and Nigel and I would DJ. The pensioners seemed really old to me when I was a teenager and I remember we would play some singles without lyrics on 33rpm rather than 45rpm so that they were able to dance to them.

At Christmas they hired a comedian, who was the first live comic I'd ever seen. Nigel and I talked to him before the show and he never said anything funny at all. I was beginning to doubt he was going to go down well, but once he was introduced and walked on stage he came alive. I remember his first joke. He was dressed as a schoolboy although he must have been in his twenties. 'My mum asked me what I wanted for Christmas,' he said. 'I said to her, I want something to wear and something to play with,' he continued and looked down at his short trousers before delivering the punchline: 'So she gave me these trousers with a hole in the pocket.' The pensioners roared. It struck me that he wasn't bothered about being funny off stage; he was saving it for where it had the most impact.

I'd dreamt of a career in comedy since I was twelve, when I saw Jack Benny on *The Dean Martin TV Show*. Dean

Martin, in a tuxedo, was on the phone at his home, which was built as a set in front of a TV audience. Jack Benny entered, also in a tuxedo. Seeing Dean was on the phone, he walked around to the sofa area. He didn't sit on the sofa though; despite being in a tuxedo, he lay on the floor and started playing dice by himself. I'd not seen Jack Benny before but I loved him immediately. This was the world I wanted to live in. It seemed so much more glamorous than the Nottingham council estate I lived on. I'd never seen a grown man do something like this before – he was having fun. All the grown-ups I'd seen up to this point seemed so formal.

I later found out that Jack Benny was so well thought of by the Marx Brothers when they were all starting out that they asked him to join them and be one of the brothers, even though technically he wasn't. But Benny's mum wouldn't allow it. The more I read about Jack Benny and the more I heard him on the radio and saw him on TV and in films, the more I wanted to be like him. By all accounts he was well liked by everyone he worked with. Despite bearing no resemblance to him in either my appearance or my material, when I was on stage performing poetry or comedy, in my head I was him.

I've written poetry since I was about fourteen, when I read a collection by Spike Milligan called *Small Dreams of a Scorpion*. I'd only known him as a comic writer up to that point and was struck at how someone so funny could also make me cry in so few words. Up until then my reading was mostly Monty Python and Spike's funny books and *Goon Show* scripts. These serious poems, though, stayed with me more than all the comedy. Even though I pursued a career in comedy and became successful, it's still the moments of pathos and genuine sentiment in all the things I've read that have made the deepest and most enduring impression.

I got to meet Spike Milligan some years later when I was in my early forties and running Baby Cow. I was asked to judge a BBC TV comedy competition alongside Spike at the Komedia in Brighton. I sat next to him on the judging panel and people kept coming up to him and asking for his autograph. 'Fuck off,' he'd say to them and they'd laugh, thinking he was joking, but he was seriously telling them to fuck off.

I told him I was very much a fan of his poems and he recited several, off the top of his head. I thanked him but felt the conversation was a bit like a performance, so I tried to communicate in a more personal manner. I was, it must be said, very tired, having worked all day in London and then having commuted back on Southern Rail. Struggling to find something we had in common, I remembered that he lived in Rye. 'I know you live in Rye,' I said. 'I live in Brighton, because I love the sea,' I continued. He looked at me a moment, then leant in and whispered, 'Henry, you're a fascinating man.' Angela now uses this riposte if ever I say anything bland or boring, which unfortunately I still do, occasionally.

In my twenties, though I had a decent job at an insurance brokers, I started performing poetry both locally and around the north, especially in Sheffield. I got to meet Sheffield bands like Pulp and Dig Vis Drill, both of whom I went on to perform with around the country, including at the famous Marquee Club in London. Pulp's lead singer Jarvis Cocker broke his legs and an arm around this time, falling from a window. I would have to wheel him on stage in his wheelchair. Morrissey had recently been wearing fake glasses and a hearing aid on stage as an affectation and I'm sure some people thought this was Jarvis going one step further. It did make me laugh when he danced his characteristic moves, but in his chair.

Sometimes I'd perform during my lunch hour or straight after work, still with my suit on. As I was performing in front of 'new wave' audiences, I needed a name to undercut any aversion to my straight appearance. Calling myself Henry Normal was a perfect way to show I was self-aware about my appearance and indeed my persona. A lot of the punk performers from the recent past had chosen strange names – Sid Vicious, Johnny Rotten, Adam Ant. And the new movement of rant poets that grew out of punk often had made-up and striking names like Attila the Stockbroker, Little Brother, John Bitumen and Seething Wells. Having a writing and performing name also helped to keep my extra-curricular activities away from my boss at the insurance brokers, not to mention the tax man. There was also a deeper significance to my choice at the time though, in that I did feel ordinary and unremarkable, lacking in character even. It struck me that to recognise that was empowering and was something I wanted to retain on my journey, wherever that would take me.

Having worked in comedy for over thirty years now, I can recognise that all the comics I've met feel in some way disenfranchised from what you might call mainstream society. I often find when talking to them that something happened to them in their childhood or early teens that made them step back from life and watch from the sidelines, trying to examine and understand how things work. Whenever you see a crowd full of people at a pop concert or on a dance floor losing themselves in the moment, you'll find none of them are comedians. The comedians are at the side wondering what is going on and making disparaging comments. There's an element of trying to retain control and an element of genuine bewilderment at other people's actions and motivations. I can't believe that an aspect of this isn't in some way connected to autism.

The name Normal was and is, of course, ironic. Sometimes I wonder if I should have included a question mark at the end. Since becoming a dad with an autistic son it has taken on a new significance. I'm never sure how people are going to react. For those who don't know, it could be seen as a name instigated after hearing my son's diagnosis. If I had chosen such a name at that point, my reasons for doing so would probably have been very different.

Back in the 1980s, it was generally thought that to make it in entertainment you had to go to London. Having been brought up on a council estate in Nottingham, my view of London was somewhat tainted by adults slagging it off. I remember a Yorkshire bloke on TV once saying, 'I don't like London, it's all big steps and little steps, you can't get a stride on.' By which I suspect he meant there were too many people. Other comments about London weren't as tame or PC. Certainly back then, working-class people in Nottingham considered themselves part of the North. Whether anyone from Manchester or Newcastle considered Nottingham part of the North, is of course open to question; people in Newcastle tend not only to think that Mancunians are soft southerners, but that people from Durham are as well.

However, one day in the 1980s while working on *Coogan's Run* with Steve, I had to go into Soho and pick up a hire car. When I got in the driver's seat something seemed strange and at first I thought someone had stolen one of the pedals.

Of course, it was an automatic. I'd never driven an automatic and had no idea how to begin. The gear stick had the numbers 1 and 2 and the letters D and N and R. I took it that 1 and 2 were first and second gears and started off through the labyrinth of streets towards Oxford Circus. Halfway across Regent Street, I stalled. No matter what I did I couldn't get the car to start again. I was straddling these lanes across the road, blocking all the traffic at one of the busiest junctions in the country, if not the world. I was fraught and completely at a loss.

Then, without being asked, strangers came from off the pavement and helped me move the car to the side of the road. 'But this is London,' I thought to myself. 'People don't just help you.' It was a revelation that shamed all my petty prejudice. It's so obvious to me now that people are people where ever they live, and in whatever circumstances.

When I'd moved to Manchester back in the 1980s I used to dye my hair black, and dressed to match. My head looked like a goth pineapple. In those first few years in Manchester, everyone else seemed to look like Smiths fans, so I certainly stuck out. I used to dye my hair myself in a very small sink and my entire face would end up stained like some sort of army camouflage. It seemed to go down well with the audience of Smiths fans, although I used to joke 'They don't laugh, they empathise'.

I remember standing on Manchester's Oxford Road when I first arrived and looking around at the huge red-brick building and thinking to myself, 'This place is too big for me, I'm going to lose my sense of self.' I was genuinely worried I couldn't cope and would become overwhelmed. Standing in Piccadilly Gardens one day people-watching, with all my cares and troubles pressing down on me, I wondered what it would be like to not have to think. At the time this seemed like it would be a relief and a blessing. The thought has haunted me ever since that God was listening and decided to teach me a lesson by giving me an autistic son. I realise how wrong that sounds in so many ways, but the incident and the thought both happened, so I can only plead guilty to 'thought crime'.

You may have noticed throughout this book that I claim to be somewhere between agnostic and atheist, although the idea of God fascinates me. I was taught RE at school and went to church. The winter after my mum died the church we went to replaced the surrounding wall, at a shilling a brick. This was in the first year that the word 'hypothermia' became commonly heard. A woman living opposite the church died. I couldn't help counting the bricks as I walked past the church and wondering how many bricks it would have taken to save her life.

I remember the first joke I wrote for Caroline Aherne. She was performing the character Sister Mary Immaculate, an Irish nun, at the time. My joke was: 'How many Protestants does it take to change a lightbulb? None: they all live in eternal darkness'. I got about £40 for that joke. You can see why I quit poetry to go into TV comedy. I also met Steve Coogan and we filmed 'the Paul Calf and the Pauline Calf's Video Diaries' around Manchester. I played a character called Darren Little who had an orthopaedic shoe. As I've got legs that are the same length, whenever we filmed I had to wear the built-up shoe and try to stand as straight as I could. One scene we filmed in a graveyard took three hours. When I saw the final scene on TV you never saw my legs at all. That is method acting for you.

When the Mad-chester scene got into its swing and Anthony Wilson proved himself a catalyst many times over, Manchester was the only place to be. A few years later, and being an exec producer by then, I sat next to Tony as he watched an early edit of *24 Hour Party People* for the first time. His comment on the film was consistent – 'When forced to pick between the truth and the legend, print the legend.' The last time I saw him was in the Atlas Bar in Manchester. He was trying to set up a scheme for young local film-makers. After listening for forty minutes I asked, 'Where are we going to get the money, Tony?' 'Oh Henry,' he said, 'You are so London!' He wasn't interested in the money. He just wanted the creativity. I love him for that.

I created the very first Manchester Poetry Festival, which has now become the Manchester Literature Festival. My favourite night was when we had Seamus Heaney two days after he'd been given the Nobel Prize. He arrived at Manchester Airport with a cheque in his pocket for nearly a million pounds, which is what you got in those days along with the prize itself. We explained to him we'd got him a cheque for £600. 'I couldn't have it in cash, could I?' he asked. He'd got no cash on him, only this huge cheque. So we went to a cash point and got the money out. When he arrived at the Whitworth Art Gallery, all 300 of the audience gave him a standing ovation.

When Angela's film *Snow Cake* opened the Berlin Film Festival I went over to support her. Standing between Sigourney Weaver and Alan Rickman I found funny, in that Alan had a slightly crumpled stoop about him, whereas Sigourney stands so upright with her shoulders back. So to talk to them both you had to adjust your height. I loved the pair of them and couldn't thank them enough as they were so supportive of the film; they even helped to cash-flow the start of filming with their own money. As I stood besuited in the plush surroundings of the film festival, with cameras flashing and champagne and celebrities all around me, I noticed Sigourney take out a cigarette. I picked up a book of matches from the table and lit it for her. For a moment I was in the movies. Here I was, once a scruffy lad from the council estate watching Jack Benny on *The Dean Martin Show*, now in the glamorous world I'd yearned for back then.

I tried to apply a little of that work ethic to our situation with Johnny but it was different. Whatever you try to teach Johnny doesn't always turn out as you might expect. Johnny doesn't always see what you consider the point, the objective or the need to learn any particular task. Even with play – actually, especially with play.

I tried to teach him to play football. I'd loved playing it as a kid. It was one of my favourite things to do. An excuse to enjoy the physicality of your body. I started as you would expect, by kicking a ball to him. I coaxed him to kick it back. He did that. I kicked it back to him and tried to coax him to kick it back to me again. He looked at me as if to say, 'I've done that.' It seemed to me that he didn't see the point or indeed feel the joy of it that I had felt as a young boy. This is emblematic of many activities we've tried to engage him in over the years. No matter how strong my or Angela's own passion, joy and wonderment for something, quite often Johnny would not be enticed. He's a little better at giving things a try these days and we can cajole him more, and through experience we are more confident that occasionally we will achieve some success.

Johnny doesn't always apply any understanding gained onto the next task, no matter how similar that task may be.

He's been going to the toilet on his own since he was eight or nine but even now he's nineteen we're still reminding him of the process and often he still forgets. At home we've put signs up that we got him to colour in so he's engaged with the words and is aware of them. Of course this is just one example, but I am told that people on the autistic spectrum don't necessarily generalise their learning; that is, if an autistic person learns to use scissors in one room they don't necessarily know how to use scissors in another room.

I was able to semi-retire recently. (I'd say 'retire' but I've been writing this book.) This has given me more time to be involved with everyday family life. Taking Johnny to college, the routines and strategies between college and tea time and less pressure at weekends to make up for time lost. I'm trying to get Johnny involved in our own garden at present. Watering and weeding, tying up climbers and general work. There's nothing remarkable or out of the ordinary about this everyday interaction but, not unlike gardening itself, mostly what you get out of it is what you put in.

TRAVELLING IN 4D

When my dad died
I was given his watch

Strange as we never
spent that much time together
absent within the same room

Our days were marked by
coins stacked on the mantelpiece
electric, gas, bread and milk

I won't leave the watch to my son
he has no need to measure hours
days are marked with meals and sleep

outside time or in perfect sync
A zone uncharted in any atlas

We are in the world as wide as it is
side by side

He chooses to walk with me
I choose to walk with him

With Johnny's arm around my shoulder
the spin of the Earth slows

Chapter 22

Autistic Portrayal in the Media

Angela and I are open about the words 'autism' and 'autistic', but these are not words we feel we need to use constantly and certainly not ones we tend to use unless there is a need. We use the words autism and autistic in front of Johnny and about Johnny. We never talk about him as though he's not there, but occasionally something will need to be clarified and the word autism or autistic cuts through the confusion.

I suspect Johnny understands he's autistic. We've both talked to him about it in the best and most honest and caring way we know how. He's nineteen now and he deserves to be respected as an adult even though he doesn't always act like a neurotypical adult. (Most neurotypical adults don't act like adults all the time when you think about it.)

What Johnny's understanding of the words and indeed the concept of autism and autistic are I don't know. I suspect he must at times notice a difference between his and other people's behaviour, but how he applies that to his understanding of the world and his understanding of himself is impossible to guess. This is a difficult subject and I suspect people hold passionate views on different ways to deal with it. Personally I try to treat people the way I would want to be treated in the same circumstances. I'd certainly want to know as much as possible and I wouldn't want people hiding something from me.

Angela is currently working on a film based on the book *The Reason I Jump*. I watched a documentary about the book with Johnny recently. It was made in Japan and featured the author, the young autistic boy, Naoki Higashida, who is not that much older than Johnny. We watched the documentary together and Johnny didn't appear that interested, but the main point for me was giving him the opportunity.

Angela and I have watched many films with autistic characters, from *Rain Man* to *Mercury Rising*, *The Black Balloon* and *What's Eating Gilbert Grape?* We've also watched many documentary films including *Mission to Lars*, *Autism: – The Musical* and *Life, Animated*, and we've watched TV shows and documentaries like *The A Word* and *The Autistic Gardener*, and every one of them has its benefits. I'm not sure, though, if Johnny would particularly like any of them and I wonder if he would even identify with any of them.

The biggest problem with all the representation in the media is that it tends very much to favour those autistic or Asperger's children or adults who are able to communicate better, rather than those who can't, or whose communications are more difficult. As an ex-TV and film producer I can see why that is. For a fulfilling story arc a series needs its characters to change. If the perception of a person's change is difficult that can be a problem for a satisfying story. What tends to happen is the autistic character is written as a secondary character so that we can follow the change in the non-autistic main character. Film and TV storytelling usually involves the viewer empathising with the emotions of the main character. If those emotions are hard to read that can cause concerns.

A good example of where an autistic central character has succeeded is the Scandinavian crime thriller *The Bridge*. Of course, the character here has to be particularly able in many areas in order to service the plot, but in my opinion it is a good attempt to represent a central character with autism on screen. The book *The Curious Incident of the Dog in the Night-Time* by Mark Haddon is a decent attempt by a non-autistic writer to tell the story from the point of view of a particular child with autistic traits. I've not seen the play yet but it seems to be doing well.

I feel that the worst aspect of documentaries is when non-autistic people try to show the world through 'autistic eyes' by overloading the sound and the use of claustrophobic camera effects. I could never pretend to know what the world looks like from Johnny's point of view. All I can do is try to show what it looks like from mine and hope that is of some use.

YOU WON'T FIND A BOX TO TICK
ON ANY FORM FOR THIS

It must have taken some time to build that wall
and there are so many walls
and there've been so many lives spent building them

We sit together
our backs to the stones
each in our own breath

No one can see what catches our eyes
only a quiet body language
You could be any teenager

I could be any dad
neither revealing superpowers of
good or evil

Your hand hovers
unconcerned with personal space
We are not afraid to touch in passing

We have arrived at an understanding
almost unnoticed
we are on the same side of the wall

Chapter 22a

Autism in the Media, Elephants and Snow Cake by Angela

I once read a book written to help screenwriters become better screenwriters. It was full of 'how to' sections, written by famous writers. At the beginning of each chapter was a list of the films that each writer had successfully made. Below this list was a list of all the film scripts they had written, that had never been made. Both lists were generally of equal length. The latter was often slightly longer than the former.

Several years later and here I am in a similar position. Currently I have had just two things 'produced on screen'; the film *Snow Cake* and a one-off TV programme starring Rhys Ifans called *Gifted*. I have, however, written many other scripts and treatments, some of which now sit in a room I refer to as Development Hell. In my head, this room is a small, sparse, cupboard-like space with one hard chair. There is a speaker hanging off the wall that continually plays tinny tracks on a loop; pan-pipe cover versions of Justin Bieber. I could weep for all my little made-up worlds trapped there.

In everything I've written since *Snow Cake*, I have been at pains to add a character who is on the spectrum. This character has either been prominent in the action or simply appears in the background of a scene. It always seems to me that whenever you see, for example, a wheelchair user on screen you know that they are there for a plot purpose. That wheelchair is going to feature later, you see if it doesn't! Wheelchair users are never 'just there' in a scene because, well, sometimes in the street you see a real-life wheelchair user. I believe that until a wide range of autistic people are more visible both out in the world and on our screens, we are probably still a long way off achieving more understanding and acceptance.

My good friend Caroline (another parent of an autistic child) and I have written several treatments for TV shows together. A few years ago we wrote the outline for a three-parter that involves a kidnap that goes wrong. Three hapless crooks accidentally take the wrong child of a wealthy family. In a bungled attempt to grab the fifteen-year-old daughter, they end up with the mostly non-verbal, severely autistic seventeen-year-old. So the kidnappers are now cooped up in a room, having to face (with shock and bemusement) what some parents live with on a daily basis – a tirade of no sleep, challenging behaviour, repetitious singing, biting, kicking, screaming, clapping, sniffing, unusual demands, sudden outbursts of joy and laughter etc. Within the first twenty minutes they find themselves beginning to seriously wonder about 'giving her back and forgetting the fucking money.'

Of course, we wanted to write something that was very positive too – and there are moments in the story that highlight the real joys that come with parenting a special needs child. I always get a kick out of writing something I've never seen before. We had never seen, for example, someone struggling to fit a sanitary towel on a severely disabled teenage girl, but these are real things that many parents and carers have to do. We both loved the idea of showing on screen a person with no knowledge or ability to cope, being thrown into this surreal world. It felt like a good way to inform and educate people. Of course, the girl's family appear in the story too. It seemed amazingly fertile ground for drama – especially having the other daughter address the elephant in the room: 'You know life would be easier if she *never* came back.'

My dad asked me if there would be anything controversial in this book. I said 'No'. But then Henry asked me if there was anything I'd want to say, that I felt I probably shouldn't. I didn't have to think very long before I said 'Yes'. Elephants in the room and all that.

There have been times in the past when I've thought about killing both myself and Johnny. I've driven along the seafront in my car with Johnny beside me and thought, just for a split second, about turning the wheel to the left and heading straight over the cliff. I even once found myself – after hearing about the funeral of a local autistic child – thinking, 'I wonder if his parents are actually, on some level, relieved.'

I have read the uproar online when the parent of a special needs child, takes not only their own, but their child's life. I fully understand the need for the special needs community to come out and loudly voice their disgust that this has happened; of course every single person's life is sacred and no one – *no one* – should take another's life against their will. However desperate they are. But a part of me thinks I might understand a little of what could have been going through that parent's mind. It may be that it hasn't got anything to do with not wanting the child in their life or feeling that life with an autistic child is a burden or unbearable. I might be wrong, but I think it might have every-thing to do with not being able to stand the fact that there will come a time when their child won't have them around to love, support and be an advocate for them, this thought being bleak beyond measure. I wonder if it isn't about loving their child almost too much. To me, us both going at the same time has occasionally felt like the kindest thing I could do for Johnny. The thought of him being left, at some point in the future, to fend for himself without me, seemed cruel. I don't have these thoughts any more, and I was in two minds about even including this segment in the book. But I have the sneaking suspicion I am not alone in having had these feelings. I also have a sneaking suspi-cion that if parents of autistic children could see more of this honesty in the media and on TV, we wouldn't feel so alone in having had them.

No commissioner wanted the autism kidnap drama.

Caroline and I also wrote a comedy animation about a team of four people with special needs who have powers bestowed on them by an alien force (which appears to them in what 'it' believes is 'the acceptable form of well-known stage and screen actor, Benedict Cumberbatch'). Not realising that they have special needs, he gives our heroes slightly inappropriate 'abili-ties'. For example, the blind one gets the ability to fly. You can probably tell that this is a little irreverent, but we thought a little irreverence might actually be appreciated in the face of a lot of 'worthy'.

Basically, the main reason that we wanted to write this was because we wanted to see a non-verbal autistic person on our screens. There are so few. We also wanted to write and see a character who our own children might recognise something of themselves in (plus one who happens to be cool and funny and gets to blow things up and defeat baddies). The producer and now friend, Stevie Lee (also the parent of a mostly non-verbal child), is trying to push this project forward for us. It has taken us eight years to get to this point. I really hope it doesn't end up in a room listening to pan-piped Justin Bieber.

Johnny has three years left in full-time education, so I imagine I have three years left to write. What happens then is anyone's guess, but I am pretty sure we will have a lot less time to work. I have been told that post-twenty-three provision is sketchy at best and in some cases poor. But issues and challenges and the need for support don't diminish in direct proportion to the number of candles on a birthday cake.

We wouldn't be happy having Johnny sitting in 'respite'-like centres, icing his name on a biscuit or being taken bowling every other day. We want him engaged in activities that are meaningful to him. I suspect we will have to seek out opportunities and help support him in these. We obviously have 'form' for doing this, but not every day, week in and week out. With the length of time it takes to get any screenplay into production, to be honest, I am not holding out much hope of seeing anything of mine completed and transmitted in the time I have left. *C'est la vie.*

Of course, my one success in getting a portrayal of autism on screen was *Snow Cake.* I wanted to write a film about someone learning to live with, love and negotiate their way around, a person on the spectrum. I think this was the first feature film I'd attempted to write.

I wrote the first draft of *Snow Cake* very quickly one Christmas, between going into the Son-Rise playroom and making dinner for volunteers. It was incredibly cathartic. I asked Henry if he'd mind me sending it off to an old friend and work colleague of his, Andrew Eaton. Andrew had made films like *Jude, 24 Hour Party*

People, *19 Songs* and *Tristram Shandy*. Henry said, 'Go for it'. Andrew rang me up shortly after reading the script. He told me he really liked it and wanted to help get it made. I was a bit shell-shocked.

I realised at this point that I needed to be very sure about what I'd written. The thing was, at this stage I wasn't. Johnny was non-verbal and the character of Linda, in the story, was VERY verbal. I had used some traits of Johnny's (like eating snow) but I had obviously invented others. I wasn't really sure if I'd written an autistic person or an Asperger's person. I suddenly remembered Ros Blackburn, who Henry and I had seen do a talk about four years earlier. I tracked her down via the NAS (National Autistic Society) and spoke with her on the phone. I was hoping that, what with her being a verbal autistic person, she'd help me clarify my thoughts and also give me some feedback.

Our first phone call was tense. Johnny was shrieking in the background, which Ros found challenging. I remember her putting the phone down because she was finding it difficult to filter out the background noise. However, we'd by then managed to arrange for me to send her a copy of the script, which she said she'd get help with to read. A couple of weeks later we met up in a top-floor office, in the building that the charity Amaze work out of. I was quite nervous. Ros bounced in. She got momentarily very excited because she thought I had a sensory toy (a Koosh ball) stuck in my hair. It was in fact my hair bobble. She then rushed to the window, where she proceeded to look at the seagulls on the roof, gleefully impersonating their cries à la *Finding Nemo* for a good five to ten minutes. I think we instantly 'clicked'. The best part of that meeting for me was when we worked through the script. I felt like a really 'good' pupil. Ros had marked out the pages and she went through her 'notes' – mostly a series of ticks and crosses, as I remember. She said things like 'Yes, I do that' and 'This is very me'. There is a line in the script where, after Linda's dog throws up, she gets into such a state she cries out, 'If it stains I'll have to move!' Ros said she'd actually said those words about something recently. That day I felt that the script had been validated. That I could say Linda was an autistic adult. Ros and I have remained in contact ever since. I really like her.

If I was to try to describe Alan Rickman's voice I'd say it was like treacle being poured over velvet. On a lazy hot afternoon. I heard it in my head every time I wrote a line that his character (initially, uncreatively called Alan) said. The thing about Alan's voice was that it could perfectly enunciate disdain, but it also had warmth, humour and intelligence. Very much like him as a person. I'd seen him on TV and in films, of course – but never imagined I'd ever meet him. When Gina Carter, one of Andrew Eaton's producers, called to say that she'd sent Alan the script and that he'd replied with 'I'm intrigued', we all tried to work out if 'intrigued', in this context, was a good thing or not.

I don't remember much about the first meeting with Alan, other than Marc Evans the director was there and that I'd stayed in London the night before with Henry, but had forgotten to pack any clean pants. I recall putting on Henry's spare pair of boxer shorts. Amazing how the brain hangs on to the most mundane of details and forgets all the interesting bits. Anyway, Alan said yes he'd love to do it. His words were 'If this script was a house, I'd say take it off the market' (to which we all inwardly squealed with delight). He also recommended Sigourney Weaver for the part of Linda. He said he'd get the script to her.

As far as we were all concerned, Sigourney was MAJOR LEAGUE and we were beside ourselves. Sigourney, it turned out, was 'in' and threw herself into making her performance as an autistic adult as 'authentic' as she could. She did a lot of research. Visited lots of schools, met Ros Blackburn in America and then spent a week over here in England working with her. They both have some funny stories about their time together. Ros, of course, had no idea who Sigourney was to start with – and certainly had no interest in pussyfooting around her, however 'Hollywood' she might be. I don't know, but I suspect for Sigourney this was a refreshing change. One day, Ros and her carer took Sigourney to a remote field and spent the day tutoring her on how to master Ros's 'autistic gait'. Sigourney finally got it when Ros gave her the instruction, 'Lead with your knees!' I love to imagine the two of them in that field, Sigourney so glamorous and poised and Ros so bouncy, yelling 'Lead with your knees!'

Apparently, at one point, Ros's mum purposely did something with the kettle to put Ros in 'meltdown mode' so that Sigourney could see what this might look like. Ros now finds this funny. They also spent a lot of time bouncing on the trampoline together.

I met Sigourney just before she went to work with Ros, in a hotel in London. I recall climbing over the settee in her plush suite and bouncing on her bed, trying to show her the way Johnny moved. I think she did an amazing job in the film. When Alan met Ros for the first time at a BAFTA Q and A evening, the look of surprise on his face was priceless. He was blown away by how much Sigourney (in character) and Ros looked alike. Were alike, I guess.

I had to go to Canada for a week to work on the script with Marc, Alan and Sigourney and be there for the read-through. This was the first time I had ever been away from Johnny and it felt like I was finally cutting the umbilical cord. He was roughly seven years old and we'd never really been apart. I flew to Canada more daunted by having to leave my son than I was about having to 'work'. Although the fact that I hadn't been in a room of 'professional' people in a work setting for years was also scary. I had of course spent the majority of the last four years dressed as Mrs Goggins from *Postman Pat* and I was out of practice when it came to speaking to grown-ups. In fact, I was out of practice when it came to stringing a sentence together in any kind of intellectual manner.

The first night I arrived, I remember there was a 'welcome party' for the cast and crew. I was uncomfortable around all the grown-ups, and missing Johnny so much that I spent the duration of it hiding in the mezzanine area and 'colouring in' with Gina's son Alfie, who was the same age as Johnny. I also remember ringing home several times a day. Looking back now I think I had quite a lot of gall, interrupting script meetings with two Hollywood legends to go off to, for example, say goodnight to Johnny, but everyone seemed to be very understanding. Marc was especially kind.

The first table read-through blew me away. Of course I had heard Alan say everything in my head, but hearing him say the lines in real life was just amazing. Sigourney chose to 'read not act' her part out, as she was saving her performance for the shoot. She actually wanted Alan to have as little information as possible about her character, so that he would genuinely be reacting to her portrayal of autism in the way he might in the flesh – coming to it as a man with no prior knowledge.

My favourite part in the whole film came from Alan. It's a silent scene with the dog. He improvised the cleaning-up of the dog vomit and it's hilarious. He was so good in *Snow Cake* – well, in everything he ever did. He was also incredibly generous. Years later he would still read scripts for me. Once or twice he sent me articles about autism. My spelling is terrible and he'd always joke in emails about it. He'd write things like 'I knew this email was from you because, well, by "throws", I think you mean "throes"'. I'd email back, 'Bad spellers of the world untie!'

Alan was a much bigger part of my life than I ever was of his, of course. His agreeing to and subsequently acting in *Snow Cake* I am forever grateful for. I have kept a letter he once wrote to me. He didn't suffer fools gladly and was very keen on good grammar. One might even consider him 'a bit of a snob', but I think he played up to this version of himself. The letter said, 'Dear Angela, I don't think a writer of your calibre should ever be an "Ange".' And I know you just read that sentence in his voice. On days when I'm feeling that I can't write for toffee, or I get knock-backs and rejections, I think back to this letter and remember Alan thought I was a writer of 'calibre'. I pick myself up and carry on.

Chapter 23
Behaviour

'What's been making you so giddy?' is a sentence Johnny has picked up from his mum. It's a question that he likes to joyfully repeat. Usually when he's excited. It's not that he wants an answer to this; he simply wants you to join in the fun and enjoy the words with him. I know I was occasionally called giddy when I was little and I know it was something that wasn't a conscious choice for me – it was more that I would be overwhelmed by, for want of a better word, joy. It's a little like when you can't stop laughing despite trying to retain your composure.

Wanting your child to have fun and connect can sometimes be at odds with coping when their behaviour becomes challenging. I'm sure this is not applicable just to Johnny. Sometimes he has a problem with appropriate play and can get over-excited. He pinches his mum's face in jest but doesn't always know when to stop, and it can be painful. He used to twist my arms and the arms of people he knows in a kind of mock-wrestling. His grip is tight now as he is a big nineteen-year-old boy who likes meat and has developed substantial muscle. He completely innocently thought this gripping and twisting was funny. If you were standing it was fairly easy to release his grip, but it sometimes hurt his mum and grandma, especially if they were sitting. I'm sure he doesn't want to hurt anyone really, but I think he likes the interaction and wants people to say 'ouch' or feign exasperation. He would always stop when your tone indicated that he had gone too far. Unfortunately this was often just slightly too late.

It was difficult to understand how to get him to stop, especially when we didn't want to discourage interaction and engagement. We tried turning the action into other games and various diversions. None seemed to work. We tried being stern to an appropriate level but often this would egg him on. We tried having no reaction at all or minimising our reaction. Then all of a sudden, I'm not quite sure how, it stopped. We still engage in physical contact, whether a hug or an arm around the shoulder on the sofa, even tickling occasionally, but the wrestling has gone. We can only hope the pinching of his mum's face will disappear, if need be in similarly mysterious circumstances.

I'm not sure when I last saw Johnny cry. It was many years ago. Probably when he was about eight and feeling ill. Angela tells me she's seen him well up since on the very odd occasion when, in pain, she'll shout at him to stop pinching her lips. When he's really upset he'll bite the back of his hand. As he's never eaten a sweet, other than an occasional mint in the car, his teeth are quite healthy and strong and some bites have been so deep that we have had to put bandages round the wounds.

When he was two it was a different matter. He would hit and bite Angela and me and anyone else who got in the way. Even though it was painful I decided that I wouldn't rise to the bait. We never smacked Johnny, although occasionally in those early years we'd shout at him out of exasperation. Later we'd always try to explain things calmly but we were never sure how much, if anything, was sinking in.

Everyone has lapses sometimes though, especially when you are tired and stressed and worn down. I remember buying him an expensive new top coat from Next For Kids when he was three or four. The first time he wore it we went for a walk in the park and he threw himself to the ground and rolled in the mud. This beautiful coat that you would expect any child to cherish was so caked it had changed from navy blue to a shitty brown. I was livid. It seemed to me at the time that he was doing it deliberately. Why, I didn't know. I shouted at him then. However, the more I shouted, the more he rolled. Whether or not he was trying to elicit a particular reaction I can't say. We took the soiled coat off him, got back in the car and came straight home

– which may well have been what he was trying to achieve. I remember on a small boat once when he was five he grabbed my sunglasses off my face and threw them in the water. I must admit I did laugh at that one. It was so outrageous, I found it comical.

Up to when Johnny was around ten, if you left him alone for five minutes you were never sure what you'd come back to. Once Angela left him in the white room where they'd earlier been playing with red paint. When she returned, the whole room looked like the scene of an axe murder. Another time, returning after having nipped to the toilet, Angela found Johnny had coloured in his private parts with black permanent marker.

He went through a stage of nicking people's chips right off their plates in restaurants and cafes. We talked to him time and time again, but he would never give us any. This, of course, is me joking about it but Johnny did steal chips and not everyone affected saw the funny side of it.

He would also climb up any ladders available anywhere. At the playground he would climb up the ladders to the slide and then just sit there. Obviously the other kids would struggle to get past him and use the slide, so Angela or I would have to climb up and coax him down. He'd climb up any equipment, however high. He didn't show any fear of heights. He was like one of the native Americans who built the skyscrapers in New York. I don't think it's a lack of a sense of danger, but more that he's agile and confident and in some way motivated. Johnny is very careful with roads and even now in the most awkwardly narrow of shopping aisles he is totally co-ordinated even though he's a big lad.

I found Johnny's phase of hitting Angela when he was around three hardest to handle. We knew at this stage that

Johnny was autistic but we didn't know how this would develop over the years, or in fact if it would develop. That's one of the scariest aspects of adjusting to being the parent of an autistic child – you don't know if there'll ever be any progress. At the toy museum in Boston on the way to Son-Rise and before I knew better, I remember I was knelt down helping Johnny fasten up his duffle coat and he hit me hard across the face. I was determined to show that this wouldn't affect me and continued to fasten his toggles. He hit me again and in defiance I continued to kneel there and just looked at him as he hit me again and again. Although it really did hurt I was hoping to prove to him my determination not to react. Looking back now, this seems foolish and somewhat masochistic.

It became apparent early on when he started speaking that Johnny had a habit of repeating the same phrase again and again for weeks. These were sometimes phrases that seemed to make no sense, like 'escalator tomato', or they were phrases from books or videos, like ' five people on the roof'. This is a line from the film *Ivor the Invisible*. Johnny repeated that for at least a month, but it felt at the time like he would repeat it for the rest of his life. That this was our life. That it would always be our life.

So when he said 'five people on the roof' we would name the people; we'd try to ask about the story, we'd act it out with figurines. We'd try any variation to expand on it. Try six people on the roof. 'Who shall we add?' Five people on something else. The top of a bus maybe? Making every mental connection we could think of, we'd try to expand on this phrase. We even tried just repeating it, which it seemed was more satisfactory to Johnny. Then one day he just didn't say it any more. He said something else seemingly random like 'Attishoo Golf', and again he'd say it over and over until that too went and another phrase took its place. My current favourite is something I heard several times just this morning, although I've no idea where it's from or if he's made it up himself. It's certainly memorable though – 'Cheese on the bone,' he's been shouting.

SAND SUSPENDED IN MID-AIR

Sand suspended in mid-air
defies the natural order

Johnny presses his teeth
against the back of his hand
to contain the excitement

My wife stands ready
as I bash the bottom of the
sun lounger once more

We can only see the effect
captured by a single frame

I'm unsure what delight
my son is experiencing

We can only see the effect
captured by a single frame.

Chapter 24
Holidays

While we were doing our Son-Rise programme we didn't take a holiday for four years. We worked in the white room through summer, Easter, Christmas, weekends, while other people were having school holidays. We've tried to make up for it since.

The great thing about holidays is that you can live in the present, which is good news for us as that is where Johnny lives, and is pretty much where the fun is. There is an easiness when we are on the beach. From a distance you wouldn't even know Johnny is autistic; we are just a family on holiday. It strikes me that if you feel like a fish out of water the thing to do is to find some water. Then you're just a fish. Finding those places and activities where Johnny can thrive is something we are always on the lookout for.

When he was around two Angela started taking Johnny to swimming lessons. I can't swim and, watching Angela struggle to teach Johnny, I would hang my head at the futility of it all. Not to be deterred, Angela carried on taking him to lessons at a local pool week after week. As the months passed it seemed to me that they weren't making any progress. She'd hold him in the water and sing to him as she poured a little water on his head. They'd play the same splashing water games and sing the same songs week after week. I'd sit on the side of the pool with the towels as Angela climbed into the pool for their session again and again, always with such a positive attitude that I was secretly embarrassed by my lack of faith. I don't know when the breakthrough came; if it was actually a certain point or just a gradual building of confidence, but within a year he had learnt to swim. Now he loves swimming. He'll stay in the pool until his fingers become corrugated like an old washboard. He even swims in the sea.

When Johnny was about six, Angela took him swimming with dolphins off the Azores. The photos of the two of them in the middle of the ocean with nothing in sight other than water and one small boat brought home to me the enormity of what Angela and Johnny had achieved. Of course, we weren't naive enough to think swimming with dolphins was going to cure Johnny's autism, but it's something Angela had wanted to do and why the hell not? I can't say it had any marked effect but I'm glad they had the experience. Even back then our lives weren't all about finding a 'cure' for autism. Enhancing Johnny's life, our relationship and just plain having fun aren't bad motivators. If that leads to him becoming more self-sufficient that's a great bonus for him and for us, as it would be with any kid.

New experiences, either abroad or at home, teach you something. An early holiday to the Isle of Wight taught me never to believe it when a brochure calls a place a 'picturesque cottage'. This one was above an Indian takeaway. It didn't even make sense. It was neither picturesque nor a cottage. When I say a holiday, it ended up as a day trip; we turned the car straight round and caught the next ferry home. I'm not averse to an Indian takeaway but as we pulled up we could see they were only just putting the carpets in what I would describe as a small first-floor flat on a dodgy back street on the outskirts of Cowes. The arse end of Cowes, as Angela put it.

Generally, though, I now love to take a leap of faith whenever possible. My experience of watching Angela in the pool with Johnny has taught me that.

The first time we went abroad as a family was to Italy when Johnny was two. A remote villa just north of Lucca. It was the first time I'd stayed in a villa and the great thing about this was you could be as noisy as you wanted and you could get up as early as you wanted. These two things were paramount as Johnny at this stage liked to get up around five o'clock and make a lot of noise, which was not conducive to staying in hotels or B&Bs. Trying to allow Angela the opportunity to sleep, I have more than once ventured out with Johnny to try to find somewhere for him to make his own dawn chorus (I am more acquainted with the comings and goings of hotel lobbies than I would have ever thought possible).

At this point we didn't know Johnny was autistic but we did know we had to manage his needs. Angela's preparations for the flight to Italy were superb. He had his favourite foods, his books, crayons, music, everything we could anticipate. The only problem we hadn't anticipated was that there was no way he would allow the seat belt to be fastened. Despite a degree of wrestling, pleas and bargaining and every other tack we could think of, he would not play ball. The cabin crew staff insisted, so we faked it, with me holding the belt in place as they passed.

Johnny loves planes now and puts on his seat belt happily. In fact, if he's in the car and you've not put your seat belt on he'll remind you stridently. He now wears his ear defenders on the plane, although occasionally a zealous cabin crew member will try to insist he takes them off, having mistaken them for headphones. I have learnt to react and explain politely, which usually does the trick.

We have developed a system now in airports and all other such places. Angela goes first and clears the way. Johnny follows and I take up the rear watching for problems. We have airports down to a fine art. Johnny has the same food every time he flies. He knows when he gets to the airport he will get certain food and when he gets on the plane he will get certain food and when he gets home he gets certain food. The more I think about it, life for him is definitely the inconvenient bit between meals.

In Italy it became clear that physical activity was helpful. Johnny had a lot of energy and couldn't sit for long periods. I accompanied him on winding walks around the villa and in a game of stepping from one chair to another around a large circular table on the patio. We drove to the beach and other places of interest but it was the walks I remember most. It was the fact that it didn't matter where we were going and what we might find. We were exploring together.

A few years down the line I had the opportunity to buy a villa and, having tried various locations, chose Portugal. There's a reason I chose the Algarve. It's quiet and unassumingly beautiful. The beaches on the west coast are not commercialised and are refreshingly natural and untouched but for small wooden cafes that seem to stay open just for us. These are all good reasons; but it's more than that. When Johnny was about six or seven we rented a villa at Carvoeiro. There's a beach just east of the main town called Praia do Vale Covo. It's a strange little beach. Directly behind, there's a concrete building that is either a hotel or apartments and looks like a honeycomb. On certain days I would consider it ugly and on others I would tip my hat to the Portuguese for making something that would last in this difficult landscape; the waves here are quite ferocious at times and have cut caves into the surrounding cliffs. This was our nearest beach and Angela, Johnny and I spent a few days here braving the surf. In retrospect Johnny coped really well with the noise of the ocean, although he was always happiest in a particular cave.

On one seemingly average sunny day, we spent the whole afternoon on the beach and sitting in the cave. As we left I went to collect Johnny. He put his arms around me and kissed the side of my head. I don't know why at this particular moment he chose to do that, but this was the first show of affection I'd ever received from my son.

In the years since, he regularly puts his arm around me. He doesn't kiss me, but then he's a boy. Occasionally he will lean into Angela and gently rest his forehead on hers, which is as near to a kiss as you can get. We do hug often to say 'Hello' and 'See you later'. I do occasionally kiss his head and sometimes try to pick him up for fun. Despite his height and weight, I can just about lift him for a couple of seconds. He takes great delight in me succeeding. Or he may just be taking delight in my delight. Anyway, he plays along. As big as he is and as grown up, he's still my boy.

THE CANALS OF MARS AT THEIR HEIGHT

An empty bottle for bashing
better than any toy
You are in control
there is no pretence at role play

This is nature unreserved
You lean forward
your brim upturned
not only the sun lights your face

This is a choice
not a compromise
this is authentic
not a substitute or a version

Expressing, playing, stimming
whatever name I give it
is only my label
and won't alter the fun one bit

If the bottle was made of precious metal
it wouldn't necessarily be any better
The red dusk complements the bright blue
of living water

You are no longer apart from the topography

Chapter 25
Christmas

We stopped doing Christmas when Johnny was about three. It was all too much for him. He was overwhelmed and fraught. The world even without Christmas must be a confusing enough place for a three-year-old with autism; then add people dressing up in a beard and a bright red coat, bringing trees into the house, eating different foods, different drinks, using different words, singing different songs, wrapping things up in brightly coloured paper, setting puddings alight, making things go bang at the dinner table, wearing paper hats, more kissing, more hugging, people being more animated and over-friendly. It must be overwhelming. Let's be honest, it is for a lot of neurotypical people.

I've never quite come to terms with Christmas myself, or New Year come to think of it. Birthdays and even weekends I've always found awkward too. It's like there's some agenda you are supposed to fit into that doesn't come naturally to me and I baulk against that. Angela seems to take all such occasions in her stride come whatever, but she was more than happy to try a change. So we decided we would stop 'doing' Christmas and instead, as a family, we'd go abroad and have a beach holiday. Johnny liked them, so that was the best Christmas gift we could give him – a beach holiday away from Christmas.

There was a big reaction when Angela mentioned on a Facebook autistic forum recently that we cancelled Christmas for several years when Johnny was younger. People were surprised, shocked even – but most of all, bloody envious. This is something a lot of people would like to do, it seems, but they fear the reaction from their family and friends. But what we found was that once we'd made it clear what we intended to do and why, people were very supportive. Three fewer people for them to buy for. And three fewer unwanted gifts of socks.

It was soon after that that we started thinking about buying a villa. The idea of owning a villa may sound glamorous but as someone who's spent Christmas Day at a villa looking down a cesspit at his own stools, let me tell you it's not. The upside to having a villa is it's a known quantity and there are things you can control. The first thing I did when we bought our place was to put a fence around it. We needed a dog-free zone as the fear of a dog wandering into the garden was not going to encourage a relaxing holiday for anyone. We lost all sharp corners, put rails over the infinity pool drop and generally made the place 'Johnny-friendly'.

So Christmas Day is for us like any other day on holiday in the Algarve. Pool, salad, beach and plenty of fish; but over the years we have started to introduce a little bit of Christmas back in, as Johnny does now have a few Christmassy videos he likes. Christmas Countdown videos on the music channels begin in October and go on to until January. Johnny enjoys Christmas CDs in the car and plays Christmas hits on YouTube. In fact he tends to play them regardless of what month it is. I woke up one lovely sunny day this August to the sound of 'Jingle Bells'. As far as Johnny's concerned any song about Santa is not just for Christmas, it's for all the year round. I can't really complain; this is just taking the idea of not being told what you can do and when you can do it to its logical extreme. For the last two years he's enjoyed choosing a tree at the garden centre and decorating it. I think what he enjoys most, though, is probably walking it back to the Christmas tree 'tip' at the end of our road.

Even now, though, Johnny knows when he's had enough Christmas for one year. In the lead up to Christmas Day last year Angela put a Christmas-themed tablecloth on the dining room table. A red one with the usual snowflakes and bells and holly and all that nonsense. Even though we were in the villa, we had a turkey dinner, which did seem odd. By this time Johnny had already had four Christmas dinners before we'd flown out to Portugal – two at school, one with family and one with friends.

Johnny coped well with the new dynamic and went along with the usual Christmas customs until the day after

Boxing Day. By this time I think we all felt the same, but
Johnny put it most clearly. On seeing the table set for dinner
with the themed table cloth still in attendance, he demanded
'Christmas off.' His mum took the tablecloth off and we got
on with enjoying our break by the sea. That was the best
Christmas present I could have wished for.

TWICE AS MANY HYDROGEN ATOMS
AS OXYGEN MOVING

I don't need to see his face to know it's him
the light has its own plans

In reality nothing is still as elements compete
A split second away there is another poem

If I want I can see a trail of silver
at the spill

or the ominous underbelly of distant concentrations
Everything I see is a reflection of this love

I can home in on the dislocation of arms
in motion

or glory in the contrast
of chemistry as liquid and gas

We may not see the same world at all
I hope yours is as full of splendour

Chapter 26

Weddings, Funerals and Religion

At weddings, inviting a family with an autistic member is probably just a tad less difficult than inviting a newly divorced couple. The fairy-tale optimism that often permeates these occasions like saccharine doesn't want to be punctured by reminders that life is not a bowl of cherries. I'm probably mixing my metaphors here but strangely enough that can be how you feel on these occasions – like a mixed metaphor or an unfortunate bit of bad grammar spoiling the prose. I've no beef with marriage, though I do have a weariness of weddings. They are a bit like Christmas but only two people get presents.

Arrive late and leave early. That's our coping strategy.
Johnny has coped with a few weddings. Usually we hang
around the outskirts and try to find something to help him
deal with the endless delay of it all. Imagine a wedding from
Johnny's point of view. Other than the food, it must be
somewhere between boredom, torture and confusion (for
me too).

Funerals are marginally better: at least you don't have to
force a smile. Johnny stood with me and Angela at my
brother Dave's funeral and insisted on repeatedly shouting,
'Peel the potatoes' – which usually means, I'd like to go
home for tea now. I know Dave would have laughed.

Dave died of cancer aged sixty-one. His wife Jan and
my three sisters and I stayed close to his bedside over his
last few days. I remember towards the end, he'd lie with his
eyes closed. My sister Angela, the youngest in the family,
leant in and asked him what he was thinking about. Dave
was the eldest and I'm sure even at the end he was just
trying to make everything easier for everyone else. 'I'm
hatching a plan,' he said reassuringly. I love that. Still a
sense of humour to the end. I can only hope I have a grain
of the stoicism both he and my dad (who died of cancer
only a couple of years later) had all the way through to
their last breath.

Johnny has been to a few funerals now. I'm sure he
knows the basic idea of death. How much he's picked up I
don't suppose I'll ever know but I asked him recently where
Uncle Dave was and he told me 'He's been dead.' There's a
plaque with Dave's name on a bench at Seaford Head. We
take Johnny there occasionally and for a family gathering
on Dave's birthday. Johnny is always happy to go there and
I think all the family find it a great way to remember Dave

and an excuse to share our memories. I like that Johnny gets to be part of that.

That said, Johnny seems to find the sad bits in films funny. Angela took him to see the musical *Our House* by Tim Firth. She tells me at the saddest part of the story when everyone was on the edge of tears Johnny was laughing so loudly and hysterically that she had to take him out of the theatre.

The idea of shielding Johnny from funerals and death seems to me insulting and counterproductive. One day I will die and one day his mum will die. Selfish as I know I am, I pray that if there is a God he'll take me first. Angela is far better with Johnny than I could ever be. But when we die Johnny will need to understand what has happened and certainly not feel that he has been abandoned. Of course, at some point Johnny will die too. How prepared he can ever be for that, no one but Johnny will know. We can only do our best to help him, as well as ourselves, make sense of it all.

I often wonder if Johnny understands what is real and what is imaginary. A couple of days ago he was repeating the words, 'Zombie aliens'. Where do you start? I suspect he'd heard the phrase on *Scooby-Doo* or some other TV show or film. I talked to him about what zombies are and what aliens are and that neither are real – in the sense that they are 'made up' and exist in stories but no one has seen any aliens or zombies that I know of. I hope he understood. I'd hate to think he would fear these things might exist and feel threatened by them at any time, or have nightmares. We have had a similar talk about dinosaurs and many other creatures from stories. Explaining that dinosaurs did exist but dragons probably didn't is just one of many difficult conversations. Then we'll watch *Blue Planet II* together, with creatures that look made-up, and I try to re-enforce that these are in fact real, although some even have me wondering.

We've talked to Johnny about how babies are conceived and how they are born. I do remember when I was first told by an older boy in the playground at school I thought he was making it up. 'Girls have an extra hole under their bottom,' he told me. It didn't seem likely to me, aged nine.

Some stories Johnny comes across need clarifying, like ones with superheroes or magic in. There are also stories set in the past with, say, pirates or Roman soldiers and ancient Egyptians; and some set in the present day, in places Johnny's only seen in books or on a screen, like Africa or the North Pole. Explaining the bits that are real and the bits that aren't is never-ending. Yes, there are apes in Africa, but no, Tarzan is not real. Yes, there were pirates, no, there was probably no kraken. Yes, there's ice in the North Pole but no, there are no elves or Santa.

Angela asked Johnny yesterday what he wanted for Christmas. Getting no reply, she tried to tease an answer out of him. 'If you opened a present on Christmas Day what would you like it to be?' she asked. 'A secret moustache,' he answered. Now whether that's because last Christmas he found a plastic toy moustache in a Christmas cracker I don't know; but anyway, it's an interesting way to describe it. Johnny has watched over fifty different and often conflicting stories about Santa. What he makes of them I have no idea. He does ask to watch them again though.

Even in children's cartoons we see death represented, in the guise of the Grim Reaper. *The Muppet Christmas Carol*, which Johnny loves, has ghosts in it, including a very forbidding Ghost of Christmas Future. Then there's God and Jesus and Buddha and Mohammed and any other religious figure. How does Johnny start to discern what is real and what isn't? But then on the bigger issues you could probably say that about any of us.

GRAVESTONES AT A WEDDING

Before God
we are outsiders on the edge

We can appear to fit in
until you look closely

My watch hangs from my wrist
My wife's dress displays birds in flight

My boy leans against the cold stone
head down

We are not really here
or we're too here

Awkward
self-conscious

Not knowing the rules
not understanding what is expected of us

Mirroring, echoing
not knowing where our edges are

Hesitant ghosts
checking our invitations

Chapter 27
Parties

When he was younger, Johnny would always 'play' alongside other children but not with them. If coaxed by an adult
he would tolerate interaction, but he has always seemed
more confident in his interaction with adults. Angela remembers an instance when Johnny was very small and we had a
friend and her son over at ours. The young boy was holding
a toy monkey. Unprompted, Johnny walked over to him
and said, 'monkey'. Angela was ecstatic – it was the first
time he'd ever approached another child and made a verbal
request. She waited with delight to see the two 'interact',

only to watch the young boy pull the monkey closer to his chest, shout, 'No! It's mine' and walk off. That's other children for you.

As Johnny gets older he tends to avoid younger children as much as possible. Probably for fear of erratic noise, and not just babies and toddlers – the otherwise seemingly charming scenario of young girls laughing and playing in the sea, squealing at the coldness of the water, is hell to Johnny. Angela and I are straight to Def Con 3 if we see a baby anywhere Johnny can't exit, like, say, on an aircraft. Angela says she bristles now if she hears a baby cry, even when Johnny isn't with her, like one of Pavlov's dogs. To Johnny, in the hierarchy of stress, kids are one level below dogs. Unpredictable behaviour and random noise appear to be kryptonite to his sense of calm.

On some level, though, Johnny enjoys parties. He will blow the candles out on any birthday cake – no matter whose birthday it is. Needless to say, he'll eat anyone's birthday cake as well. We had his college class round to the house for his sixteenth birthday for a party. Now a party with around ten autistic kids is not like your usual party. Getting them even to stay in the same room is almost impossible. Once we did manage to get them all around the table for food we were treated to a very funny rendition of 'Happy Birthday'; half of them had their fingers in their ears and half would sing only when everyone else wasn't singing.

A game Angela has instigated on a few occasions when the class have been over, the success of which surprised even her the first time, is the Dressing-Up Game. It's a game she used to play at parties as a child. You have a bin bag full of outrageous dressing-up clothes and all the kids stand in a circle. They walk around the room and when the music stops, the one standing in front of the bag has to pull out an item and put it on. A bit like musical chairs. So there she was with a room full of between eight and ten children with special needs, and to her amazement they all stayed in the same room together, focusing on the same activity, for about twenty-five minutes. Once the bag was empty then they posed for a group photo. The smiles on their faces in the picture said it all. This game has now been played three or four times and each time the enjoyment is evident. If you listen to Angela talk about it you'll soon realise she considers the application of the 'Dressing-Up Game' to parties for kids with special needs to be her greatest contribution to mankind.

Everyone, it seems, likes dressing up. We hosted a music-themed quiz night recently at our home with about twenty friends in fancy dress. Angela was the quiz master, dressed and made up as Amy Winehouse, complete with fake tattoos and pretend cigarette. She looked great and had gone to a lot of trouble to set up the evening. We don't have that many friends round very often as we are never sure if Johnny will cope. We gave him plenty of information in the days leading up to the quiz and got him involved with the preparations. Johnny has at times sported very cool sideburns, so I came up with the idea that he and I could both come as the Blues Brothers. A couple of weeks before I explained to him that we were going to grow our sideburns to dress up and showed him the video of John Belushi and Dan Aykroyd in character at the end of the film performing the song 'Everybody Needs Somebody to Love'. Johnny took to singing lines from the song around the house, so I knew he was enjoying the idea.

Angela bought a couple of pairs of sunglasses and a hat from the fancy dress shop. They only had one hat, so I wore a similar one we already had that Johnny sometimes wears. I went to the supermarket and bought him a white shirt and thin black tie. He had some smart black trousers already, although he'd never worn them (he's not called upon to dress formally very often). So on the morning of the party we shaved, keeping our long sideburns. Then thirty minutes before our guests arrived I helped Johnny get ready. He put on his black trousers and white shirt. I tied his thin black tie for him. He put on his hat and sunglasses and he looked really cool. The great thing was, though, he absolutely loved it. We even wrote JOHNNY in felt tip across his knuckles and HENRY across mine, to copy Jake and Elwood in the film, which really tickled Johnny. He didn't even want to wash it off the next day.

First to arrive were his grandma and granddad as Stevie Nicks from Fleetwood Mac and Rod Stewart. The weird-ness of seeing his grandparents in wigs, you might have thought, would have fazed Johnny, but no. Let's face it, the very concept of a fancy-dress party on the face of it seems illogical and I wasn't sure how Johnny would react to seeing familiar people now dressed up in what to him must have been illogical costumes. He doesn't know Stevie Nicks or Rod Stewart, not that any of our looks were accurate enough to have made perfect sense even if he had known the celebrity.

Angela took some photos and Johnny delighted in getting involved. Over the course of the next thirty minutes friends and family arrived as the following – Abba, Dr Hook (complete with eye patch), Ginger Spice, Lady Gaga, another Stevie Nicks (to add to the confusion), Adam Ant,

Björk, Britney, Dusty Springfield, Siouxsie, David Bowie, Dolly Parton, Madonna and others I can't remember – or possibly didn't actually recognise. Despite the heightened noise of people greeting and enthusing and getting food and drinks, Johnny wandered around the periphery enjoying the atmosphere. Everyone complimented him and he looked comfortable having his photo taken. Angela and I were relieved, but more than that we were so proud and impressed that he was not only coping but really enjoying the event.

The quiz was to get under way after his usual bedtime, so I asked him if he wanted to go to bed. He confirmed 'bed' without any hesitation, so he said a big 'goodnight' to everyone and I took him up the stairs. We closed the bedroom door, quietening the noise from downstairs, and I started to help Johnny get out of his costume. 'What's wrong with me?' he said.

He often repeats words and phrases from films and I couldn't be sure that this wasn't just a phrase he picked up, but the timing and the nature of the phrase stopped me dead. This is not a phrase I could remember hearing him say before. 'What's wrong with me?' he repeated. It was like time stopped and my head filled with so many things I wanted to say. It didn't matter whether it was something he was just repeating, I reasoned. Of all the questions or phrases he could choose why would he choose this one now? There were so many things I wanted to explain to him. There before me in this quiet room was my nineteen-year-old son, going to bed at a quarter to nine rather than joining in with our family and friends in a night of fun and laughter. He looked so grown up now in his shirt and tie. He looked smart and cool and he stood there taller than me, asking the most difficult question in the world. I just wanted to hug him and kiss him like he was a baby again, all sixteen stone of him, but he was a man now. I squeezed his arm and said the only words that would come to me. 'There's nothing wrong with you,' I said. 'You're my son and I love you.'

Johnny got undressed, put his pyjamas on and cleaned his teeth. 'Do you want a story?' I asked. '*Finding Nemo*,' he requested. We lay on the bed and I read him the book. Then I closed his bedroom curtains and said goodnight. I walked down the stairs and into the living room, where the quiz was in full swing. As I had helped set the questions, my role was keeping the scores. Our guests were having a great night, Angela's personality was shining through and I could see the quiz was a great success. I sat in my Blues Brothers costume and put my shades back on. At the end of each round I totted up the scores and announced the leaders, but in reality I was still upstairs standing in front of my son trying to find words. Even writing this today I'm still standing there.

GUADALUPE AND THE NAVIGATOR

Trying to explain Jesus
to my son I realise
there is what I believe
and what I want to believe

These walls feel as old as hope
and my heart aches for a miracle
or the allowance
of the possibility of a miracle
somewhere
under the possibility
of heaven

I wipe my eyes embarrassed as
my wife returns from the gift shop
leaflet in hand

The donkey we saw in the masonry
is a bull
to signify St Luke

The angels on the ceiling
slaves stolen by the *infante*

I give the guide to a young English man entering

I'm not aware if he has a son

Chapter 28
Perspective

When you first have a child you are probably optimistic, even though there is a chance that child will grow up to hate everything you stand for. They might be a criminal, a drug addict, a despot, a bully or a racist. They might grow up to be sexist, homophobic or just generally intolerant of other people. They might be a bloody miserable git all round. They might end up in a loveless marriage, or live a life unfulfilled. They may lead a life of physical pain. They might struggle with disability. They might be lonely or abused.

They might end up committing suicide or self-harming. They might always lack confidence and suffer from low self-esteem. They might feel awkward and misunderstood. They might feel misjudged and mistreated. They might become ill or suffer from all manner of terrible accidents. Their life might be one of hardship and tears, like so many that have gone before. Still, when you have a child I'm sure there is some sense of optimism. My son is autistic. I'm not sure yet whether any of the above will apply to either him, myself or Angela. I remain optimistic.

RECLAIMED

My camera can't capture the breadth
of this wind-teased ocean
or the authority of volcanic mounds
that fall away far beyond the beach

180 degrees of untamed depth
180 degrees of fire made solid

Johnny pinches his mum's skin
playful in this physical domain

Small barnacles polka dot
black boulders on the beach
smoothed by abrasion

All this ground upon which I stand
is just a bigger rock rising out of the sea

I am anchored in the present by family
We whoop and shout into the high wide sky

For a full 360 degrees our world
remains beautifully autistic

Chapter 28a

Looks, Persistence and Paddling Like Hell by Angela

These days, to all intents and purposes, Johnny lives the life of Riley. I would say that fifty per cent of the time he is fully connected with us, thirty per cent of the time he is reachable and twenty per cent of the time he is completely in his own world and any moves to connect with him could be counterproductive. I wouldn't want to demand his attention when he's 'off somewhere'. He needs some time out, like all of us, although this time out, it seems to me, is even more important for him. I am happy with these statistics when I think about how far we have come. And when I think about the quality of the connection we do have. I am also aware that one can be genuinely happy with the present situation yet still want to 'reach for the stars', i.e. achieve more or dream bigger. The two states are not mutually exclusive. Don't let anyone tell you otherwise.

After our four years of staying inside doing the Son-Rise programme when Johnny was very small, we are now always out and about. We take him to restaurants and abroad several times a year. I once did a writing exercise with a group of people where we had to jot down our ten favourite moments, ever. It became clear that, for everyone, the majority of chosen 'best bits' involved being out in nature. I have reached an age now where I can tell, even while I am actually engaged in an activity, that this is going to be one of the best moments of my life. I have had several of these moments on beaches and in the sea with Johnny. There is a certain freedom you get when the sea stretches out before you and you can swim, shout and jump around, yelling loudly to the sky and the waves. Johnny gives us the excuse to embrace this sort of behaviour. It's impossible not to join in with him as he physically engages in his own inimitable way with the natural world around him.

Here might be a good place to add something about being looked at. We can't go *anywhere* without being stared at. Even when we're not joining in with our son and his exuberant ways, Johnny, sporting his red ear defenders, shouting, clapping and moving the way he does, means that we can never just blend in as a family. I have to admit sometimes I find it tiresome, even though most people tend (after a split second of sussing out if

271

there is any possible danger to them) to give us a smile. It's hard not to smile when you see Johnny laughing and clapping. A few people are less impressed. Some people are downright miserable. I always think the way people respond to Johnny gives you an instant window into the way they experience the world. I once got very upset because, as we entered a shop, a man pulled his two small children into him as though protecting them from a terrible evil. Johnny was being loud, but he was happy. He has never, as yet, hit a stranger. He has never, as far as I know, made any move to touch a stranger. Apart from a bald man in ASDA once. But his head was *very* shiny. Oh, and there was that young woman standing outside a shop in the Lanes, dressed entirely in a rubber jumpsuit. But to be fair, it *did* look like very inviting material to have a feel of. To give her credit, after her initial shock, she was completely fine about it. Luckily it was just her arm.

We face being studied if Johnny is getting anxious, or if he's having a whale of a time. It doesn't matter which. Little kids are the worst offenders when it comes to gawping. Henry tells me that little girls always look at my hair anyway (it's big – basically it hasn't changed since the 1980s) but as we pass, you can see children's mouths literally fall open as they try to make head or tail of Johnny. It's as if they haven't seen anything quite like him before. Does . . . Not . . . Compute.

I don't know exactly what I'd like their parents to tell them. Sometimes I think it's simply 'Stop staring.' Sometimes I think it's 'Why don't you give them a smile? I think he's autistic. We'll google autistic when we get home darling, but it's nothing to be frightened of.' Sometimes I think it's 'If you want to look that's fine honey, but it's just a young man whose brain is wired differently.' Sometimes it's 'Go and say hello! Look how happy he is. Isn't it great to see someone enjoying themselves so much?'

Sometimes (after a really early start) I want to use a misquotation that Johnny loves to shout from the film *Flushed Away*. Sometimes I imagine myself quietly whispering into their ear, 'Get lost you pink-eyed freak'.

I'm joking, of course, but Henry has pointed out that I have to be sensitive here. We have to give small children the same allowance of imperfection that we allow our own son – and ourselves. He's right, of course. Children may not instinctively understand special needs or disabilities and differences can be frightening for them. I recall when I was about five I saw the back of what I thought was a young girl in a shop in Cromer, but when she turned around, she had the face of an old woman. It was the first time I'd seen a dwarf and I burst into tears.

Still, I really would like something great to say in answer to the ogling. The trouble is, I don't feel clever enough to come up with the perfect response on my own. Perhaps we need a group effort. Maybe the National Autistic Society could run a competition? I'd genuinely like to have a polite, short but effective spiel. Something that's not too heavy but does the job. I've heard that some people hand out little cards with a bit of information on them. I like this idea, but I couldn't be sure that I wouldn't, at some point, have had 'Get lost you pink-eyed freak' beautifully embossed on a few of mine.

The thing is, the world isn't going to change or become kinder regarding our children if we're invisible and not around to help the learning process in any way – even if it's just being there to provoke discussion. So we never shy away from going out in public.

Johnny also goes shopping, swimming, walking, to the theatre and to art galleries and partakes in a whole host of other activities. To be honest, I've sort of made a rod for my own back because he now expects to have an 'outing' every day. He needs to. Because this is our routine. I must confess, I had an additional ulterior motive when instigating these activities originally. As well as them providing interactive and learning opportunities, I've always felt that if I tire Johnny out enough during the day at least he'll sleep at night! Not realising, foolishly, that lots of physical activity now means that he is as fit as a racehorse, and so needs ever more physical activity to reach that elusive state of being so worn out he'll sleep through the night. It's a vicious circle where he just gets ever-fitter and I get ever more fit to drop!

I'd like to point out here that one of the most important things I've learnt during the last nineteen years is to be persistent. By which I mean, try things with your autistic child but don't be put off if your child doesn't immediately 'take' to these things or if they seem initially overwhelmed by them. I have found, in our experience, that going back to an activity – for even just a short time – gives your child the chance to access it again, and maybe the second time, or third time, or fourth time they might feel able to take part more because they are less overwhelmed and feel more at ease in a familiar environment.

Many of the activities Johnny loves now have taken years of sticking with. Of increasing the time spent doing them little by little. I clearly don't mean dragging your child kicking and screaming somewhere. But maybe just be aware that perhaps your child might need a little longer than the average to understand what's expected of them, what is on offer and how much fun something might be. And to understand that small steps can lead to giant strides. I have found over the years that I've also said the phrase 'We're going to quit while we're ahead' a lot. I've felt that finishing up an activity on a high – leaving Johnny perhaps wanting more and therefore with a positive memory – has been very productive. It means he is always keen to go back.

Of course, every activity mentioned above is meticulously planned. 'Planning to fail is failing to plan' is our family motto. Along with 'Please Send Chocolate' (that's just mine actually). If you ever see a family with autism having a lovely time out somewhere, be aware that we are proverbial ducks, gliding along the surface, while our feet are paddling like crazy underneath. We are trying to hold it all together, while being prepared for any situation we can imagine. And any situation we can't imagine. In our case, this means anything from always having a small plastic toy on hand for Johnny to bash and bite, to knowing where the nearest place is in which we can access his favourite food (and which will be open and not too busy), to making sure that no one says anything remotely negative to anyone else (even an insult hurled out of the window at another driver), because Johnny always reacts to a negative tone of voice whether it's directed at him or not.

We are on our guard 24/7 to head off any meltdowns that we can, while accepting, of course, that some we can never head off, and understanding that sometimes a meltdown may be exactly what Johnny needs to relieve a build-up of stress. We are also aware that we can't always be on hand to 'protect' Johnny in life and that therefore he actually needs at times to be given the opportunity to acquire the skills to manage and come through difficult moments by himself. It's a juggling minefield, if you can picture such a mixed metaphor.

Here might be a good place to also add a little advice if you are reading this as a friend or family member of someone with autism. Be on time. If making plans to visit or meet up with anyone with, or looking after someone with, autism – please turn up at the arranged hour. We have routines and expectations to adhere to. Sometimes just getting to the point where we are able to greet and spend time with you has taken an awful lot of effort.

The ability to wait and fill time doesn't always come easy and things can fall apart pretty quickly if what is supposed to be happening at a certain time doesn't.

On a similar note, if things start going pear-shaped, get out quickly. Don't feel the need to be polite, or faff around trying to rearrange another date, or even, actually, offer help more than once. Believe me when I say that in these situations the most useful thing you can do is say, 'OK, I'll leave you to it' and then just go. Check in with us later by all means. If we need your help, we will take up the offer – but frequently it's easier for all concerned if we are just left to work through anything ourselves. We tend to have form and can be much more effective if we are not also worrying about having to negotiate an extra body. Do not take any of this personally either. We will love you even more for your understanding, thoughtfulness – and absence.

I once read that parents of autistic people have higher stress levels than front line combat soldiers. This I can believe. I also, incidentally, believe that every country in the world would be better off if it were run by parents of special needs children. If we had any spare time, that is. We are collectively a group of do-ers. We get up early and we get stuff done. We rarely complain. We fight for what we believe in. As a tribe, we tend to be non-judge-mental. We have an inordinate amount of patience and we can laugh at ourselves and the world. We have become extremely good listeners. And did I mention, we get up early and WE GET STUFF DONE? (We also may repeat ourselves occasionally, through lack of sleep.) But above all else, we know and appreci-ate the value of kindness. I doubt there would be many wars with us at the helm.

Chapter 29

Poached Egg (for example)

A quote that's stayed with me for many years is from an alien. It's from an episode of *The Outer Limits*, a great old black and white US sci-fi series I watched as a kid. An alien was cleaning a toilet. 'How demeaning,' said another character. The alien looked up and said, 'Does the job demean the man or the man demean the job?'

Including Johnny in activities is something we try to do even with the most mundane of tasks. As an example, let me explain his cooked breakfast on holiday. When we're in

Portugal, Johnny has a poached egg on toast with tomatoes every day. As I'm lying blissfully in bed, the shutters on the windows down completing the blackness, without warning a hand will reach around the door and switch on the main light. This is between 7 a.m. and 8 a.m. depending on heaven knows what.

'Poached egg,' is Johnny's morning greeting. No 'Good morning' or 'How are you this morning?' or 'Sleep well?', simply 'Poached egg.' A clear instruction as to what Johnny wants. It's not that we haven't tried instilling manners and niceties into his conversation, but Johnny has never quite grasped this use of 'please' and 'thank you'; instead they are things he says as a call and response when corrected. If you ask him a question like 'What day is it?' he might sometimes get it wrong and say 'Tuesday' when it's Wednesday. If you say 'No' or 'Try again' he could very well say 'Tuesday please' or 'Tuesday thank you'.

Rather than get straight up we tend, even now, to invite Johnny to sit in bed with us and we elicit a bit of conversation or sing a few songs together. Usually we talk about what we are going to do today so Johnny is aware of and comfortable with the schedule and sequence. Then, having already been up several times in the night to attend to him, Angela gets fifteen minutes' rest while I follow him into the kitchen.

So there are two objects to any job with Johnny. One is doing the job – in this case making breakfast. The second is to encourage interaction and self-reliance. It's always easier to sustain my son's interest if there is food involved, so I make the most of it.

First job – Johnny put your sandals on. The floors are solid and hard and a big lad who likes jumping about can easily hurt his feet.

Second job – Put the blinds up. These are electrical so only the press of a button is required. But all these little jobs depend on communication and understanding. What is easy now wasn't always so. Even the simplest of tasks need to be modelled at first. Like a lot of autistic people, Johnny often takes things literally. Angela once said to him, 'There's some socks in your drawer, can you bring them here?' He arrived back two minutes later holding the entire drawer of socks. Another time she regretted asking him to 'put these toilet rolls in the toilet for me.'

I ask a lot of questions, as casually as I can, during this process. 'What shall we do first?' 'Pan,' Johnny will say. So we get out the egg-poaching pan. I'll give him one of the cups for the eggs from the pan tray. 'Where's the margarine?' 'Fridge,' says Johnny and he goes and gets it, puts a bit on his finger and lines the inner surface of the cup. Often at this point we'll sing a made-up song, 'Bring Me Your Finger', to the tune of an old pop song. This always makes Johnny smile.

Next I present Johnny with the eggs and he chooses one: 'This one'. Now, the eggs may be all the same and he'll probably eat them all anyway but that's not the point. It's all interaction. Sometimes Johnny will crack the egg in, sometimes he'll say, 'Daddy do it.' Water in the pan, gas on, pan on gas, lid on. The egg is cooking. We are now on a timetable. Johnny wants the egg to cook faster than it does. 'White,' he'll say. 'Yes, it needs to cook,' I'll explain and we proceed with our routine to fill in the time. Johnny is much better at waiting these days. Let's face it, even the best of us can get frustrated whilst waiting. However, there's no need to create a problem when you don't need to, so we keep talking.

'Are you having a big tomato or little tomatoes?' I ask next. 'Little tomatoes,' is the usual answer. 'How many?' 'Three.' Johnny selects three tomatoes and washes them, then places them on his plate by the cooker.

'Right, let's set the table,' I'll say. 'What do we need?' 'Knife and fork,' he'll reply. 'What about Mum and Dad?' He'll take the right number of utensils from the drawer and start to set the table. Now you are probably baulking a little at how mundane this task is and how perfunctory the conversation. That is precisely the point I'm making here. But the trick is to enjoy the simplicity. We've already engaged in over twenty interactions and the egg hasn't even cooked yet.

This is so different from being in a room with Johnny when he was little. For one thing, back then, if he could he'd leave any room you were in asap. Here now, though, we are engaged in a task together without any confrontation, building a bond and enjoying each other's company. Well, I suppose Johnny could be anywhere on a scale from toleration through appreciation to enjoyment; but I say enjoying as he always seems cheerful during this process.

Between us we'll lay out all the table. By then the egg white is usually turning 'white' and Johnny knows this is the signal to put the toast in the toaster. We'll normally do a countdown together as we wait for the toast. When it's ready, Johnny will spread his dairy-free marge on the toast and I'll pop the egg on the toast. We sit down at the table and eat breakfast and enjoy a small task done together.

Johnny always eats his cooked breakfast in a particular way. He wields his knife now like a surgeon. Something at first I thought he'd never learn to do even basically. He's very precise. He always starts by cutting the egg white around the yolk. He de-pips the tomatoes and leaves the toast untouched until the end. I suppose we all have our own way of doing things. I like to combine variations of the different tastes. A bit of each flavour on its own, then a bit of egg white with toast maybe. Then perhaps egg yolk with tomato, egg yolk and egg white, tomato and toast, egg yolk and toast, egg white and tomato. Then on to three flavours – egg white, tomato and toast. Going through all the combinations. Finally all the different tastes on one fork. Let's face it, if there is a genetic predisposition to autism there's no real mystery as to which side of the family Johnny's comes from.

I find with most tasks that, if you take the time constraint out it and put the emphasis on joining in, they can be useful as interactions. Johnny likes jigsaws and simple computer games and, when you think about it, they are only tasks to be completed. I suppose it's about making each task fun or interesting and getting a sense of achievement.

Making poached egg on toast with your own son may not be considered worthy of any award or lauded in the media, it may not be remembered by posterity, but it is enjoyable and I personally find it very satisfying.

WHAT WOULD I HAVE DONE BETTER?

My head is on upside down
Iron filings on opposite poles of a magnet

I can feel but I can't think
and even then it's confusing

Without imagination
monkey bars are just bars

Pyjamas, it appears, can be worn any time of day
Everything money can't buy I don't understand

I'm searching for clues in old memories
as if the answer was there all along

The world outside my brain is too big
in every direction

I could stare at yesterday for ever
and still not understand

What would I have done better?
Everything

Chapter 29a
Another Way of Looking at it by Angela

In the early days of Henry's TV career, when Johnny was very small, I'd find myself attending countless 'do's and award ceremonies' where I'd have to contend with the dreaded question, 'What do you do?' My reply, 'I run a home programme for our autistic child,' always seemed to leave the recipient glassy-eyed and not really knowing how to answer. And in true 'media world' fashion, realising that I was in no way able to help them better their career, they would swiftly move on. At these sort of events, I frequently felt very, very dull indeed.

We don't go to many of these kind of evenings any more. Henry prefers to stay at home with a cup of tea and an Eccles cake. If I get the chance of a night out, I'd rather go and 'do' kara-oke with my mates. Our life at home means our feet are firmly kept on the ground (or the trampoline). Having Johnny has given both Henry and me a grounding in the art of putting things in perspective and being able to prioritise. The BAFTA we have on the sideboard in our dining room, for example, doesn't compare to Johnny's Silver Duke of Edinburgh Award certificate on the fridge. The fact that Johnny has no interest in either should prob-ably give us all food for thought. Like most of us he does enjoy praise, but he is fundamentally a man who lives in the present. No need to keep harping on about past glories. He is happiest in water or out in nature. Moving his body and flapping his hands, interacting with this great big beautiful planet of ours, in a way that doesn't necessarily put 'being social' or receiving a piece of paper someone has signed to say how well you have done some-thing anywhere near the top of his 'things to achieve' list. If indeed he has a 'things to achieve' list.

For Henry and me, shiny baubles and lunches out with famous people are all very pleasant, but there's nothing that can compare to the feeling we get when our son masters something new. Even the smallest achievements are big events in our house and are the real things that should and need to be celebrated. I can't tell you the number of times my heart has soared when I've seen Johnny try something or say something he has never done or said before.

Just the other Monday while we were in the car waiting for the horses to go past (Brighton has a racecourse that stops traffic), Johnny shouted out, 'Come on!' I don't know what you'd call that – a command? An exclamation? A comment? A glimpse of how he was feeling? Whatever it was, it was a first. It was unprompted and it was expressive. I couldn't wait to tell Henry. This is the sort of triumph that tops a positive business meeting. It may even be what sets us special needs parents apart from the parents of 'regular' kids. We notice the smallest of successes and are eternally grateful for them. They may seem minuscule and not really what you'd consider 'worthy' of voicing in conversations that involve other parent's recounting, for example, their children's exam grades.

Them: 'My son got an A* in maths!'
Me: 'That's great! Johnny offered me a crisp today – without me even asking!'

Perhaps our children's triumphs feel harder won, especially when we're thinking of the effort it might have taken them with the many challenges they face.

I used to feel a bit desperate sometimes when I was in the company of my friends who had regular kids. They are all extremely lovely but there were times when I'd feel I just had nothing to say about Johnny. They were telling funny stories about what their son or daughter had said or done, and I had no stories. How could I, when Johnny didn't really say anything that I could make sense of? He just didn't really interact with people in ways that gave us anecdotes. It was another way in which I felt bereft at that time.

On the plus side, I should add here that Johnny not really having a lot of language means to me that we almost have a deeper level of communication. We can't rely on words but there is often a real feeling of understanding between us that goes beyond the verbal. I find it hard to describe – telepathy sounds just too weird and new-agey (next stop angel card readings!), but we are very tuned in to each other. Perhaps it's a case of senses over-compensating. Or perhaps I have just spent so long watching him intently, trying to figure out what he's feeling and translating for him that something passes between us these days that means our lack of 'conversation' doesn't matter quite as much as it used to. Not, perhaps, that it ever mattered to him.

Like Henry, I cannot say how Johnny feels about his autism. For him I suspect he feels no separation. Being autistic is just how he has always experienced the world. It's not an 'added' thing. I do wonder, however, if at times he isn't acutely aware that he is 'different'. That other people his age aren't always accompanied everywhere by their mums. But perhaps – just maybe – it's that he sees us neurotypical people as the odd ones, i.e. in the minority. Because for such a lot of his time growing up, he's been around other people with disabilities. Maybe he feels that these are his tribe; these are the folks he feels more comfortable with (when they're not making loud, unpredictable noises, of course). Perhaps he can relax more around his own kind of 'normal'? Because they aren't always making demands on him?

We once had a visit from a very beautiful twenty-year-old girl who was on the spectrum. It was really interesting to see her and Johnny interact. She was nervous about coming in, but as soon as she saw that Johnny was sitting watching *The Little Mermaid* she keenly joined us. The two of them 'hit it off' and they ended up dancing around the hallway together. It was the first time I had felt the urge to joke to my son, 'Oooh, Johnny's got a girlfriend!' (in that way that parents like to embarrass their children). I don't know if they found each other physically attractive, but it seemed to me that they felt a connection, perhaps a recognition of a kindred spirit. I am hoping she will visit again some time. Of course, it may be that if she did, Johnny would have no interest in seeing her a second time. He is very good at confounding expectations!

I try not to dwell on the fact that Johnny is unlikely ever to have a 'romantic relationship' with anyone. I would of course love my son to experience all the highs life has to offer. I do wonder, when he watches his favourite animated films, with the countless princesses and princes kissing at the end, what he makes of it all. In fact I wonder this about a lot of things in life: the man dressed as a zebra playing the piano in the centre of Brighton/golf/why we only tend to have pancakes one day a year/how you can expect anyone to learn to spell anything correctly these days when there are shops called Fones 4U – what does Johnny make of it all?

I do remember once standing in the shopping centre with Johnny when he was younger and looking at a gang of teenagers. I recall having the reassuring thought that although my son might not be able to do a lot of the things they could, at least I probably wouldn't ever have to worry that he might get a girl pregnant, overdose, drink-drive or experience a broken heart. Swings and roundabouts.

I know from the outward signs that sometimes being Johnny can be stressful and overwhelming. And at other times it appears exhilarating and liberating. As far as my own experience of Johnny's autism goes, I can no longer say if it is a good thing or a bad thing – 'a gift' or 'a curse' – it just is what it is. Johnny is simply Johnny. I have no idea where his personality ends and his autism takes over. Or if his autism defines his personality. All I can say, from an outsider's point of view, is that often he seems filled with what I can only describe as 'the sheer joy of being alive'. I am both relieved and envious.

Chapter 30
What I Carry With Me

I was born at 34 Seymour Street, off Carlton Road, Nottingham on 15 August 1956. It was in the middle of the Suez Crisis, so when asked, I joke that I was a war baby. Let's face it, one way or another we are all war babies. My dad would always refer to the district as Sneinton, though I believe technically it was the less well-off St Anne's and this was my dad putting a posh spin on it. If you knew Sneinton in the 1950s and 60s, though, you'd realise it still wasn't that posh. All the houses on Seymour Street were back-to-back terraces and there was still the wreckage of bombed-out buildings like missing teeth along the row. My earliest memory is being on my own aged six with a plastic fire engine, moving it backwards and forwards along a windowsill for what seemed like hours. The more I think about this vivid memory the more I wonder if I'm on the spectrum.

When I was around six I fell while playing in the debris of a bomb site. I found an old gas mask that must have lain hidden there for a decade and a half. Foolishly, I tried it on. Even more foolishly, I breathed in. I don't know if that's what gave me pneumonia but I was so ill around this time my mum later told me she had thought I was going to die. All I remember is being allowed to miss school and snuggle up on the settee in the 'best room' and watch the telly. I was never normally allowed in the best room. No one was allowed in the best room. It's ridiculous nowadays to think that a room would be set aside and never used but in those days it seemed to be a matter of pride. The television was quite small, 12-inch at most and black and white, of course. The film I recall watching while ill was *The Alamo* with John Wayne, a story of resistance against the odds. I survived pneumonia but was a little weaker in the chest afterwards.

Despite having a brother and three sisters, I played on my own a lot when I was a kid. I had friends at school but I did spend hours in my room making a papier-mâché mountain for my Airfix soldiers, or playing with a chemistry set or collecting stamps. I would spend hours lowering and raising my Action Man on a makeshift winch out of my bedroom window. I sometimes even played football on my own. Kicking the ball against a wall or keepy-ups. I was tongue-tied, or short-tongued as they used to say, and had to have a piece of tissue under my tongue removed to help me speak.

As I'm told is common in ASD children, I did have trouble understanding my bowels and bladder, more so than I think would be considered usual nowadays in a neurotypical child. I had a plastic sheet until the age of six and distinctly remember pooing my pants and shaking it out of my short trousers' leg and into the gutter. Not a pleasant thought; but I'm trying to be honest here and I'm conscious some of this stuff may be relevant and resonate with others.

My mum was very warm, loving and tactile and had a lively sense of humour. I remember once her taking my sister Linda and me to the dentist's when I was around six. We were to have teeth out or filled and would need gas, as was administered at the time. 'What flavour gas do you want?' Mum asked my sister. 'Orange flavour,' she said. 'And what flavour do you want?' she asked me. There was no hesitation. 'Fruit cake,' I said. 'Right,' said Mum. When we got to the dentist's both Linda and me sat in the two dentist's chairs. The dentist approached Linda first with the anaesthetic and she soon fell asleep. He then turned and came straight over to me but I could see he hadn't changed the gas at all. 'No,' I shouted, 'I don't want orange flavour!'

My dad was generally at work. A somewhat stereotypical northern working-class man of his generation and not one to interact with his kids in those early years. He doesn't appear in many of the photos from this time. Quiet as he always was, I realise in retrospect that he was there but was usually the one taking the photo.

The door to our house in Seymour Street was bright pink, while every other door in the street was painted corporation green. We owned our home and Mum insisted the door wasn't green. There was no front garden. The front door opened straight onto the pavement or 'corsey' as it was called locally. Consequently, although our house was half way up the street, you could see our door from the bottom of the road. We had an outside toilet down the bottom of the garden. No toilet paper, just a copy of the *Daily Mirror*. You could put the big questions of the day behind you. Treat celebrities with the respect they deserved. We also had a tin bath that you had to fill with the kettle if you wanted hot water. This image seems like a relic from a generation before, I know, but was still very much alive in the provinces during the Swinging Sixties. The kitchen was ten foot square; no fridge, just a larder; no drier, just a mangle and a clothes line. If it rained you dried the washing on the clothes horses in front of the coal fire. There was no back garden, just a stone-paved yard.

The first time I was conscious of injustice was around the age of five. I'd gone with my mum to the public bath house on the suitably named Bath Street. This was a large public utility for people without their own facilities at home to wash clothes. The forerunner of a launderette but run by the council. The machines were quite big, sturdy, one might say industrial. I wasn't allowed in the main functional bit so I had to watch through a window in a waiting area. It happened when mum got to the drying section. There was a large machine that acted as a continuously rotating mangle. Mum helped the woman in front of her with her sheets. It was difficult on your own to load the sheet into one side of the mangle and then run round and collect the sheet on the other side. Easy for two people, though, and they shared a joke or two while working. For twenty minutes Mum helped the woman. Then the woman left. To do our sheets, Mum had to operate the machine by herself. Small as I was, I knew this was wrong but there was nothing I could do to help. I had to stand and watch. I remember crying out of frustration. If you were to see me at this point you might well think I was just a naughty or spoilt child.

My sister and I walked to school and back unaccompanied along the main road from the age of five. Children weren't indulged in those days. The classes at school were one teacher to over thirty kids and individual attention was rare. Lessons were mostly learning by repetition and set text. How an autistic child would survive I can't imagine. Before things got more PC, anyone different was often mercilessly mocked by children – and by many adults. Words like 'weirdo' and 'mong' were common parlance. A kid with round National Health glasses, as I had, was the extent of integration of special needs.

Once when I was eight I was riding my bike along the main road when I heard a clunk. I thought nothing of it and climbed the hill to the top of our street. Turning back down into Seymour Street to complete the circuit, I realised my brake cable had snapped. I was picking up speed on the cobble stones, heading straight back for the traffic on the main road. I had to make a decision. I turned in to the pavement and flew over the handlebars. I landed face first on the concrete slabs. A quarter of my front tooth broke and pushed through my top lip, leaving a scar. My face bloody and arms and legs grazed, I was nonetheless alive. I was told I couldn't have my front tooth capped until I was an adult. Up to the age of twenty I had a broken front tooth so until then I smiled with my mouth closed, head down. Even now I don't often show my teeth when I smile, especially in front of a camera.

When the council started knocking down the back-to-back housing in St Anne's, Nottingham, we moved to a council estate on the edge of the city. 32 Baythorn Rd, Bilborough, seemed like heaven after St Anne's. We had a kitchen six times as big, and a garden with actual soil at both the front and back of the house. We even had a bathroom upstairs with a toilet, and downstairs we had a second toilet, for some reason just outside the back door. Being working-class as we were, I don't think the council trusted us to shit inside downstairs in the 1960s. You would never build a house like that nowadays. It's like they were trying to lure us in and teach us to do our toilet in the house gently, by degrees.

I was relatively gregarious up to the age of eleven. One day in January I came home from school for dinner anxious to get back there as it was double games and we were play-ing football. The house seemed odd and full of people I didn't know. I had to wait for my dad to come home, which was annoying as I was going to miss out on football and the sports teacher was very strict on lateness. My dad finally arrived and sat me and my sister Linda on each of his knees. He told us that there had been a car accident and our mother had died. Linda didn't take it calmly and screamed like only a thirteen-year-old girl can. Long hair and gangly arms and legs all over the place. Dad tried to comfort her and I was passed over to some woman I didn't know. I sat confused by it all. I didn't understand. It wasn't until some time later, sat alone on Mum's bed, that it sank in. Whatever it was I felt that day has stayed with me all my life. It's difficult to describe, so we have to give it names like 'loss' and 'grief', to attempt to understand.

If my mum hadn't died I would probably have been a greengrocer. She ran a little business selling eggs and fruit and veg door to door from the back of a van around the local council estates. It was successful and we had one of the most 'well-to-do' houses on our road. Once she died, though, the house and our finances and clothes all went downhill.

The first original joke I remember making up was during the 'egg round'. I used to skive off school on Thursdays and Fridays to help Mum. She didn't seem to mind. We were in Nuthall, a private housing estate in Nottingham, on a street called 'Edgeway'. My mum was talking to a customer and I was anxious to get on as halfway through the round I usually got sweets and often a superhero comic. I tried to interject politely. Both women were talking two to the dozen and something occurred to me. Proud of my discovery, I exclaimed, 'I can't get a word in edgeway.' They both laughed and shook their heads in mock despair. But there it was – albeit a bad pun – I was up and running.

The other incident from those rounds that stays with me is when a brick smashed the window of our old Bedford van. The entire windscreen shattered and, trying to drive home even slowly, my mum couldn't see as the wind was fierce against her eyes. I watched her fight and strain to keep going. I'd not seen my mum in pain like this before. Eventually she stopped. 'Run and get your dad,' she said. I have never run so hard in my entire life. My ten-year-old chest was burning. Two miles with one thought, one purpose. It felt like the most important task of my young life. It's not often you get that sort of clarity of purpose, I've found in the fifty years since. Coming to terms with your child being autistic is another such challenge.

LOOKING CLOSELY AT MY FACE IN THE PAST

There's someone else in my kitchen
He's younger than me
He's wearing my clothes
His hair still has colour

He is fooling himself with organic soup
and orange juice
The declaration 'free' is turned from his sight
The word 'pure' is there to be found

Holding onto white bread in his left hand
In his right steel reflects light
The palette of the sun and sky
appear pale

The world around him seems out of focus
His head bowed
eyes closed
as if in prayer

From this angle I can see that he is not alone
Does he feel the same as I do?
Does he know it's all going to be alright?
Does he even know that?

Chapter 30a

Most Probable Future by Angela

No one knows their denouement. In an ideal world, Johnny would miraculously overnight acquire age-appropriate abilities, Ryan Gosling and Michelle Pfeiffer would respectively leave their partners and develop sudden, obsessive interests in two middle-aged writers from Brighton, and world peace would break out. This is, of course, not impossible, but it is highly improbable.

The most likely course of events for us, I believe, will be that Henry (who is thirteen years older than me) will die before me. I will eventually become too old and frail to manage Johnny and he will move into supported living arrangements. Apart from my parents, I only have very distant relatives, the vast majority of whom are older than me. Most of my friends are older than me. So I imagine that if I live to a ripe old age, I will go into a home and spend most of my time alone. A bit like going full circle, if you remember the description of my youth. Johnny will probably not come and visit me very often, if at all. Not because he won't want to, but because he will be in the care system – and the care system runs on timetables, staff availability, whether the minibus is booked/working and other people's priorities. I will most likely die alone. Johnny may or may not come to my funeral; I don't know how aware he will be or what choices he will be able to make at that stage. Or, again, if he'll have someone available to support him if he wants to. My son's well-being will predominantly be the responsibility of strangers.

My friend Karen's two daughters Ruth and Ursula and my cousin's daughters Martha and Lily have all expressed the desire to keep a watchful eye on Johnny in the future. I am pretty sure Henry's sister Linda's sons Laurence and Mike will too.

When Ursula and Martha made their offers I cried, with relief and in thanks for their generosity. I am crying now as I write this. We have made a will. But somehow it doesn't seem to be enough. It's not a firm guarantee that Johnny will be OK and, actually, 'OK' is not enough. He will be financially secure, we have made sure of that, but I want him to still be able to do all the things he loves doing. I want him to be able to paint, go on holiday, eat his favourite meals, dance to hits from the 1980s on Vintage TV every night. I want him to have someone who will continue to read Ivor The Engine stories to him in a bloody awful fake Welsh accent. You can write all this down in a letter of wishes, but it's not a legally binding document, and no amount of paperwork can ensure that someone will love your child. Even if they do, of course, they are never going to love them as much as you love them. This is true of all children, I know, but not all children are so vulnerable.

You will probably forgive me when you read this, for preferring to live in the present and of not dwelling too much on the future. But don't think that I am not aware that burying one's head in the sand is cowardly and probably not in any of our own best interests. The only way I can really get through thinking about this 'most probable future', is a) by imagining that Johnny will be surrounded by good people and b) by reminding myself that yes, I will be dead, but in the grand scheme of things – in another hundred years or so – Johnny will be dead too. Everyone reading this book now will be dead – and, not to put too fine a point on it, eventually all their children will be dead as well. So there's no point in worrying about anything, really.

The only thing to do is what Johnny does: live in the moment as much as possible and enjoy everything we can.

Chapter 31

Friends, Romance, Boredom, Loneliness and Other Things I Don't Know About Johnny

There are so many things I still don't know about Johnny. I don't know if he gets bored. I don't know if he gets lonely, or craves romance or friendship. It's difficult to know the truth of these matters about anyone, of course, including yourself.

I can't remember being bored very often as a kid. There were times on a Sunday when nothing much seemed to be happening and there was little distraction. Of course, Sundays back in the 1960s and early 1970s were very different to what they are now. Shops weren't open and it seemed the whole world was just in a corridor waiting for Monday. Most of the time though, even on a Sunday I had something to occupy my brain. Even though I had friends at school, the abiding memory of my childhood seems to be of me being alone. Company was not something I would actively seek out, more something I would accept and find comfort in. Certainly after my mum died, I would walk a lot and began reading more and writing to amuse myself.

I find it difficult to define loneliness. There are certainly times in my life I have felt alone and wished for company. It had to be the right company though. Not just anyone. Like most people, I expect, I have felt most lonely when in the wrong company. I do wonder then how Johnny feels.

I still have friends from when I was nine. Nigel Kirkwood, who lived two doors away, I lost touch with for many years, but have recently been able to spend time with. Social media means it's often easier these days to trace people whose addresses and phone numbers you've lost and who've moved (often several times) since you last spoke. I know for certain, though, that in the years I didn't see Nigel, I still considered him a really good friend. If for any reason he needed help, I wouldn't have hesitated to offer whatever I could, as I would for my own brother. I know in my bones he would do the same for me.

Angela finds it strange that I have such strong feelings for certain people but make very little attempt to contact them.

There are many friends, both men and women, that I've met over the years who I still hold a great affection for. If by chance I were to meet them, I'm sure we would talk as though it was only yesterday since we last spoke. In fact this happens often so I know it to be true. But despite being a man who has run a successful TV and film company and has stood in front of many audiences and cameras, underneath I am still quite awkward in a lot of social situations. I'm never sure what is expected of me and I'm always worried I will leave people insulted or disappointed. It is therefore easier to be on my own, or with Angela and Johnny, where I feel confident.

There's always something puzzling to me about the rules of 'doing social'. I'm never sure of the mode of operation, the *raison d'être*, other people's motivations and intentions and quite often the basic object of the whole exercise. Strangely enough, being at work or on stage is easier, as the rules and the answers to all those other questions are more easily defined.

Angela asked me recently whose funeral I would go to. We went through a list of my friends and acquaintances, family, work colleagues and a list of her friends. Some of my answers surprised her. 'But you've not seen them for years!' she said. 'It doesn't matter,' I said. 'But you wouldn't know anyone at the funeral,' she said. 'It doesn't matter,' I said, 'it's between me and them.' 'So why don't you call them and meet up with them while they are still alive??!' she asked. 'They've got their own lives to live,' I said, 'I don't want to bother them.' I genuinely don't see why the fact I have an affection or respect for someone should mean they have any time for me. My feelings for them aren't diminished at all through absence, so I suspect theirs aren't for me. It seems logical to me then that Johnny may well have strong feelings for people without needing to seek them out or display his feelings.

Romance and sex are trickier to understand. I'm sure even as a teenager with my hormones going wild, it was as much friendship as anything else I was seeking in a romantic partner. 'Someone you can do nothing with', as Winnie-the-Pooh might say. The sex is partly a confirmation of the special relationship. A shared intimacy that can create a bond. I remember as a teenager never being able to gauge the strength of someone's feelings, especially my own. I had trouble working out how to act. I would be too stand-offish and then too familiar. I would talk constantly to avoid awkward silences. I would try too hard and often miss obvious signals. At the moment, I find it hard to imagine Johnny navigating such relationships.

Out of respect for all the women I've had a relationship with, I'm not going to go into detail here. They gave me some beautiful moments, some painful, some exciting, some I regret and some I cherish. I wish I'd been kinder and more caring, more handsome, more intelligent, had a better body, been better at sex, had a better personality, been more successful and generally been a better person – but at the time I was doing my best.

I was very lucky to meet Angela and for us to stay together. I would love Johnny to find such a friend, who he wanted to spend time with. I would love him to find a girl-friend. I know it's important to keep an open mind but it saddens me to think he could well miss out on this aspect of life. I'm conscious, though, of using my expectations and my definitions of happiness and fulfilment to set some sort of template for Johnny; his life will probably be very different from mine and what will make him happy and fulfilled could be very different too. Not less or lacking, just different– and quite possibly better in many ways.

FRIENDS, ROMANS, COUNTRYMEN, LEND ME YOUR EAR DEFENDERS

The gentle vice
that keeps your head in place

Vault doors on the Safe Room
The clasp securing the jewels

Sonic drawbridges
guarding side gates

Binary black holes
holding a centre of gravity

Flood defence
against the rising waves

Matching comfort cushions
Personal Echo Chambers

Dual air locks on a space station
Shields aligned

The world
on mute

Chapter 31a

The People You'll
Meet by Angela

We are very fortunate to have reached a really good place on our journey so far. Although I am always aware that things can change. Several people I know have found themselves in the situation where they have had to put their children into residential care. I know that bad schooling, puberty and a mix of other specific obstacles that each individual child found challenging, brought about in each case a perfect storm that meant they just couldn't remain safely at home. This has nothing at all to do with any lack in parenting. Or not doing the 'right thing'. We have just the same chance of this happening to us. All of us. It is a tightrope we walk every day. Hence we appreciate every day. I try to remember that the only guaranteed things in life are death and the fact that everything is in flux. So when things are going well, I appreciate what we have – and when things are not going so well, I focus on the fact that everything is in flux.

Actually, I have found there is one other sure-fire thing you'll experience as a special needs parent: a whole host of new people will come into your life. Many of these, in the early days, will be 'professionals'. Sadly, few of them will be much use. The one or two who actually believe (rather than just say) that you as parents are their best resource – are generally the ones to hold on to. Don't ever forget that you *are*, without a doubt, the people who know your child better than anyone else. If something doesn't feel right, say so. I used to be a teacher of deaf students many, many moons ago before having Johnny. At parents' evening we teachers would sit at our desks and there would be certain parents who you would all privately roll your eyes about and hope weren't on your list. The ones who were demanding and overly interested in what you were doing and why. The bolshie ones. I realise now, of course, that is PRECISELY the kind of parent I later had to become myself in order to get the best for Johnny. It is good to always be polite and respectful – but really, don't take brush-offs or half-answers or vaguely promised plans. Be strident-stroke-annoying in your persistence. The squeaky wheel gets the oil. If you end up causing a bit of eye-rolling, then so be it. For some teachers these days, having so much paperwork to do and targets to meet, it may be the only physical exercise they get.

Other parents of children on the spectrum can also become a lifeline. Seek them out. You will not click with all of them, but the ones you do feel an affinity with, hang on to like grim death. Two of my closest friends who I've met along the way, Caroline and Julie, have autistic children. There is something invaluable about not having to explain everything to them. There is something invaluable and precious, too, about the time 'off' we get together. There is something unsaid about our connection. I'll be honest – we often have a real laugh about the various surreal predicaments we find ourselves in. This is a release. We also often find ourselves marvelling at how different our lives are from the lives of other people who we jokingly refer to as, *'not knowing they're born'.* Other parents of children on the spectrum also just know how to 'be' around your child and make you all feel welcome in their houses if you ever visit.

It should be said, though, that even spending time together with these friends and our children doesn't always work out. Some time before we went to Ireland with Johnny to have a break and possibly catch up with David Mitchell, who I had been working with, I remember having a conversation with him that summed up what it's like getting together with other families who have children on the spectrum. We suggested that our two families might meet on the beach. However, we were all completely prepared for the possibility that it would actually only be for a very quick hello, with the rest of the afternoon spent a mile apart, playing with our respective offspring and, every so often, waving over at each other.

Once a year, Julie, Caroline, another friend called Julie and I get to go on a busman's holiday; we have four days off together at the villa in Portugal. Even though the three of us with autistic children end up talking about them way more than we probably should, it's a real recharge of the batteries. In preparation, of course, before we go we spend a good deal of time ensuring everything is in place for our kids. Not unlike a military operation. Once there, however, we cannot physically be responsible for anything at home, being seven hours' travelling time away – so we let loose, swim naked in the sea and dress up in wigs and false eyelashes. At some point during each holiday, we look at each other in astonishment and say, with equal measures of guilt and glee, 'Can't believe we've got away with this again.' If only this sort of break could be available on prescription for all carers. I am not being flippant here.

If you have the time and energy (you know what, forget having energy. You probably won't have any. Ever. Again. I swear by chia seeds on my cereal in the morning but I have a vague suspicion they are merely a placebo) there are all sorts of new activities you could end up trying, to help expand your child's interests and abilities and their world. I am also very aware that money is a huge issue for families with special needs members. Henry and I are patrons of the Brighton charity Amaze and the figures on how much more a family with special needs requires are staggering. I know we are very fortunate in our circumstances but if you need to and feel able to, it is worth exploring charities, bursaries and crowd funding.

This means that as well as educational/health professionals and parents, you also might have the good fortune to meet other people who, without your child's additional needs, you would probably never have come into contact with. In our case, we've met art facilitators, circus performers, musicians and animal 'whisperers', to name a few. They have all had one thing in common – the ability to connect with and engage Johnny, without ever speaking down to him. They have kept their expectations of and aspirations for him high.

Over the years, it is these different, often 'slightly left-field' people who have entered our sphere for some reason or another, who have made a huge difference, not only to Johnny, but also to our world, making it all the better and more colourful just by being in it. These individuals are few and far between but when we find them, they are like gold dust. They have no idea quite how much they mean to us, I'm sure. Of course, over time, they come and go. But their impact remains for ever. They spark inter-action and growth in our children and for our kinds of families I think their effects are beyond profound.

It means the bloody world to us parents to have someone speak to our children in a respectful, fun, appropriate, encourag-ing way – while also helping them access new experiences, skills and means of expressing themselves. These people are great adverts for human beings. I hope you get to meet one or two similar characters on your journey. Doing so leaves you a little more hopeful in the knowledge that when you die, there *are* some brilliant people out there who 'get' your kid. And on a good day, you can choose to believe that it might – just might – be these sorts of people who are looking after your child when you've gone.

Chapter 32

Some Things I've Learnt

Angela has a glass jar in which she keeps handwritten notes of moments of joy that occur throughout the year. Then at Christmas she opens the jar and is reminded of those moments. I love the fact that she not only allows herself the possibility of joy, but expects it and even plans for it. I've met many people in my life. Some have a sense of humour and some have a sense of fun. These are very different attributes. Angela manages to combine a quiet stoicism with a great sense of humour and is full of fun too. She is an inspiration to me.

They say that speaking in front of other people is one of the most common fears. More common than the fear of spiders or snakes. Some people would rather do anything than have to talk in front of even a small group. We are a strange species, that we should be afraid of other humans. But Johnny appears not to be afraid of other human beings. Whether he's interested in others or not, generally it seems he does not have an inbuilt fear of strangers. My guess is that he regards people exactly as they are; mostly he's not wanting anything from them, he's not trying to sell them anything and he's not interested in their opinion of him.

I remember a while back Angela and Johnny got on the bus down on the seafront and she said to him, 'Go upstairs while I pay,' and he went upstairs and she paid. When she reached the top of the stairs there was nobody on the top deck apart from one man, and Johnny sitting right next to him. I love that; to me it's further proof that he's not afraid of people. Certainly not as afraid as the bloke on the bus with a six-foot-three stranger wearing ear defenders sitting next to him.

Another thing I've learnt from Johnny is to enjoy silence. It's quite easy at times to fill every available moment with chatter and noise. Whether it's the radio or television or music or whatever, we all seem to have a constant soundtrack to our lives. With Johnny I've been forced to be quieter and so it's given me the opportunity to embrace and enjoy that quiet space.

The biggest thing I've learnt, though, is to live in the present. Johnny shows no interest in the future or the past beyond the practicality of the next week. He'll tell you what's happening today and sometimes he'll map out his next seven days, but more often than not he'll just exist in the moment. I'll often give Johnny a list of what we're going to do, so I'll say, 'We're going for a walk, then we'll come back and have hummus and then you can watch the circus on DVD then we'll do a jigsaw and have tea and listen to music and have a bath and go to bed' and he'll usually say, 'Walk'. Whatever the list, he's only really interested in the first thing. If I said, 'Johnny, we're going to go for a walk then you're going to have your absolute favourite food and we're going on a brilliant adventure and you're going to meet all your favourite people and it's going to be great and it's going to be the best time ever,' he'd still say, 'Walk'. He's interested in the now, not your promises for some possible future.

I've spent much of my life trying to learn from my mistakes, trying to ensure I do things better next time. I've also spent so much time like a meerkat, looking out for danger, trying to anticipate and head off problems. The ability to enjoy the moment doesn't come naturally to me. Being with Johnny, though, you are forced to slow down and experience it. That's a great gift.

I love to see the change in people when Johnny enters a room. It's funny, even people who generally seem frosty or rigid let down their guard a little. I often see a kinder side to people. Sometimes even the mention of him can bring this on. That's a lovely testament to humanity. It certainly shames me into optimism at times.

I've learnt to allow other people their imperfections, however annoying they can be. Even the kids I used to want to decapitate for causing Johnny pain by screaming on the plane for no reason or crying crocodile tears in order to get their own way. Not to forget those kind souls who make an extra effort to be friendly when I'm with Johnny who wouldn't otherwise give me so much as a smile if I was on my own.

I can't write this entire book without mentioning the word 'cure'. The whole idea of a cure for autism is a contentious one. Cure is a word I'd have used fifteen years ago. It's not a word I use now. I've found that autism is a different way of interacting and perceiving the world. I'm now not sure you could take this condition entirely from my boy without losing something of what is essentially him. Like any parent, I just want to see my child grow and take care of himself and learn to cope with life's stresses.

I remember seeing my dad checking the pools coupon every Saturday teatime. I'd sit there with my sister Linda, who'd prod and tickle me, out of Dad's sight. When I reacted Dad would shout at me to be quiet. The pools were a serious business. It made Linda taunt me even more just for a laugh. My dad never won the pools but spent his life just one score draw away. I remember picking his old jacket up in the hallway one day and it was so heavy with betting slips from all the horses he'd backed that never came in. Like all the chances he'd missed were weighing him down. As I grew up I decided I would never bet on horses or do the pools or even buy a lottery ticket. I didn't want to spend my time and money waiting helplessly for things to come my way. I decided I would only put my time and money into something where I could affect the outcome. Bringing up an autistic kid puts that thought very much at the front of my mind. Whatever my luck and whatever the outcome, I needed and continue to need to take action and be responsible for those actions.

My dad, like a lot of working-class men in Nottingham at the time, smoked over forty fags a day. I sometimes joke with people I see lighting up that 'he smoked right up to the operation'. He used to smoke Embassy cigarettes. At the time a packet of twenty would have a '5' coupon inside and a pack of ten would have a '2' coupon. If you sent in your coupons you could obtain gifts from the catalogue. Every couple of years we would count the coupons. He had thousands of them. Every '5' would have cost him 50p and every '2' cost 25p. I remember looking at the floor covered with coupons and seeing how much money he'd literally burned. If ever there was a lesson on taking control of your own destiny, for me that was it. The fact that he died of cancer only added injury to insult, to rephrase the old saying. My dad liked a drink every now and again, though never to excess (and let's face it, if you're trying to cope with five kids on your own you deserve a drink). I've never been one for alcohol so he'd have enjoyed the irony of my having a beer named after me by a Nottingham brewery; last year Castle Rock brewed the Henry Normal beer. Angela told me not to drink too much of it before driving home or, as she said, I'd 'literally drink myself to death.'

I loved the documentary *Life, Animated*, about the young autistic man who has a love of Disney cartoons. I'd thoroughly recommend it. There's a line in that film that always makes me cry. The father, on discovering his son would talk directly to a glove puppet, lifted it up and asked, 'When did we get to be such good friends?' This, to me, is the most perfect response. As well as the line itself, I say many variations of this line to Johnny. When did you get to be so clever? When did you get to be so handsome? I like the fact that as well as being positive, it allows Johnny the opportunity to reply and express himself.

I love watching Johnny get absorbed in his art and his engagement with people, which has come on so well. I love watching him swimming or walking along a beach. I love watching him bravely try something new. They say to be brave you have to have fear. Given the obstacles Johnny's overcome, he is one of the bravest people I know.

Looking back on the journey we've had together I have learnt to be grateful for the small victories and minor breakthroughs we have had and continue to have as the years go by. Where once I'd have been too ambitious with a neurotypical child I had to stop myself from underestimating Johnny.

From Angela, I've learnt how to be accepting while supportive, even to allow myself a tentative optimism for the near future. I've learnt that if we don't worry about the far future for now, but live in and for the present, then hopefully there's more fun to be had for our 'normal' family.

Recently, arriving at the farm for his regular day working with the horses, Johnny saw a small wooden podium in the grass, discarded after a gymkhana. He'd have ignored this when he was first diagnosed, but now we watched as he playfully climbed to the top and held his arms up high.

FIRST PRIZE

As you climb the podium
we applaud
there is no grand speech

We are the only witnesses
if you discount
the shrubs and the sky of course

This is for fun
but motivation is there
balance and coordination

You are the hero
you have overcome
you are ready to play

There are no medals big enough
no metals shiny enough
to do you justice

Two wooden boxes
on a piece of grass
make you taller

But
you are already taller
you are already taller

Chapter 32a

Small Epiphanies and the Fear of Trolls by Angela

Things I have learnt (aka IT'S THE SAME DOG)

I have managed to learn a few things on my forty-eight trips around the sun. Don't eat in a restaurant that has actual photographs of the food on the menu, for example. My sister-in-law Linda lives by the rather interesting motto, 'If it's wet and it's not yours – don't touch it'. The Dalai Lama has taught me (not personally), that it is good to be kind whenever possible – and, of course, it is always possible. An old school friend, Katie, recently told me that 'failure is not the opposite of success – it is often one step closer to it'. Which I like a lot. And another old friend, Jason, says, 'Put in "If your aunt has balls – she's probably your uncle."' I could go on. However, there are only really three life lessons I'd like to mention in my closing chapter.

I have often been asked, 'What would you tell other parents if you had the opportunity?' Well, this looks like possibly the best opportunity I am going to be afforded, so here goes. I hope that what I offer up might be useful to you in some way, even if purely as food for thought – digested and then discarded. I think we all have an effect on the world and the people we rub up against. Even if it's simply to cause a quiet mental note of 'I'm not going to live my life like that'.

Number 1
This is what I wish I could say to every teacher, classroom assistant and person who comes into contact with an autistic person.

Never assume that if a person doesn't communicate verbally or in a 'regular' manner (or is someone who outwardly looks and expresses themselves 'differently'), they don't understand what is going on or being said around them. Always be mindful of this. Also, be aware that every act could be an act of communication.

Number 2
When working with your child, focus on one goal at a time. For example, during an activity in which you might be trying to encourage speech, don't worry about 'teaching' coordination or sequencing or pointing or handwriting at the same time. Likewise, if you are encouraging turn-taking, don't try too hard to elicit appropriate speech as well. Neurotypical people find it difficult to multiply numbers while walking. It is much easier for your child or young person to concentrate on one thing at a time. Make your

intention clear, to yourself, before you start. What *exactly* am I working on at this point? To me, having a focused intention is helpful all round.

Number 3

YOU CAN CHOOSE HOW YOU FEEL.
ABOUT EVERYTHING.

No one else can make you feel anything. You are in sole charge of your own feelings.

This is what has had the most profound effect on my life so far. And in turn, I suspect, on Johnny's life. I know Henry has also mentioned this briefly earlier.

Discovering that you can choose how you feel shouldn't really have been a revelation, but it was. I have the Son-Rise staff to thank for teaching me this, as it is one of the core principles of their work. Realising it, was no less than enlightening for me. I have now reached a level of 'enlightenment' that means that these days, whenever a friend comes into a room saying, 'So-and-so made me really angry at work today', I reply, 'No they didn't. You made yourself angry.' Which is probably really annoying for them. But hey, they're choosing to be annoyed with me. They could just be thankful. ☺

The whole principle was first described to me along these lines: we as humans function using a STIMULUS→BELIEF→RESPONSE method. For example, we see something – the STIMULUS – like a dog barking on the street. Our BELIEF kicks in, and we all have different beliefs, mostly based on our experience. So my belief might be: that dog sounds annoyed. His bark is very loud. I don't like the look of him. Maybe when I was younger, a barking dog tried to bite me. My RESPONSE might then be: right, I'm going to cross over the road to avoid him. However, someone else might hold the belief: aww, that poor dog looks like he needs a pat. He's probably lonely. Maybe this person grew up surrounded by dogs. So their response might be to cross the road towards the dog and go and show him a bit of love. It's the same noise. IT'S THE SAME DOG.

The point is: we can change our beliefs. None of them are set in stone. And when we change our beliefs – we can then change our responses. The really profound thing to me is, we are totally in control of our own feelings. I wish I'd been taught that in school.

I recall really committing to this idea following a particular incident when Johnny was very small. I had spent forty minutes cleaning up Johnny's play room. He had smeared poo everywhere. It was all over him and his bed and the walls. I changed him and the bed. Washed down the walls and floor. I went downstairs to put the washing on and by the time I had gone back upstairs, he'd weed. Everywhere. I changed him again, cleaned the room and stripped the bed. I went downstairs with the next load of washing. I distinctly remember standing at the sink thinking, 'I hate my life. I can't cope. I can't do this any more.'

I had been up since 2 a.m. I felt like everyone else I knew was out there, enjoying their freedom and having fun, while I was reduced, to put it bluntly, to cleaning up shit and piss. With the added prospect that this was going to be my life for ever. And I decided the only way that I was going to get through it was to choose to feel OK about it. Come what may, as bad as it was going to get, for as long as it was going to take. So I decided to believe that I could cope. That I could continue to 'do this'. That I was going to feel OK about my life. Not 'all-out great' (for now) but just one step up – OK. It's only when you get to a profound moment like that, that you really understand the significance.

I chose to start gradually. The morning had been really challenging but I was now going to believe that the rest of the day would be much better. And if it wasn't, that I would be fine about it. My life was not the life I had planned (remember those handmade biscuits?) but never mind. From now on, I would be happy with my lot. I am not sure how long it lasted that first time, but I think we had a good afternoon. It does take a long time before 'deciding to feel positive when faced with bad things' becomes your default setting. Seventeen years later I still sometimes have to remind myself.

The thing is, life is much nicer this way. But more importantly I think, above all else, I am much more effective for and with Johnny when I am in a positive frame of mind. When Johnny is feeling stressed, anxious or biting himself, it doesn't help if I start feeling upset or sad for my son. It just doesn't.

This is not to say that I don't ever feel down, or bad, or annoyed. And a severe lack of sleep will always amplify any problem. Two years ago, for example, after taking Johnny to a cookery course for special needs kids, I came home and cried. He was by far the most special of the children – by which I mean he was way more challenged than any of them. It was a stark reminder of all the things my child can't do and that on the scale of disability, Johnny's difficulties are extreme.

Occasionally other things throw me. I recently had to have a lengthy conversation with the council on the phone about the fact that Johnny isn't able to vote. They kept sending reminders to fill in a Register To Vote form with his name on. I kept filling them in and writing a note to inform them that Johnny is officially 'mentally incapacitated' and therefore not legally able to put a cross in any box.

After the very nice man on the phone reassured me that he'd taken Johnny off the list and that I wouldn't be getting anything else through the post, another one arrived, two weeks later. Yet again, another literal reminder of something that our son isn't able to do. *He has no right to vote.* I had to laugh at their complete inefficiency. Well, I didn't have to, but I chose to. I am now always aware that I have the power to decide exactly what I'm going to spend my precious minutes feeling. And what impact my choice has.

In addition to this, I have also tried to stop worrying and fretting. When I used to get an hour off from running the Son-Rise home programme I would whizz into town to get banking and things done and I always remember my journey home was miserable. I'd be driving back, whittling about what I was going to find on my return. Would Johnny have been stressed, or have bitten himself or hit the person I'd left him with? If so, would the person ever want to come back again? Much of the time, though, nothing too major had occurred. Nothing that couldn't be dealt with. And on more than one occasion a really great time had been had by all. So I'd just literally wasted my last twenty minutes off imagining dreadful scenarios. Even if what I had imagined had happened, there would have been nothing I could have done about it. I often think back to those drives home and remind myself that worrying about 'what if's and 'might be's is mostly daft.

I have Johnny to thank for so many things. He has been an inspiration and a great teacher. He has helped me put everything in perspective. Taught me what to prioritise. Opened out my world. Without him I definitely wouldn't be the person I am today. I hope in turn that we have been good parents so far. If I could take away Johnny's anxiety and the moments in which he is over-whelmed I would. If I could give him the language to be more able to express himself, I would. If I could make the world a kinder place for him to be 'different' in, I would. But I certainly wouldn't want to 'cure' him of his autism. Not now. Now I understand that it is intrinsically tied up in the threads of his DNA with his personality. I would have no idea who he might be without it. And when I see him so joyously interacting with the physical world around him and experiencing life in the extraordinary way that he does, I can't imagine anyone wanting to take that from him.

I hope that you've enjoyed our Adventures On the Spectrum. If you are reading this because you also have an autism connection, then I wish you and your family all the best. If you are reading this and you don't have an autism connection, then I wonder about your recreational reading habits but applaud you for getting this far. I hope it's been interesting to you and I also wish you and your family well.

I have struggled with the question: Should we even be writing this book? When our son isn't able to give us his permission to tell our joint story? There is also always a risk when you put something out into the world, especially these days. We all have to brave the trolls and the people who feel they know more about your circumstances than you do. The days of constructive criticism, it seems, are long gone. But anyway, here we are. In print. Baring (nearly) all. Awaiting the comments, likes and possible poo emojis.

Writing this *hasn't* been easy. Aside from exposing our lives, it's actually been a trial to remember everything. I put this down to the heady mix of nearly twenty years of broken sleep, the perimenopause and probably too much alcohol in my younger days. When I *have* remembered events, they have usually come back to me at around 3 a.m., so I've been forced to fumble for my phone and make a note in the handy NOTES section, because the likelihood of me hanging on to these memories until sun up is practically zero. (I stopped drinking alcohol around the time Johnny was diagnosed as I felt I needed to be alert at all times. For the last fifteen years or so I have been pretty much teetotal. Nowadays if I even have the odd half a glass of anything, a couple of sips in, a red blotch appears on each cheek and I start to resemble a child's drawing of me.)

To be frank, I am terrified about how all this will be received. I have frequently wanted to say to Henry, 'Let's just *not* do this, shall we?' But I think back to an email that was forwarded to me by my agent after *Snow Cake* came out. It was from a parent who I had never met. In it she wrote about how she'd been having a hard time with her autistic son. She was tearing her hair out, finding him very difficult to be with. She sat down to watch the film and when it was over, she told me that she felt compelled to go upstairs to her child's room where he was sleeping . . . and kiss him on the head. That was the best review I could have hoped for.

If this book, which we offer up with tired outstretched arms, is even a little bit helpful, insightful or encourages just one person to feel a bit more connected with another human being – or even themselves – then it will have been worth the effort, additional sleepless nights and stress-related eczema. This is of course my own perspective. I suspect the publishers are aiming for slightly higher numbers.

I mentioned to Johnny that we were writing an account of our lives together and that we hoped he'd be OK with this. He smiled and said 'Yes.' We do not know if he really has any understanding of what this or anything else we talk to him about really means, but we continue to speak to him as if he does.

Thank goodness he didn't say no.

Chapter 33

How We Got to this Book

We have tapes of Johnny growing up that I can't watch yet as they are too painful. These are tapes shot on camcorders in formats that no longer exist except in specialist tape transfer labs. One day I may have them converted on to memory sticks and maybe I'll pluck up the courage to watch them. It was hard enough living through those moments once, though.

Writing this book had a similar masochistic feel at times. Some of the experience is still raw. My brain may have anaesthetised itself to many of the memories with the passing of years. The most useful stimulus has been photos. We have hundreds of photos of Johnny growing up. He was a good-looking kid (I'm biased I know) and we now live in the age of cameras on phones, so Angela has regularly taken photos of Johnny since he was born. Before even, if you count pregnancy photos.

When I was young photos were taken once a year at school, on holiday along the prom next to the pier by a bloke in a stripy jacket, at weddings and christenings, or, when Polaroids became fashionable, just standing in the house marvelling at the invention. I'm told that in Skegness each year I would run up to the photographers on the promenade to ensure I got my picture taken. I have no such pictures now so I can only assume we never bought them. Somewhere perhaps there are countless images of me as a toddler, looking delighted, lost amongst all the other unwanted snaps.

As Johnny had always lived in the same house in Brighton, we decided that we would never move. Instead, a few years ago we decided to rebuild the house with an eye to practical living with Johnny for the rest of our lives together. We enlisted the help of an architect and we set about thinking what would make our lives, and particularly Johnny's, easier, more practical and more enjoyable. There were simple things like ensuring the doorways were all high enough. With Johnny being six foot three and possibly still growing, that seemed logical. We had taller toilets put in to help him, even though a regular-sized person can feel a little like an elf sat on the large-scale plumbing.

We ensured there was a room off the kitchen for Johnny to do his art, complete with en suite and shower should he get messy. We had glass inserted in the adjoining door so Angela could keep an eye on Johnny while she was cooking. Next to his bedroom we built an adjoining room where he can hang out, watch TV and chill on his own. There are no sharp corners anywhere. Everything is built to be robust and to withstand a sixteen stone lad jumping on it. Everything, that is, with the exception of Angela and me.

We had the garden relaid with a flatter lawn, a hut for picnics, a sturdy swing, and, using the old front door, a secret passage through to Johnny's trampoline. Several autistic people we've met seem to enjoy trampolines. I'm not sure if it's the intake of oxygen, the weightlessness, the sheer fun or something else but Johnny loves it.

We moved back into the rebuilt house on 2 July 2014, my dad's birthday, and almost a year after he died of cancer at the age of ninety. With the fairly recent death of my brother David from cancer still very much on my mind, I thought I'd take the opportunity to sort out my family photos, which I hadn't looked through in years. I have hundreds of pictures and they exist in a combination of photo albums and loose in boxes.

I decided to sort them out in terms of who was in each picture. This is probably my autistic side coming to the fore. I had a box for my family, a box for Angela's family, a box for friends, a box for photos of Johnny on his own and a box for photos of Johnny with me and Angela. As I began sorting I became intrigued by the box of photos of me, Angela and Johnny. What did this haphazard selection of images say about us and our relationship? Certain photos made me feel much more emotional than others. Why was that? What was it about these images that could make me feel joy or anger or sadness or loss? Why did others make me feel nothing?

I felt compelled to write my thoughts down and these thoughts became poems. I hadn't written poetry for over twenty years. I'd not set out with the idea of writing poems, but it seemed a natural way of processing this experience. After I'd written a few of these early poems I showed them to Angela. They were quite raw and maybe somewhat basic. Angela did feel that those first attempts were on the whole quite depressing and often repetitive (she does not shy away from honest criticism). Her favourite phrases were, 'That's a bit "nothingy"' and 'That's half a poem.' Sometimes she was being generous there. Anyway I stuck at it and after a year I had a variety of poems and still some nothingy, half poems.

I simply wrote, not thinking much about where it would lead or of any literary or other merit. I continued to put my trust in the worth of one concept – truth. If I could be true to myself, this work would be worth something, if only to me. Even if no one ever saw this poetry, the act of creation and the experience and understanding gained would justify the endeavour. I tried never to force the issue. If a photo was not inspiring, I moved on to the next. Sometimes, however, even no reaction was interesting. Why no reaction?

For most pictures I'd ask: What do I like or not like about it? Can I remember what I felt at the time? Who took the picture? Where was that? Why did we have a picture taken? What happened before or after? Then I'd move on to look at the details within the picture. Each detail can lead to a question or an emotion. It was really the emotion that most interested me.

Angela and Johnny always go shopping on a Saturday morning, so after working in London all week it was lovely therapy for me to have Saturday mornings to myself, looking at family photos and writing. I was worried, when I started, whether the whole business was self-indulgent, but

I convinced myself that this was the universe I know. This is the only part of the universe I have seen and I'm retelling the story from the one point of view I truly have: my own. And although a lot of the subject matter covered was personal, I felt sure there were other people contending with many of the issues raised and I hoped they might find something useful within the poems.

Angela has mentioned that we are patrons of Amaze, a special needs charity in Brighton. They were very useful in helping us understand the local facilities when we first found out about Johnny's autism. For the past few years we've helped them put on an annual comedy charity event called the 'Big Cheer'. Some of the great comics who have worked with Baby Cow have performed alongside up-and-coming Brighton comics. The show has raised both money and awareness. So last year I offered to put on a special poetry night for them called 'Photos With My Son' and we booked the small room at the Komedia in Brighton. The capacity of 100 seats sold out quickly in advance and all I needed now was to put on a show. I'd not performed an evening of this nature for over twenty years.

I greeted everyone personally on the way in to the venue, as I wanted to dispel any idea of this being anything other than an ordinary bloke telling a true story about his family. I'd seen so much ego and artifice in my years of working in comedy and TV and I didn't want this communication to suffer from distancing in any way. I used a slide projector connected to my laptop, together with the photos that had inspired the poems, and set about performing for two halves of forty-five minutes each. It was quite emotional for me. It was the first time I'd read any of these new poems aloud to anyone, even myself. I arranged for the director, Dave

Lambert from my office at Baby Cow, to film the gig on two cameras and I've put some of the show up on YouTube. If you type 'Henry Normal Photos with my Son' into YouTube's search engine you can watch it. You will see from the footage it's quite raw. I am on the edge of breaking down at several points, but I managed to get through. In the end I was on stage nearly two hours. From the reports I received afterwards it was a success, but I was both physically and emotionally shattered. I won't deny that there was an element of therapy for me in doing the show. I think there's an element of therapy in writing this book too, and in telling any aspect of this story to others.

Adrenalin is great for when you are on stage and it sustained my energy until the end of the show, but it also meant I never got a wink of sleep afterwards. The next day was when it really took its toll. It was like not having done any exercise for twenty years and then doing a two-hour workout. Approaching sixty, as a family man with a successful business, it did seem odd to me to be motivated to even get on stage again, but having not performed for such a long time, I found that this whole experience was different. Unlike the first time round, I wasn't trying to be famous or earn money or get laid, even. I was trying to communicate and express something about our family life. Nothing earth-shattering, nothing pushing the boundaries of art, nothing unique, but to me it felt worthwhile. If I had only ever done the one performance and nothing had become of it, this to me was a contribution I could make beyond looking after my family. I'm not a qualified doctor or a professor but I am an experienced dad who happens to be able to write a little and is willing to stand up in front of people and engage.

Lemn Sissay, who has been a friend of mine for over thirty years now, had come along to the gig. I'd met Lemn in Manchester and we had toured together with John Bramwell, aka Johnny Dangerously. The performances we did were some of the most enjoyable of my life and the chance to hang around with these two creative and funny men was such a joy. I always admired not only Lemn's talent as a poet and performer, but also his courage. At the time, at most of the places we played, he was the only black person in the room; sometimes the only black person in the town. Lemn had just recorded a BBC Radio 4 show with the BBC radio producer Ed Morrish and suggested my name to him. I met Ed, a quiet, thoughtful and personable man, and immediately trusted him. He suggested a possible half-hour show also with BBC Radio 4.

I didn't want to make the show at all if I couldn't make it well. It was a challenge getting the right balance between comedy and insight. I submitted a guide treatment and crossed my fingers. Sioned Williams was now the comedy commissioner at BBC Radio; I'd met in her previous job as commissioner for ITV. She is astute and very experienced and my only worry was that she might find the subject matter leant too heavily on autism and might need to be lighter for this particular comedy radio slot. But, without asking for any alterations at all, she gave us the go-ahead and the stage show became a thirty-minute radio show. We recorded it back at the Komedia, but this time in the main room, which was packed. Of course, it being for radio there were no slides; instead I'd included a few sound effects to add to the audio experience.

The show *A Normal Family* was transmitted on 31 July 2016. The way I described it in the show itself was 'some serious poems, some funny poems and a few jokes. A bit like a poetry salad with me as a tosser.'

I was really encouraged by the response to *A Normal Life* and also to *A Normal Family*, which followed soon after, also on Radio 4. Not only did *A Normal Life* get chosen for 'Pick of the Week' and 'Pick of the Year', but *A Normal Family* won a Silver Aria. But it was the response on social media I found most heartening. In particular a lot of people were asking for copies of the final poem from the show. I'd recounted the story of meeting the psychiatrist at Son-Rise when Johnny was little – the one who said none of us feel good enough. And I also mentioned I have a photo above my computer where I write. It's called 'Pale Blue Dot' and it was taken from the *Voyager One* space probe as it left the solar system. It's quite a big picture and in the middle of all the blackness is one pixel of pale blue – that is the Earth. It's like the furthest selfie ever taken. And on that one pixel are all the hopes and dreams, all the pain and joy of everyone that has ever lived.

I find this photo very grounding. The final poem was then, as it is now:

A PRAYER FOR THE HESITANT

A pale blue dot
amid a family portrait

This is your home planet
you are where you were born to be
breathe

The world is your living room
you are amongst friends
your ancestors, your family and
over ten thousand saints look down

Nobody means you any harm
not even God or nature
you can choose not to fear

The universe expects nothing
Every single thing is more than nothing
You have already exceeded expectation

If you forget me
my name
this moment
remember only this
you are good enough

imperfect as we are
you are good enough

With the success of the radio show, I was asked to write this book with the same title. What started as a reaction to sorting out my photos has set me on a path of trying to bring some awareness and understanding to the everyday world of living with an autistic member of the family. I had not thought before writing those first poems that I had anything to say to the world, but writing about our everyday adventures has reminded me how much joy and fulfilment Johnny has brought into our home. It's reminded me of the great qualities both my wife and my son bring into this world. But most of all, it's reminded me how lucky I've been to share this journey with Angela and Johnny and why I love them.

On hearing that we'd been offered a book deal, Angela said to me, 'Why would anyone be interested in our story? We aren't anything special.'

'I think that's the point,' I said.

Acknowledgements

We would like to thank Sarah and Andrew Pell for all they do, plus looking after Johnny at times so that we could meet our deadline for this book. Also Linda Hallam, Karen Gazeley and Caroline Bell for their support and thoughts and Kate Hewson at Two Roads for her help with every-thing, especially our terrible grammar.

We would also like to say a big thank you to the follow-ing people, without whom we would have not have been in a position to write this account:

Firstly, to everyone who joined us on our Son-Rise Programme: Valerie Carroll, Lisa Newman, Lindsay Hughes, Lee Harris, Nick Taylor, Julie Everton, Jonathan Hearsay, Natalie Barrazone, Julie Curry, Cheontell Barnes, Cath Mason and anyone else who came and went but who now, after years, in our befuddled state, we can't remember. We are eternally grateful for their time, energy and openness and for braving all the bites, whacks and kicks. They helped empower Johnny – helped him find his voice. Quite literally. He may well have found this eventually without their inter-vention; he may well have done better or not progressed at all – we will never know. But we firmly believe the young man he is today can be traced directly back to the love and support he got during those years spent running around a white room.

Lisa Newman continued working with Johnny on a Friday, for a total of twelve years. We had no idea, that day we stuck a poster up at the university, that a friend of hers would see it, tell her about it and that she'd turn up on our doorstep asking questions and would eventually become part of our family. Sometimes taking a leap of faith in an idea that you're not really sure is going to work is more than worth it.

Also many thanks to Dido Fisher, Tom Cook, Persephone Pearl, Tony Hallam, Angela Carroll, Jan Carroll, the Gazeleys, Julie Gill, the Son-Rise staff at The Option Institute, Jane Root, Ros Blackburn, Johnny's teachers and classroom assistants, the other parents of special needs children we have met who have offered their advice and support, the Myers, Lyndsey Posner, Lemn Sissay, Phil Greenwood, Sue Winter, Jo Offer, Sharon Wennington, Andrew Eaton, Marc Evans, Gina Carter, Ed Moorish, Carl Cooper, Penny Shepherd, Teresa Sowerby, Stevie Lee, Jeremy Dear, David Mitchell, Jerry Rothwell, Jonathan Merrill, the NAS and all the staff and volunteers at Amaze.

Lastly we'd like to mention you, the person reading this line right now (unless you're one of those people who goes straight to the back of the book and scans the last paragraph before deciding if they're actually going to read the rest of it).

Of the million and one things you could have chosen to do with your time, you decided to spend some of it with us. Thank you.

About the Authors

Henry Normal is an English poet, writer, broadcaster and film and television producer. He was Managing Director of Baby Cow Productions Ltd, which he set up with Steve Coogan. He co-wrote *The Royle Family* with Caroline Aherne and Craig Cash, and has recently written three acclaimed Radio 4 shows, *A Normal Life*, *A Normal Family* and *A Normal Love*.

His poetry collections include *Staring Directly at the Eclipse*, *Raining Upwards* and *Travelling Second Class Through Hope*. He lives in Brighton with his wife, Angela, and their son, Johnny.

Angela Pell is a writer for film and TV whose credits include *Snow Cake*, starring Sigourney Weaver and Alan Rickman, *Gifted*, starring Rhys Ifans and the upcoming adaptation of Naoki Higashida and David Mitchell's *The Reason I Jump*.